Dr Lawrence Blair was brought up in Mexico where he took his first degree. He wrote his doctoral thesis on contemporary mysticism at Lancaster University. He now writes and lectures, and sculpts Pythagorean crystalline forms which depict the geometrical connections underlying such esoteric arts as the Tarot, the I Ching, palmistry, astrology. He lives in West London.

Lawrence Blair

Rhythms of Vision

Paladin

Granada Publishing Limited
Published in 1976 by Paladin
Frogmore, St Albans, Herts AL2 2NF

First published in Great Britain by
Croom Helm Ltd 1975
Copyright © Lawrence Blair 1975

Made and printed in Great Britain by
Richard Clay (The Chaucer Press) Ltd
Bungay, Suffolk
Filmset in 'Monophoto' Ehrhardt 10 on 12 pt

Contents

To LYDIA and LORNE
and all those who are aware of
riding the high wave of change

Acknowledgements

Grateful acknowledgements go to Professor Ninian Smart, for his fastidious nursing of my doctoral thesis; to David Croom for patiently helping me to communicate its basic contents to a broader public; and to Clive Entwhistle, for generously checking the manuscript. Sincere thanks are also due to Dr Lyall Watson and Theodore Roszak for their enlightened encouragement. I am also deeply indebted to the many unsung hierophants of Aquarian thought who have generously allowed me glimpses of their different gardens of insight.

Special appreciation also goes to Larry Welz, for conjuring up 'The Sleeping Continent', Pat Butterworth for her splendid drawings and Keith Critchlow for his abundant geometrical imagery. Thanks to David Tansley, John Michell, Dr James Hillman and Theo Gimbel for their bountiful inspiration.

The illustrations on pages 139 and 140 are reproduced by permission of Danniel H. Kientz of Psychotronic Research Institute, 720 Beaver Street, Santa Rosa, California 95404 and The Trustees of the National Gallery, London.

The photographs of Rose Macauly on pages 156 and 157 were taken by David Anthony.

Foreword

This is a difficult book. And an important one.

Difficult, because it expects us to question our most basic beliefs, those tidy interpretations of reality that we have all learned to make in common and to accept as exclusive fact. And important, because that is precisely what we now need to do.

Reality has become unreal in the sense that there is no absolute truth, but rather many versions of it and all of them equally valid. Lawrence Blair surveys all the currently popular sets of perceptions and, gently and wisely, lures them out into the open where it can be seen that the power that gave each its initial impetus is now being 'calcified by the patterns of form'. He suggests that this is altogether unnecessary and that we need to see ideas and beliefs not as immovable objects but as vehicles of growth and change.

I like that very much.

Off the coast of Japan are a number of tiny islands where resident populations of macaques have been under continuous observation for more than twenty years. The scientists provide supplementary food, but the monkeys also feed themselves by digging up sweet potatoes and eating them dirt and all. This uncomfortable practice continued unchanged for many years until one day a young male monkey broke with tradition and carried his potato down to the sea where he washed it before eating it. He taught the trick to his mother, who showed it to her current mate, and so the culture spread through the colony until most of them, let us say ninety-nine monkeys, were doing it. Then one Tuesday morning at eleven, the hundredth individual acquired the habit and, within an hour, it appeared on two other islands in two physically unconnected populations of monkeys who until that moment had shown no inclination to wash their food.

I believe that ideas in human societies spread in the same kind of way and that when enough of us hold something to be true, then it becomes true for everyone. I can see no other way in which we can reach some sort of meaningful consensus in the limited time that now seems to be at our disposal. Lawrence Blair I think agrees. He says that 'when a myth is shared by large numbers of people it becomes reality'. I desperately hope that he is right and that we can find a way of using our ideas not as stumbling blocks but as what he calls 'tuning forks for freedom'.

That vision alone makes this book worthwhile and I hope that one of those who reads it turns out to be a hundredth monkey.

Bermuda   LYALL WATSON

1   Leavening Awareness

When the ancestors of the Blackfoot Indians awoke to being naked and lost in a world of so many things they asked Old Man, their Maker, how they should live. He told them to pray, to sleep and to listen carefully to the animals which appeared in their dreams. In this way, their legend goes, they derived from their sleep power which stilled fear and, from the creatures of their dreams, knowledge of how to hunt, and build fires and shelters; and they flourished.

Today, in a culture which has lost its capacity to dream, we are without those mythic looms whereon the outer world of economics and science is woven into the same fabric as our inner world of death and the significance of life. Our few remaining myths – of 'progress', 'education', 'achievement' – articulate only the outer world, and shroud us from the deeper mystery which, on solitary nights, can occasionally be heard lapping at our foundations, reminding us of death and chaos. We keep out the night, suspecting there is no life in it; we guard against thinking too deeply, fearing what we cannot see, for we cannot trust that the invisible has meaning or that the universe is ordered even in areas that we cannot control. Yet how much do we control, and how much meaning is wrested from the universe with the conscious grasp?

'Religion' derives from the Latin *ligare*, 'to connect'; *religare* means to reconnect ourselves to what underlies our existence. Since each of us is different, the points of reconnection differ as widely as do individual temperaments. Everywhere in the natural world, creatures are linked with meaning – they flourish into what they *are*, like the proverbial lilies of the field, without reaping or toiling. Only in the mind of man is there darkness and imbalance.

Carl Jung writes, 'Religion is nothing if not obedience to awareness.' Yet am I *aware* of my existence, or is it always obscured by my cluttered universe of facts, of the dates and breakfasts, hopes and pains which hold me in their grasp? But to loosen this grasp, I must first be aware of what *is*, rather than what I would like, or have been conditioned to believe exists. This book unfolds a spectrum which can help leaven our awareness of who we are, and of the miraculous aquarium of time in which we swim.

First of all we are *aware* that something is wrong, that we are no longer *homo ludens*, the man who sings and celebrates with laughter; nor are we the creatures through whom the supernatural continually reverberates. We cannot see the seasonal movements of the lichens across the continents, as did the Red Indians; feel in the blood, as they did, the migrating herds, the shoals of fish. We of the cities scarcely gaze up at the night sky any more, and when we do what we see is flat, pinpricked like a board – not coiling with suns through deep dimensions of time. It is generations now since we were close to the immediate symbolism of poetry, the cyclical pulse of birth and death; could see the spirits and subtle energies which permeate ourselves and our environment; and could knowingly touch what was infinitely Greater, rather than cushioning ourselves from it with talk of God.

Our time is distinguished by its isolation from the miraculous. Angels, as Peter Berger puts it, have been reduced to a rumour, miracles are largely obsolete, and we are blind to the fact that for a brief span of years we live on the brink of the 'Numinous' – the sage's word for Luminous Eternity. The windowless room we inhabit in ourselves excludes the Aweful, the Divinely Outlandish; the closest we come to it now is in our fascination with disasters, volcanoes and death on a grand scale, monsters – like Barnum and Bailey's whale in a tent, where crowds could queue to see the rotting leviathan dragged from the deep seas. Yet these tawdry dramas somehow echo in the sleeping soul a world of boundless amazement from which we have become estranged.

Immunized against the radiance of our existence, we are aware of only a fraction of the spectrum of vibration in which we have our being – while all about us nature breathes in regular rhythms, the tides drawn about the earth, the sap *ascending and descending* the stems of the vegetable world, the strange radio-electric emanations from space monitored by the astronomers. Even our bodies, eyes and voices reflect these rhythms, and by touching our own wrists we can actually feel the universal beat of our blood.

We can sense that even the health and beauty that remain in our bodies are but an echo from the primal days of strength and sunlight. In the crowds milling in the streets we see faces weighed with a pain and myopia of which the sufferers themselves are unaware. The further we get from those ancient days, the more our bodies decline, they bend at the back, the lustre fades from the eyes, and love becomes a sexuality no more powerful than a spasm in the genitals. Compare ourselves, our domesticated culture, to the beauty of wild creatures, of vine-snakes or cougars! For what profane ceremony are we distorting and fattening ourselves, breeding away our fire? We inwardly know that we are now the Shadow People, fallen from grace, cast from the Garden of Eden of the inner self – the self which knows the richness of the subtle world – and that we are banished to the wilderness of externals.

But what has happened to make the Universe appear chaotic and fearful if it is not simply that our perspective, our 'angle of vision', has become misaligned? If we can but change our ways of 'seeing', and alter our habitual focus from the outside world of endlessly ramifying and unrelated facts, we can discern an extraordinary order underlying the apparent chaos. This order is in the movement of *energy*. The most apparent thing about energy is that there is nothing else. Its rhythms are not only outside and within us, but they *are* us, from the oscillating particles comprising the atoms of our bones and eyelashes, to the rhythms which web and flow in our minds. Energy moves in cycles, or wave motions; it is never at rest, and it is always everywhere, appearing in countless hierarchical modes – like the waves on an ocean breaker, the ripples on those waves and the flutings on those ripples: each being part of an organic flux, but played in a different key. The differences between blue and orange, F sharp and E flat, even between a circle and a square are differences only in wave motion.

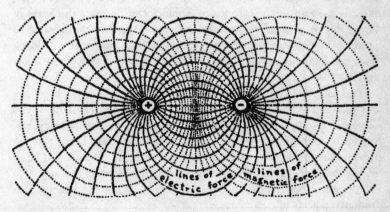

1. Field diagram of electrical polarities.

Thought-processes, myths and symbols, are no less than different modes of energy, exhibiting patterns which parallel the crystalline forms of nature. Thus to alter our focus from the chaos of ordinary thought to the *reconnection* with awareness of these patterns of energy which constitute the universe, both mythic and empirical, is the first step towards discerning the new forms of re-ligion. Since we are dual creatures, 'feeling' as well as 'reasoning', this reconnection with universal rhythms not only unites our otherwise warring faculties of emotion and intellect, but begins to link our own personal lives with the entire underlying harmony of meaning which permeates existence. It is this harmony, and its connections, which we shall explore here, from the interplay of galactic tides in our universe to the perfect geometry of the crystals in our blood.

2. The symbiotic polarities of Yin and Yang.

Energy – like the pendulum – moves between extremes, troughing and peaking within the confines of its particular vibrationary rates, or modes. Growth, which is simply energy ascending through different modes, moves through the eternal play of action and re-action. First there is the effusion of Life Force, around which accrete the fibres of form; this in turn is 'reacted' against, destroyed and transcended to produce a higher, more complex crystallization into matter. Watch how the bamboo grows, knots at the full moon, grows and knots again.

This pulse between gravity and levity, entropy and vitality, breathing out and breathing in, is as discernible in the galaxies as it is in the affairs of men, for our myths too, our 'ways of seeing', break in cyclical rhythms on the beach of time. Ages of Romanticism break through Reason, become in time mere airy superstition, and are curtailed again by the fashion for facts. It is in the present crest of cultural change that we discern a new fabric of myth, one which unites the 'feeling' and 'rational' aspects of our nature.

During the Middle Ages the cultural focus was predominantly on 'feeling', or inner experience, where angels and devils were as real – if not more so – than people. But this reached a peak where the empirical world of everyday facts was so neglected that the counter-swing began, and gradually, with the Enlightenment, the 'feeling' myth seceded to a rationalist focus on reality. The authority of the Church, which had endorsed the medieval cultural myth, now gave way to the authority of Science, which endorsed the myth of technological progress, of the alleviation of inner suffering via outer means; and gradually the world of objective facts became more real than people. But as the following chapters will show, a new counter-swing of myth has begun, for the inchoate lava of growth – of energy in a new mode – is eroding those rigid thought-forms which have acquired such an alienating power since the first revelations of the scientific enlightenment. It is this new fabric of myth – to which each one of us contributes – that suggests a way of synthesizing our opposing worlds of reason and feeling.

It has been said that the kernel of 're-ligion' is its poetry, the sling which throws us beyond the confines of our usual myopia. This music moves from the inside outward, rather than the reverse, from 'feeling' rather than fact. This book is written in the same vein, and the 'facts' contained in it should only be taken as touchstones to personal meaning, rather than as additional components in the ramification of chaos.

Since we are tracing the connecting threads between our inner and outer worlds, we shall explore those dream and legendary symbols which ancient civilizations, attuned more closely to the world we are re-discovering, have left in their legacies. More particularly, we examine those points at which the higher reaches of science are progressively corroborating the existence of an 'invisible world' long maintained to exist by seers and mystics.

In Chapter 2, *The Mirrors of Myth*, we begin with the way we *see*, exploring the myths in which our perception is caged, and those which free us to see anew. There is the interplay between the 'outer' myths of science, and the 'inner', subterranean myths of vanished wisdom, of visitors from space, and of hierarchies of spiritual power. In *Astral Logic* we turn to the Universe to observe how time and space, from the most distant galaxies to the most immediate atomic particles, are suffused with the rhythms which move the tides, the rings in trees, the chemistry of our cells; and how the scientific myth of cosmology begins to blend with the lost myths of occultism. We then move to *Number and Form*, the languages of energy, to see how numerology and sacred geometry –

the 'divine grammar' of the ancient magicians – still express the primal modes of force. Entering their structure is an end in itself, rather than a tool – as in ordinary mathematics – to an end *outside* the self. We see how energy is trapped in such shapes and numbers as the Egyptian pyramids, the Pythagorean solids, the Druid observatories and the golden mean ratios which are so integral a part of spirals, minerals and sacred architecture.

Vibration takes us to the different expressions of energy in our immediate environment, the music of crystals, plants and human beings; the links between vibration and form, the resonance woven through trees, the movement of water; the shedding of colour and sound from the sun into the symphonic mantle of the earth. We examine those points at which the frontiers of the 'subtle environment' are being broached by the new scientists of the invisible. We see how disks of sand vibrated at certain frequencies produce 'mandalas', the sacred shapes which are at the heart of nature and of human worship. We see how plants have 'aetheric' nervous systems which respond to music and human thought-forms, and how the human aura itself can be photographed to reveal the colours and moods of the psyche. Even the rhythms monitored in the human mind show that the visions of consciousness are themselves *woven with vibration*.

In *Fringe Medicine and the Subtle Anatomy of Man* we return more closely to ourselves. Our own bodies, as well as the consciousness they contain, are seen to be merely force fields – refrains, like all existence, in the harmonic flux of energy. True medicine, like religion, is seen merely as a re-tuning of our tapestry of vibration to the overriding energy from which we spring. 'Dis-ease', either of body or of belief, disappears with re-alignment to what is already *there*, but which we are unable to see. The growing adherence to 'fringe' psychiatries and medicines can also be seen as a barometer of the shifting cultural awareness, which is moving from viewing man and the universe as determinist machines to seeing them in the context of a web of interrelated forces. The human body, like the electro-magnetic bodies of the sun or the earth, has with our present knowledge expanded beyond its physical confines, revealing the subtle human faculties beyond the five senses: the auras of the 'aetheric' body, and its organs – the 'chakras' – of religious tradition, the streams of 'qi' energy which the acupuncturist traces – all of which emanations parallel and fuse with the energy rhythms of our planet, and beyond.

With *Maps of Self-Discovery* we move to the psyche, to the subtle grammars which are being disinterred from the occult heritage and show themselves to be keys to ordering our present expansion of knowledge. The Tarot and the I Ching are seen as highly condensed codes for perceiving the trans-temporal – but immediate – universe of higher modes of energy. Here too are the 'body languages' of palmistry, phrenology, physiognomy, which show that the psyche – its individual nature and temperament – leaves its imprint even in the flesh, in the palms of the hands, in the lustre of the eyes.

In *The Religions of Experience*, we move inwards still further to the anatomy of sacred commitment, to those multiple groups which seek to re-align themselves with the source of universal energy via their different symbol systems. And finally, in *Time Now*, we re-examine this brief moment of our existence in history, experiencing the incipient world view where the transcendent evolutionary future of man begins to gleam beneath the rubble of technocracy.

To re-align ourselves with energy requires a complete stilling of our habitual responses to external and internal stimuli. This is true in order to think or feel anew, let alone to *be* anew. This 'stilling', this permitting again of the neglected faculties to respond to Force, may occur under countless circumstances and guises; through shock or grief, through love and religion, or through sheer spontaneity – a kind of sudden earthquake of revelation with no discernible cause.

I was 'opened' – as it is called – into an esoteric group called Subud,[1]* and although it could have been any one of the long catalogue of occult systems whose symbolism and exercises flower into changing forms, this particular group, though better than some and worse than many, led indirectly to the discoveries unfolded in the following chapters. I shall therefore begin by describing it, both in terms of how I experienced it and in the historical and symbolic context in which it reached me.

Being 'opened', I was told, was simply the submission to a Divine Force, which I could receive and should respond to in the presence of others who had already received this 'contact' and were practised in the submission and response to it. This practice was called the latihan – the Indonesian word for 'exercise', since it originated with the Javanese mystic Bapak Muhammad Subuh.

As I stood in the latihan hall before some eight of my 'brothers' prior to my opening, I felt a great tide of dread surround me. Already there

* Superior figures refer to chapter notes at the end of the book.

was a 'force' there, and it was fear. The occult realm was as full of demons as it was of angels (the child in me whispered) and here I was about to surrender unconditionally to a supernatural force of unknown origin. What if it released the whole chasm of terrors which, since early childhood, I had managed to bury? What if I was offering myself up to the great entropic powers of chaos?

We were asked by the 'helper' – the only hierarchical step in Subud between Bapak and the members – to remove our shoes and watches and to stand quietly while he read a statement from Bapak that I should try to receive the power with sincerity, trust and submission (all rather vague terms to me); that I should try not to think nor be disturbed by the actions of those around me, but to respond to any movements which might be prompted by my inner self. There was a silence, and the helper said: 'Begin.' Almost immediately people around me began to hum, to vibrate, to cry and even to cartwheel. I was petrified, partly with fascination, since the sound they made together touched some deep memory in me.

Much of the fascination was in seeing people reveal the personalities they normally concealed. The psychic constrictions usually masked by ordinary people were here exposed. The helper remained quite still in front of me, his face expressionless, while tears ran from the corners of his closed eyes. There was no hysteria, no outer contact between us, just a strange rhythm to which each was responding according to who he was. Only towards the end of the half-hour session did I begin to experiment with what I imagined submission to be. Almost immediately, my eyelids began fluttering. This normally happened when I was tense, and could instantly be stopped by consciously relaxing; but now the more I relaxed the more they fluttered. As soon as I willed them to stop they would do so, as soon as I surrendered they began again. I was just beginning to feel a kind of cerebral effervescence when the helper said, 'Finish.' People were quiet and dazed for a while, then they gradually put on their shoes and watches, nodded goodbye and filed off home.

That was it! I was none the wiser, but I felt in some sense changed. My evening meal was so good that I ate it with special care – nor could I speak as much as usual. I went to bed early; the sheets were infinitely soft, and the night carried me away into its protection as it had only done before in distant memory. Something odd had happened, and I did not know what.

It was at this point that I sought more explanation, some framework into which I could fit the experience I had embarked on. Subud began in 1934 when Bapak, a humble Javanese accountant, out walking with some friends, was struck by a force. Those with him saw a light enter him from above, and Bapak himself describes experiencing a vibration so disturbing and intense that he thought he was dying. There was no choice but to surrender to, rather than resist it; at which he sensed a deep change in himself, as if all the cells of his being had been re-polarized in some way. He later discovered that he could resist the force at any time by an effort of will, but that at an inner gesture of submission it would seize and vibrate him again. He further found that once he entered this state of latihan the force could be received by anyone else in his presence who consciously opened themselves to what they imagined the source of it to be. This experience thus spread by a kind of invisible contagion, and today there are some 12,000 people throughout the world regularly practising the latihan.

Nobody, not even Bapak, could tell me quite what the force is, but it was called – presumably for the sake of convenience – either the Divine Life Force or the Power of God. The purpose of the latihan, I was told, was gradually to awaken and throw into relief that inner nature of man which is usually suffocated by his inherited and self-acquired conditioning. Subud maintained that it was neither a teaching nor a religion, but merely a 'receiving', one which differed little from those previous divine influxes – in Mormonism, Sufism, Quakerism – about which were later to accrete the fibres of religious dogmatism.

I was reminded that the force of the latihan permeated the 'whole self', and was too great for the mind alone to understand, at least until the interior faculties – either atrophied or barely developing in contemporary man – had grown to a degree where the intellect could perceive what was happening. Thus all efforts were required to still the mind and to prevent it from interfering with the process of growth. Submission involved giving all that we think we are to something completely 'Other' – in this case to an Energy which activates the inner nature, and through its purifying process tends to move and vibrate even those parts of us which we cannot see, which are 'out of mind'. Thus, depending on the individual's particular inner knots or distortions, he might outwardly jump or cry or roll on the floor during the purifying process of the latihan. The more practised the Subudian, the more interior his latihan; so that his body eventually barely moved, as the process was directly vibrating his inner feelings.

Although there was no teaching in Subud, there were certain

protective guidelines, the primary one being that the latihan should not be practised more than half an hour at a time, two or three times a week. The reason for this was that in contrast to certain concentrative techniques of meditation the latihan was a receiving through complete non-doing, and the nature and strength of the force which came through would, if bathed in too often, be sufficient to disrupt and traumatize the patterns of the psyche and the nervous system. Excessive latihan – and once you had acquired the 'technique' you could practise it anywhere and at any time – carried the danger of 'spiritual crisis', a common condition in the literature of all living religions.*

Although the latihan is usually performed in groups (because, like the light produced by a collection of solar cells, the power is somehow greater than the sum of its parts), it remains a purely subjective experience, and very little can be said *about* it except for its brief history, and what it is believed by its practitioners to do. The difficulty was to distinguish between what it was actually doing to me, and what I was led to expect it would do.

Several weeks after my 'opening', once I was more accustomed to the exercise, I found I could wander around the latihan hall with my eyes closed and still avoid knocking into other people, the supporting pillar or the walls because I could feel them like a pressure on my skin at a distance of several feet. But as soon as I began experimenting with this, I lost the faculty – as if it were some by-product of a process occurring at a much deeper level in me than normal curiosity.

Each latihan was an exercise in learning how to submit the will, and all that I thought I was, to something which at times could be felt as powerfully as a flood tide. Not only could it be stopped at will, but it could also be started. Sometimes it started itself, waking me at night, or vibrating me when I was going to school on the bus. This could be indulged with virtually no exterior signs, but I was warned against doing it in public lest other people, in a 'quiet condition', be unwittingly 'opened' also. My chemistry had been changed in some way: certain preferred foods became unpalatable, certain colours and music were now jarringly offensive. Films or books, when they became sentimental, would bring a lump to my throat and tears to my eyes. Horror films, which I had always relished, became horribly real and although I knew that both the sentiment and the horror were shallow games, they

* Subud crisis cases have since become recognized by psychiatrists as similar to, but differing from, schizophrenia, and have been referred to in the *Lancet* and various other medical journals as the 'Subud Syndrome' or 'Subud Psychosis'.

touched my feelings so strongly that I was often an embarrassment to myself and others.

A duality emerged, as if I were gestating a powerful embryo which felt and responded to situations before I did, but which could nevertheless be ignored.

The latihans themselves were not necessarily pleasant. For a period of months I had feelings of nausea during the latihan, but could not surrender enough to be prepared to vomit on the Subud carpet. When I exercised alone next to the lavatory, prepared to give everything I had, I retched, but nothing came up, and after several such latihans the sickness never returned. It was as if an emotional knot, symbolized as a very real desire to vomit, had been dissolved. There were also periods of intense cramp in my left foot, which only occurred during latihan and could only be cured either by stopping it or by entering more deeply and being carried past a severe threshold of pain. I came to recognize the cramping, during any situation, as a signal for receiving – for shedding my armour and responding to the situation, either spiritual or everyday, with this inner and enigmatic faculty which was awakening.

Some latihans brought back the full taste of forgotten memories, like psychoanalysis, particularly those wounding or amazing experiences of early childhood which had since been buried by the years. One such memory flooded back of when, aged three or four, I was walking down a London street with my mother. I remembered that at that time I seldom took in the tops of things – the tops of cupboards, the roofs of houses; these were all of what was to come, what was still out of reach. I was annoying my hurrying mother with a dilatory independence. I stopped at some steps which led up to the gothic doors of a church; I faced it and gazed upwards to levels of windows and carvings; looking further I saw the steeple and, like lighted methane, I went up with it – all the way up to the top and beyond in an incandescent flight. It was my mother's voice which called me down again; she was twenty yards ahead, and it took me a few moments to rediscover who she was and who I was before running after her.

A vivid series of dreams from about the same age came back to me, of when I could fly with outspread arms, and how, as the weeks passed, I could only glide. One night, as I was gliding down a long staircase, my feet touched one of the steps, and as I awoke I knew with a great sadness that I would never fly in my dreams again.

Some of these memories which returned during the latihan with their full colour and emotional impact could not be outwardly placed, but seemed to have happened in sleep, or under anaesthetic. They may even have been inherited experiences – like dying pleasantly in a sunfilled room with people weeping around me.

Four years after my opening a lot had happened externally; my step-father had died, I had travelled and worked my way round Europe, America and Alaska, and I was still doing the latihan, which in its own way had progressed through a broad and often painful terrain. After the first year or so of quite dramatic Subud experiences, I entered a long drought period when the latihan seemed excruciatingly boring, and was more like ordinary life – except for the irritating setting of my contorted and moaning 'brothers' – than life itself. This, I was told by the helpers, was a period when the latihan was working on the contents of my mind itself. But after some six months the force came back, though with less of its initial intensity. I realized I understood it no more than at the beginning: I continued because I liked it, and recognized some absence in my diet if I stopped. Perhaps, I thought, it was some kind of addictive weakness, was merely a pap of no real sustenance which I childishly retained to postpone the real business of living. Thus, when it was suddenly possible to go to Cilandak, Bapak's home and spiritual centre on the Indonesian island of Java, I went with a cultivated air of cynicism, to get to the bottom once and for all of the mystery to which I seemed addicted.

I arrived at the time of Sukarno's overthrow, shortly after the abortive communist coup, and was the only foreigner at the Subud complex, which consisted of Bapak, his wife and family, and five other satellite families who had been with him since the time of his first experience – all now guarding themselves day and night against various foraging armed political factions. At that time *Wisma Subud* – as it is now called – was a group of simple Dutch colonial buildings set in an oasis of frangipani trees beyond the city limits of Jakarta.

They were fasting from sleep at the time, sitting on the verandah until around five in the morning before going to bed. Bapak would join the three Javanese helpers, who were equivalent to disciples and had been with him since shortly after his first experience, and they would talk quietly together, unwilling to translate much to me – or would just sit silently for hours while the aromatic night washed over us. Bapak was a tall, straight-backed man, with an awesome presence and a face like a bespectacled bullfrog. There was no sense of personal contact with him, he seemed to see dispassionately through me, and was altogether too mountainously distant to emanate that powerful enveloping love which sweeps the followers of certain Indian gurus off their feet. Whenever he appeared I was compelled to stand, something which annoyed me since there was no outer compulsion to do so. I even decided to force myself to remain seated, but on each occasion I could hold it for only a few moments before rising like an air balloon.

They were all enigmatic and barely communicative; the food was appalling and the bathrooms malodorous and crawling with mosquito larvae, but the area was alive with a powerful and mysterious quality. As I gradually joined them in the fast, and was sleeping some four hours in every twenty-four, the boundaries between sleep and wakefulness became blurred to a point where the weeks became like a powerful dream in which it was quite natural for extraordinary things to happen.

When, in the early hours of the morning, the burden of remaining awake became very heavy, I was told it would be lightened if I sat next to Bapak, but when this failed I should give myself to the power of the latihan. Sitting next to Bapak allayed the desire to sleep for a further twenty minutes or so since a kind of tide of emanations could be clearly felt from him, and although these did not cease, the novelty did, and I would go alone into the large Dutch barn which served as the latihan hall.

On one such occasion I stood in the middle of the hall: high above me I could see the slightly lighter star-filled rectangles of the windows which contrasted with the darkness around me. I raised my arms, and offered myself to the Power. Instantaneously, I felt myself in a different kind of body; I was black and slippery, mis-shapen like a tadpole gargoyle. Though bowed, I was still looking upward, and I saw the windows cloud into the total blackness of my environment. I was naked in some kind of vibrationary liquid, and I saw and felt large luminous bubbles swirling upwards round my skin. Like some obscure creature which normally inhabits the black depths of the sea, I was caught in an upcurrent, and was ascending at great speed through layer upon layer of diminishing pressure towards an intensity of light too dreadful to imagine. I was so terrified that I immediately shouted 'finish!' The current died away, the windows gradually reappeared above me and I stood shaking and now totally awake.

I returned to the others on the verandah and sat down in a state of shock. For some time we were all silent, then Sudarto, one of the helpers, haltingly said that there were times when the inner self was brought to the brink of its capacity to experience the light, and although from here one had a hint of the reality and strength of the other world, to pass beyond it could still be dangerous. Bapak then told me I should sleep now, and for the first time I realized that they knew much more than they ever disclosed.

When I slept I had the first of a series of vivid dreams, which took three nights to unfold. I was at the controls of a light aeroplane about to take off on a runway with tall trees at the end of it. My mother and brother were behind me, and although I knew I could not fly, they were quietly confident that I could make it. It was night-time, and the cockpit light was on, its reflection in the windows making it hard to see out. The control tower kept saying I could take off, but I could not find the light switch, and I knew there were more important controls than that!

After several nights I told this recurrent dream to Sudarto, who simply said I should take off! The dream returned, and though I remembered his advice in my dream, the fear of killing myself and my closest people was of course no less vivid than if I had been awake. I revved up the engines – still unable to see clearly – and could even feel the heartbeats quickening in the chest of my sleeping body. Only when I had decided to go, and was rolling down the runway, could I suddenly find the light switch. Without the glare of the cockpit light I could see out, and the last of the dreams finished with my just clearing the trees at the end of the runway. Immediately I awoke with the realization that I had begun to fly in my dreams again – although no longer the flight of a child merely with outspread arms: I had left the ground and taken again the first leap back into the aether of inner experience.

Sudarto later told me that the inner self is gradually strengthened so that it can break the chrysalis of the ego against whose walls we generally see only our own diminutive reflections. Once this veil of inherited and acquired myopia is torn, we can glimpse the vastness of the real world. It is the fear of this reality which makes us curl more tightly in the chrysalis, but the purpose of all religions – the essence of living – is to break it so that man can gradually respond to the immense spectrum of outside energies to which he is rightfully heir.*

I realized that here in this distant oasis of power there were people who had become inwardly alive, who had put as much time and effort into those areas of psyche and spirit as we in the West put into technology. Before sleeping, eating, making love – all the fundamental gram-

* Macrocosmically, we see how entire cultures maintain these eggs of self-reflections, stubbornly seeing them as the 'real world', and respond with fear and censure to the broadening world views of such troublesome seers as Socrates, Christ, Galileo and Darwin. But all chrysalises, like skins, have their season of shedding.

mar of living – they would briefly abandon themselves to the force so that they could respond each time afresh from their awakening centres and become progressively freer from the bonds of habit.

I once watched them use the faculty to test whether a visitor was in fact arriving on an aeroplane, the flight number of which had been cabled in advance. The airport was an hour's humid drive away over rutted roads, and after testing together, I watched three of them quietly ignore the flight arrival time, and drive out to meet a different plane the following day. I was with them when the astonished guest came through customs with profuse apologies about the misinformation in his cable. But these people continually stressed that the Force was to use us, rather than the reverse; that the latihan was essentially a worship, as indeed all living experience could become, and the quickening of the psychic faculties was simply a fringe benefit, and one to be used with great care and humility.

I watched one of them choose a songbird at the market for his family, carefully sensing each creature beforehand – 'receiving' how it would be inwardly for the bird, how for its new environment. From this I noticed that the animals, plants and families of many of these people had been chosen for the blending of their vibrationary qualities by a palate beyond the intellect, and that they flowered in a kind of symbiotic interdependence. Their lives were centred around guidance received from this strange harmonizing power, which ordered and enlivened the understanding by continually creating, destroying and re-creating. They were committed to a dangerous game, with the ultimate stakes involved. Many of them had already experienced the traps and demons, revelations and dark nights of the soul which are part of the universal grammar of spiritual evolution, and which can be found in differing guises throughout the world's religious literature.

A new degree of commitment was required of me and, like my first 'opening', I began hesitatingly to experiment with living by 'receiving'. The experience was just a taste of what it could be like. Saying grace or prayers had always been a hollow repetition during my childhood, but here was a new meaning. One asked and thanked for nothing, but merely surrendered to a clearly sentient power, and went ahead with the slightly altered chemistry. In the case of food, receiving before eating meant that I either lost my appetite – though not the capacity to choose whether I would eat anyway – or discovered a subtle and exquisite hunger, though not necessarily for what was in front of me. Thus the question of free will was thrown into clear relief: I could choose the part of myself to which I owed greater allegiance. Receiving before sleeping either awakened me more, as if my body were declaring that it was not yet ready to sleep, or I would sink swiftly away to an area where the dreams were soft and lucid and could be remembered clearly next day. In this way the channels to the inner world were kept clear for information which could then be acted upon by the conscious self.

Although I actively disliked some of my 'brothers', I found as a result of the latihan that we were all connected in some way in an area beyond that of social communication. Some latihans were a journey through a magical fairyland of sound and feeling; soft and gentle, to a rhythm beyond my own. I was back in the filtered sunlight of childhood, and by the end of them I was in such a daze of warmth and stillness that my heart expanded far beyond me with a feeling for which we only have the word 'love'. My early weeping and shock at the sentiment and horror of the cinema caricatures had been the first signs of the release of a constricted heart. I was like the lungfish, trapped so long in a desiccated sheath of clay; the rains had come, and the awakening flesh smarted at the first thaw.

People became transparent as I saw the disparity between their outer persons and who they really were. It became more difficult to lie, and to be lied to, since the emphasis of the experienced world was shifting key. Tired terms like 'heart' and 'love' and 'the brotherhood of man' began to burn with a different meaning. My family in particular was sensed as the closest cell in the single palpitating organism of people, a unity quite unaffected by geographical distance. We all practised the latihan now, and although people of other esoteric groups give more lucid experiences of their family unity, any major inner event in one of us could be felt by the others, either awake or in dreams. There have been various occasions when one of us would send a cable asking simply: 'All right, what's happened?' to find it crossing with another describing what had.

There was thus the world of my own experience, and the subjective imaginative context of where it was leading, and the hints and interpretations given by the long-time Indonesian helpers, which, although neither dogma nor teaching, were often obscurely clothed in the symbolism of their own culture. I had arrived with a reserved cynicism in order better to judge whether I was addicted to folly, and my judgement had been blown off its feet; I left feeling I held by the tip of its tail a mystery of vast proportions. The inner world was *real*, I just did not know anything about it yet; but I had a loom on which to weave the disparate threads of my experiences, and a key for interpreting the new dimension of dream symbolism I had embarked on. In Cilandak I had been cradled in a power beyond my own, and, while there, was capable of things not yet mine. Shortly I was to return to my normal obscure vision and ineptitude, but with dim intimations of what lies behind personal religion.

For weeks afterwards, as I visited the other cities in the East I had planned to enjoy, I merely sat in cafés or my hotel room, feeling the earth move. No adventure could be more delicious than what I briefly carried with me. I was stoned, in love and, as with the revealed church spire of my early childhood, I had lighted into an area of uncontainable possibility; but here too I was soon to be called down by the voice of the temporal world, into the body of my actual capacities.

But it was these experiences which made me think that Subud was not alone, that among the wide variety of contemporary esoteric groups there must be others who, via their own particular symbols and exercises, were also discovering the lost world of inner dimensions. Within a year I had returned to England to research for a doctoral thesis on contemporary mysticism and alternatives to orthodox religion, in which I sought to map the outlines of this emergent continent from scraps brought back by inward travellers.

The field revealed itself to cover an enormous spectrum ranging from paraphysics, fringe psychology and medicine, through spiritualism, gnostic and magical groups, to Islamic, Buddhist and Hindu meditational transplants, and many others. All these ways – and each appeared tailored to particular temperaments – involved the multitude of traps and revelations which characterize the journey to self-discovery. Many of them appeared superstitious, cranky or downright hysterical, but they could all be seen to mirror the psyche in its many stages of unfolding.

So I began to map the field, using my own exercise as a touchstone in sorting the great and apparently conflicting variety of symbolic vehicles. Then a shadow appeared in my own faith; something was wrong. When my Indonesian euphoria had worn off, and I was now regularly trying to apply the receiving in the latihan to every aspect of living, I still retained in my subconscious the image that Subud was a group structured in such a way that the men at the top could lead me to a greater understanding. But as the organization grew, it became encrusted with the first layers of a Subud theology. Bapak's suggestions, and his descriptions of his inner world, became for the brotherhood injunctions, predetermined maps of everyone's inner world – even before the individuals had experienced them. What had been parables became 'facts', and for many Bapak became God on earth, even if this conflicted with the personal receiving of the latihan. What had simply been guidelines in the areas of habits and morality, hardened into rules, and the helpers' groups began to assume the first pedagogic attitudes of a priest class. Once again, it seemed, around the first influx of naked evolutionary power, had begun to calcify the patterns of form. I was reminded of Mephistopheles' remark to the mythical Dr Faustus that the flock of sheep is a fitting symbol for the followers of Christianity because they bleat along behind the Shepherd blindly avoiding the terrible gift of freedom which Christ really brought.

The forces now at play in myself were painful and disturbing: the carefully suggested doctrinal guidelines, which had initially served as a protection and orientation prior to my own capacity to experience meaning in the latihan, were now a constriction. If these teachings, coming from people clearly much wiser than myself, had borne fruit, who was I to see their limitations? Was mine simply an ignorant ambition to pursue a personal world view, one which avoided the pressure of the increasing discipline entailed in obeying other people's rules?

The Subud symbols, which were once malleable enough to reflect my own experience and to nurture me to my present precarious faith, were now hardening, and though I continued to practise the particular meditational exercise which fate had given me, it was now the gems of insight picked from the enormous and largely subterranean esoteric revival which increasingly articulated my own experience – gems which would have been less vivid had I not experienced a painful and at times fanatical commitment to one particular group. It was now the cultural phenomenon as a whole which had most meaning for me, and the thorny maze surrounding that castle was the fabric of symbol itself.

Man has been described as the 'symbol-making creature', and the history of cultures, as well as of individual growth, is the continual replacement of one set of symbols – believed to disclose 'ultimate significance' – by another. People are still killing and dying for symbols alone, mistaking them for the real goal, instead of seeing them for what they are: merely compass needles, organic maps which change as the evolving position of the self, or the culture, changes. People commit suicide because, with the collapse of their personal symbols of orientation – and before discerning the next symbolic layer unfolding in the psyche – they mistakenly feel it is the world of Meaning itself which has collapsed.

It is the esoteric groups (and here I include those small enclaves of scientists who, via their symbolic systems of biochemistry and astrophysics, are also pressed against the chasm of the unknown) which are microcosmic symbol kilns, where world views are formed and shatter, and have to be re-worked and fired again. It was through the personal trauma of distinguishing between what had become orthodox Subud injunctions and what appeared to *myself* through the latihan, that I began to recognize the same processes in other movements. There were those for whom the group symbolisms – whether the lotus feet of the Maharaj Ji, or the orders of Flying Saucer captains – were absolutely real, and there were those for whom their symbolisms were transparent, and recognized merely as vehicles of growth and change, perhaps with an inbuilt obsolescence.

Hubert Benoit, in his *Supreme Doctrine*, writes that Zen '. . . compares all teaching with a finger that points to the moon, and it puts us unceasingly on guard against the mistake of placing the accent of Reality on this finger which is only a means and which, in itself, has no importance'.[2]

It was thus quite suddenly that I recognized among the confusing array of esoteric groups (and scientific theories) an extraordinary thread of significance, one which traces the indistinct outlines of a continent of new meaning. Each group, despite the apparent lunacy of its symbols and exercises, contributes in some part to an emergent map. The esoteric revival on the one hand, together with the higher abstractions of science on the other, could suddenly be seen as a field of symbolism flowering through the aridity of technocracy; responding to a rhythm which utterly changes the view which most of us hold of ourselves and our environment.

2 The Mirrors of Myth

If we have the imagination to suppose that the world is not as we see it, nor our flesh, nor the purpose of our lives, then where do we look for the chance to see them afresh?

When Magellan's expedition first landed at Tierra del Fuego, the Fuegans, who for centuries had been isolated with their canoe culture, were unable to *see* the ships which anchored in the bay. They were so far beyond their experience that, despite their bulk, the horizon continued unbroken: the ships were invisible. This was learned on later expeditions to the area when the Fuegans described how, according to one account, the shaman had first brought to the villagers' attention that the strangers had arrived *in* something, something which, although preposterous beyond belief, could actually be *seen* if one looked very carefully. We ask how could they *not* see the ships – they were so obvious, so 'real' – yet others would ask how *we* cannot see things just as obviously real.

Everything we see, even in the physical world, involves a *non-seeing* of something else. We know that perception, whether visual or cerebral, involves the filtering out of thousands of competing stimuli to retain that which has 'meaning'. Whereas seeing is conditioned by 'meaning', meaning itself depends on a tacit, pre-established frame of reference, an adopted blueprint of possibility into which the 'seen' things must fit.

We must of course have a blueprint, a 'paint-by-numbers' canvas, or else we would have no framework for meaning and could see nothing at all – or else everything together, like white light before it is separated into colours by a prism. But for most of us, and particularly as cultural groups, our blueprint is fixed, has no un-numbered squares for possible unimaginable colours, and is not flexible, as is the eye, to alter focus and see anew.

These focal depths which condition what we see as real are, like the Fuegans', shaped largely by our culture and its myths, and are usually as far from our minds as the microscope is to the man looking through it.

Thus 'myth' and 'legend', assumed by the rationalists to be false history, are a very real part of our perception, and condition the 'ceilings' of our capacity to know: for *meaning* is not in the dry facts of an event alone (either past, present or future) but in the deep layers beneath the phenomenal world with which the 'facticians' of history, or the present, deal. The secrets of these timeless layers are trapped in the crystalline languages of myth and legend, and although to many they appear simply as dry bone-necklaces, passed from generation to generation and worn about the necks of the bards, to those sensitive to the music of symbolism they are resonant with memories of the different breeds of creature which roam the fields of time and the human psyche. In all cultures, and today no less than in the past, we are arched by myth, though it constantly changes countenance as we ourselves change, like our reflections in a mirror. Like the pre-determined 'blueprints' which condition our vision, myths may either reveal vistas beyond our wildest imaginings or else, if they have outlived their time, restrain us from moving into new areas of knowledge.

Our inherited myth, which has supported the growth of science, is that the world is 'out there' and we are 'in here' trying to see more of it. We think that to see reality 'as it is' can only be done 'rationally', and *homo sapiens* (as his self-styled name implies) is he who *knows* – knows how objective and 'realistic' he has become by scorning the childish consolations of the subjective world, that slippery slope to self-delusion.

This 'rationalist' myth in which we find ourselves constrained has already outlived its time, and is due to be sloughed off like an old skin – as we can see by re-examining how 'objectively real' is even the most immediate of worlds.

The philosophy of science, and its corollary, science fiction, have an uncanny knack of anticipating empirical discoveries; they have even been credited with causing them. For several generations they have theorized (and fantasized) about such 'secondary' qualities as colour, smell and sound not being inherent in physical things, but in us. It took Bertrand Russell only 15,000 carefully fitted words in his *The Problem of Philosophy* to establish that we are 'only immediately aware of our sense data', and that 'the real table, if there is one, is not immediately known to us, but must be an inference'.[1]

With the advent of neurophysiology and the psychology of perception, these theories became 'real'. Sir John Eccles, as a result of his Nobel prize-winning research on the physiology of the brain, describes how colour is perceived via retinal cells which have specific 'coded' photo-receptors, and how, because it is along *these* lines that the impulses reach the brain, the illusion of colour explodes in the mind. 'It must be recognized,' he writes, 'that colour appears in the picture as an experience deriving from specifically coded patterns in the brain. There is no colour in the outside world.'[2]

The once unassailable reality of the outside world began to crumble with the discovery that it is not colours, odours or sounds which are carried to our brain by nerves, but merely pulses of energy – all of the *same kind* of electrical potential. The amplitude is the same for each nerve, whether optic or auditory, and the difference of the things we experience depends not on the difference of what 'touches' our sense-organs, but only on the *rate* at which the pulses flow, and on the places *within the brain* that they reach.

Eccles's empirical work inside the cranium thus led him back to philosophy, and he later wrote: 'It is generally believed that [the reality of the external and objective world] alone provides a sound basis for scientific investigation. However, this objective-subjective distinction is illusory, being derived from misunderstanding and misrepresentation.'[3]

Art and anthropology have since shown that colours – particularly on the borders between the primaries – are highly subjective, and the perception and naming of them varies greatly with cultural fashions. It has been argued, for instance, that there are various other reasons besides the fact that there is no word for 'blue' in ancient Greek to suggest that the Greeks saw blue only as a different shading of green, and not as a separate colour in itself. Very few animals see colours at all, and the process of evolution appears to involve becoming aware of a wider spectrum of energy pulses. Alice Bailey,[4] the early twentieth-century mystic, has described how a sudden evolutionary lurch in man's early history suddenly rendered a world of shadows lambent with colour.

It is because colour-blind people are not blind to colours, but merely see them differently, that they less easily project into the 'coloured world' the assumptions that are tacitly held by colour-seeing people. They are consequently used by the military forces of most nations to detect camouflage.

The discovery that these 'secondary qualities' such as colour, sound, smell, etc., are really 'within' us rather than 'within' the outside world has gone unnoticed by many, while causing considerable tremors among the philosophers of science. One of these, G. W. K. Mundle, who was at pains to retain the objective reality of at least the *shape* of an object, asked plaintively: 'When one looks at a tomato, it is a *single* visible something which has the colour and the shape; so if the colour is in the observer, how could the shape be outside him?'[5]

Sadly enough, the shape is not either – as we can see from the art critic Anton Ehrenzweig's descriptions of the philosophical problems of drawing a head from two different angles: 'Turning from full face to profile causes every single feature on the face to change beyond recognition in terms of abstract form. But in the total likeness no change occurs. The recognition of real objects is not dependent on memorization of their many formal aspects. Understanding of reality comes *before* the appreciation of abstract forms.'[6]

It is the part played by the *expectation* of the viewer which is the essential one, and art, at its best, is greater than life because it plays games with the focal depth of our reality, scything into the essence of what is 'unreal' yet totally meaningful.

The implications of this evolution in thought – every bit as commanding as the Scientific Enlightenment was in its time – is that things are not as they appear – since they appear only as we expect to see them. This framework of 'expectation' is the substance of myth; and releasing ourselves from obsolete myths opens us, in turn, to broader, more vital and more *useful* ones.

The quality of light, for instance, as revealed by sensitive photo-electric eyes, changes from second to second throughout the twenty-four hours of the day. Similarly, the human body, in texture, colour, weight, is constantly changing – with every meal and thought. Yet when an intimate friend has changed more in a week than a glancing acquaintance has in a year, we seldom ask just *how* we continue to recognize him. There is no physiological button in our brains, like a computer, which lights up and says, 'That fits, that's my friend.' All perception relies on fluid symbols of equivalence, rather than exactitude, and we take what we 'see' as symbols on to which we project what we already anticipate in our heads. It is when our 'projection apparatus' is caught off guard that we occasionally, for instance, see a stranger reflected in a shop window before realizing with a shock that it is ourselves – at which point what we think we look like hurriedly forms in the glass. To attempt to delay that formation is a meditation in itself.

Our inquiry into the outside world is thus never pure, but always mixed with what we think ourselves to be. In science – ostensibly the most objective of pursuits – we readily see how the anthropomorphic images in our own minds are projected outside us. Our ships and motor cars take on gender and character; the more carefully we peer at the 'faces' of our meters and dials the more we see our own faces. At the still more abstract levels of 'objectivity', electrical circuits 'reject' some signals and 'accept' others; atomic particles 'attract' and 'repel' one another, rather as do people; they 'experience' forces, are 'captured' and 'escape', and so on.

There are good grounds for the awesome theory that scientific discovery is the *projection into matter of the exploration of the human mind*; and that all our worlds are lived within us, illusions of lesser or greater power, maintained by the weight of corporate belief, but are seen as 'out there'. What is 'real' is what we make real, even the colour of the sky or the shape of a tree.

Thus when a myth is shared by a large number of people it acquires not only as great a power as 'objectivity' has over us, but becomes reality itself, even producing tangible objects. Physiological as well as emotional limits are extended once we know they are sanctioned by possibility. Levi-Strauss mentions that: 'The thresholds of excitement, the limits of resistance are different in each culture. The "impossible" effort, the "unbearable" pain ... are less individual functions than criteria sanctioned by collective approval or disapproval.'[7]

Mount Everest, once the mountaineer's impossibility, is now far booked up ahead by expeditions with the Nepalese Government. Barely an Olympic mile is run any more in over four minutes. The unthinkable thirty years ago, in the form of a colour TV set, may actually be glowing in our living rooms.

Myths, although irreplaceable tools for forging new horizons, have a built-in obsolescence. Our present rational myth is one of considerable paradox, inherited from Humanism and the Enlightenment – which in turn were reacting against an over-subjective and intangible 'truth'. This reaction eventually bore a bitter fruit, and man found himself in a wasteland of statistics and facts without meaning, the heart of his own feeling left behind somewhere in his history, abandoned by the collective allegiance to 'outer' knowledge as the prime criterion for truth. And God, who was really the Great Unifier of 'meaning' and outer experience, moved beyond the cultural focal depth – into invisibility, and eventually into non-existence. The present hole in our rational myth can be seen by observing how irrationally 'rational' man lives his life. Find a man who lives by reason alone, who knows what he wants and hourly and consistently builds towards that end! Even the Apollo space programme, often cited as the supreme monument to the powers of reason, is stimulated by the desire to explore and experience. Our reason is at best a tool for achieving the ends of a subtler, unexamined vitality which are not in themselves either 'objective' nor truly 'real'.

But where, with science, is 'reason' taking us if not back to the grounds of vitality?

We already know that sense-data cannot be the surfaces of physical objects, since they are merely a series of atomic particles. Researchers into biochemistry and nuclear physics are already aware of Arthur Koestler's paraphrasing of the Second Commandment: 'Thou shalt not make unto thee any graven image – either of Gods or of Protons';[8] for symbols are merely fluid and expendable tools which in no way accurately represent 'reality'.

With the realization that the abstractions of science are purely symbolic but may give birth to 'real' and everyday objects, comes the reverse image that the world of everyday objects is no less symbolic, and for its perception and meaning relies again on abstractions. To train ourselves to see the physical world as purely symbolic is as difficult as it is for the physicist to formulate in everyday language what is glimpsed as decidedly 'other-worldly'. We see this with the problem in sub-atomic physics which Bertrand Russell put thus: 'matter is a convenient way of describing what happens where it isn't.'

The various mathematical models which come close to crystallizing the enigmatic behaviour of the electron, for instance, do so at the price of being unintelligible in terms of space, time, matter or causation. It was nevertheless for this enigma that Heisenberg won his Nobel Prize on the *Theory of Indeterminacy*, which Oppenheimer describes as follows: 'If we ask ... whether the position of the electron remains the same, we must say "No"; if we ask whether the electron's position changes with time, we must say "No"; if we ask whether it is in motion, we must say "No".'[9]

Yet nuclear reactors are already churning out millions of kilowatts a year, so that your lights may glow to read this book by.

It is now, when the limits of rationalism have been reached, and consequently also those of its language – which is tied to the world of everyday experience – that our mythic projections are falling on naked space which can only reflect the 'a priori' patterns of subjective symbolism. These archetypal symbols are the same tools with which man articulates his comprehension of transcendent states of consciousness.

The medieval alchemists, who sought to distil gold from the elements, are often derided as pseudo-scientists whose superstition and wishful thinking corrupted their reason. But Carl Jung pointed out that alchemy can only partly be taken as chemistry, since the alchemists did not see the substances they manipulated as 'objective' in the terms that a chemist would have done until recently, but as filled with the projections of psychic and unconscious symbolism – as instruments of *meaning* which mirrored the tranformation of the psyche; little different, in fact, from today's new scientists. Yet many people still argue that our projections into, say, electrons, which are both there and not there, and black holes in space, where particles travel faster than light, where causes happen *after* their effects and time moves backwards, are more 'securely' founded projections than those of the alchemists.

One may ask, what have such scientific theories to do with *me*? What possible bearing can Einstein's unifying theory of space and time have on my own days and nights, and am I really to believe that this immediate world is not here? The fact is that it is still here but – as the Vatican is still here after the discovery that the earth is not the centre of the universe – its 'hereness' has undergone a profound change. For if science, the buttress of our cultural orientation, is aware that we change our reality according to our capacity to see afresh, then the effect must bear more deeply on our personal lives than any number of motor cars and washing machines. For the object of research is now no longer nature, but nature exposed to human questioning. The question is what we see, and the question turns out to be what it is that questions. In von Weizacker's words: 'Man tries to penetrate the factual truth of nature, but in her last, unfathomable reaches suddenly, as in a mirror, he meets himself.'[10]

For this reason the higher reaches of scientific symbolism, in their sudden defiance of Aristotelian logic (such as 'being and not being at the same time', 'being in one place and omnipresent simultaneously'), are paralleling the 'religious' language of deep subjectivism. Einstein commented that the highest edifices of scientific thought have been purchased at the price of *emptiness of content*. The atom is as porous as the solar system, and it has been remarked that if we eliminated all the unfilled space in a man's body, and collected all the protons and electrons into one mass, he would be reduced to a speck the size of a mustard seed. Yet these atomic particles which constitute what we call 'mass' have no coherence relative to space, only to each other; their unity *overleaps* space. Meister Eckhardt, the medieval mystic, writes that when the spirit turns away from all things that 'have become', it turns back into its origins – the eternal image of the 'unbecome'. The only constant in our physical as well as psychic universe is movement – movement in emptiness. All the phenomena of nature, its laws and systems, are relative only to one another – not to space. We may know one wavelength's proportion to another, but not its absolute length. Motion has no frame: it is cradled in the void which makes all motion possible. What is, is but a movement in what is not; thus Lao-tse wrote:

Clay is moulded into vessels,
And because of the space where nothing exists we are able to use them as vessels.
Doors and windows are cut out in the wall of a house
And because they are empty spaces, we are able to use them.[11]

The 'life' of this emptiness is described in the Upanishads – the sacred Hindu literature – in a similar vein to that of contemporary science:

> That moves and moves not;
> That is far and the same is near;
> That is within all this and that is
> also outside all this.[12]

From the early days of rationalism the examination of nature through ever larger and ever smaller lenses of glass progressed until objective vision reached a barrier, where form dissolved into the 'Cloud of Unknowing' of oscillating particles and gas. It has been remarked that the key discovery of scientific man was not steel – the obvious choice – but glass, through whose lenses he saw that he was not alone, or Chosen, either in the microscopic universe, or among the nebulous galaxies of light; that God, despite His limitless reverberations, did not lie *outside*. Glass, through whose stained panes colour was woven into music by the medieval masons, became the extension of man's eyes – the mirror of his soul – which finally drew him back into himself again, in the direction of God.

'In religious experience also,' writes Aniela Jaffá, 'man meets himself, or rather, he meets *the* self. The distinction between appearance (the subjectively experienced psychic image or content) and an "objective" reality hidden behind it calls for deepened insight and heightened consciousness.'[13]

It is now, when the 'I' and the outside world are no longer so separate, when the myth of Objective Fact evaporates to reveal the vastness of things as curiously related to myself, that religion and science begin to blend. Like the tiger and the antelope in times of drought, they are both now required to meet shoulder to shoulder at the same waterhole, to drink from the same vast repository or archetypal symbolism.

John Bleibtreu, describing how biological research reveals symbols which totally alter our concept of space and time, remarks that:

Once we acknowledge the world as being subjectively perceived, we must also acknowledge that the world varies with an individual's sensibilities. Are there sensibilities of which we are unaware? Do we receive a 'knowledge' of the world and the order of things from sources of sensibility that are as yet inaccessible to the intellect? Every myth, including this new one of science maintains that we do . . .[14]

While the new myths of science are becoming more transparent with the projections of the human mind, beneath the surface of the culture a different, ancient brand of myth has broken through. These are the inner myths of occultism, which all answer the need to shatter the limitations imposed by the dogma of reason, by the facts which, brick by brick, have walled up our forgotten 'sensibilities'; and they are powered by what Rudolph Otto calls 'the *feeling* which remains where the *concept* fails'. Their language is that of symbols, the supreme mediators between different worlds of experience.

'Only the symbol awakens intimations,' writes J. J. Backhofen. 'Speech can only explain. The symbol plucks all the strings of the human spirit at once; speech is compelled to take up a single thought at a time . . . only the symbol can combine the most disparate elements into a unitary expression.'[15]

It is the unifying power of these symbols which emerges in the esoteric myths, for whereas science has begun to *see* itself, as in a mirror, subcultural currents are moving towards *experiencing* the self. True to the biblical quote: 'In times of great change, the people revert to the Old Gods', people are now reaching inwards to the symbols of the distant past to test how clearly they may still resonate the interior universe. For whereas 'myth' is the screen on to which we project our concepts of the rational and temporal world, at a different and deeper level it is also myth (and legend) which articulates the atemporal, or timeless world which encircles both the infinite past and the infinite future.

It is this kind of myth – beneath the screen of rationalism, and sensed with the faculties of 'feeling' – which nestles in the hearts of us all. Like the virus, which sleeps as a mineral for thousands of years until the right chemical conditions surround and resurrect it, so too are the eternal myths passed among us for thousands of generations – inert and purely legendary – until the time is ripe for them to flower into life. Like the paleontologist who assembles decayed and unknown bones until the unthinkable diplodocus roams, alive, through the jungles of our past, we too can now assemble the disparate bones of legend into the living giants of eternal meaning.

These subjective myths and legends are putting forth ever stronger shoots from the dark recesses of our culture, and though they blend and intertwine in myriad variations we can detect three essential themes: the Garden of Eden, Star People and the Invisible World Myths.

1. *Garden of Eden myths* see mankind, over recent millennia, as having degenerated from root-races and cultures of great spiritual and technological knowledge which flowered in a golden age of antiquity, and which were destroyed to be reborn (perhaps many times) in aeons more distant than the limitations of today's science would let us believe. We can see that anthropology, for instance with Dr Leakey's work at the Alduvai Gorge in South Africa, has in the space of the *last ten years* extended the hypothesized age of man from one million to over two and a half million years – and with every year our origins recede in time. Thus ten years ago our view of our origins was as 'mythic' as those of today's anthropologists – neither more nor less 'real' than the esoteric myths of Adam and Eve or Atlantis.

We know that by today's accepted time-scale, if the entire age of the earth, from the time it cooled down enough to support life, were reduced to the scale of a twenty-four-hour day, man's emergence on the scene would occupy less than the last minute. But beneath the confusion of the rational theories about our ethnic origins spring the esoteric myths of the early 'root-races', the primal seedlings of humanity, which inhabited the now lost continents of Atlantis, of Mu or Lemuria in the Pacific, and of the once warm and fertile polar regions.[16] But all these were destroyed by sudden cataclysms which plunged Atlantis and Lemuria beneath the waves, and the polar regions into ice and snow. These unheavals are still traceable in local myths from Indonesia to Mexico. Velikovsky's explosively titled books[17] argue that such Armageddons have occurred various times in the earth's history – the most recent one being less than 200,000 years ago, altering the earth's axis and leaving the north pole in the area of what is now S.E. Asia. The physical footprints of this myth begin to materialize, from the decaying coral reefs off Spitzbergen to the coal deposits in Antarctica which are evidence of that continent once being mantled with tropical forest.

Mammoth tusks are still washed up on the beaches of Arctic islands. The Leningrad Museum has defrosted perfectly preserved mammoths from the snows of Siberia with freshly-eaten semi-tropical flora in their stomachs. Analysis in mountain ranges of certain crystals polarized along the earth's magnetic field at the time of their formation points to the earth having suddenly changed its axis – perhaps several times – well within man's (even present) paltry reckoning of his age.

To filter out the data of one framework of myth means that another acquires greater power and reality. Charles Fort, the nineteenth-century American eccentric, amassed 'facts' which, because they did not fit the tacitly held framework of science, were ignored by it. The Fortean Society continues his work today, collecting objects, photographs and those brief and mysterious references which occasionally appear in the papers and drop forever from sight because they cannot – despite the fascination they hold for us – be *placed* in the context of how we think existence works. The Society's data range from the bones of humanoid giants to the perfectly tooled pieces of unknown metal discovered in coal seams thousands of feet beneath the earth's surface.

It is these inner myths which hint that the vanished civilization of our globe – the Egyptians, the Aztecs and the Mayas – were masters of a different order of knowledge; they were adepts in the science of vibrationary harmonies, and their aim was simply to attune themselves to the energies which our century is only just beginning to counternance. They did not try, as we have done, to keep the universal energies at bay, to separate themselves from nature with machines and industry. On the contrary, their knowledge involved a science so advanced that it had far outstripped the impedimenta of technology, and man himself was seen as the only 'temple', the prism which mediated all energies.

It is here that we sense the roots of wisdom behind the saying 'knowledge is freedom'; for this was not the knowledge of linear rationalism alone, but the knowledge of the 'irrational' dimensions which are just as real but which require subtler and more elevated human faculties than reason to discern them. For 'freedom' is simply freedom to be *ourselves*, to find our equilibrium in the multi-dimensional web of life. It was the 'eating of the apple' of linear and rational knowledge which gradually blinded us to the deeper dimensions which unify the earthly and universal harmonies, and which curtailed our freedom.

It is in these Garden of Eden myths, which have their parallels in many different cultures' stories of creation (when man walked with the Gods among the Elysian fields of sunlight, 'naked' of the pretensions of rational separatism), that we detect the scent of our timeless potential

– our latent capacity to integrate our outer and inner worlds. This promise, which in myth we may project into the distant mists of linear time, is really immediately *here* in eternal and mythic time; for all the faculties of knowledge are this instant locked in the sleeping miasma of flesh and psyche which we call ourselves, and the Valhalla of integration is not so 'distant' as we might suppose.

Myths of the Olmec and Maya Indians of Mexico tell of their forbears originally coming from the East – across the Atlantic – bringing with them the 'cosmic knowledge' which was the seed of the great Meso-American cultures. The knowledge is reflected in the pre-Hispanic exactitude of calendars, astronomy and the awareness of cycles, from a time before the religion became corrupted and the 'sacrifice' of the 'heart' to the life-giving power of the sun degenerated into the literal tearing out of human hearts on the Sungod's altar.

On the other side of the Atlantic, Egyptian mythology – reverberating down the centuries to Plato – speaks of the bringing of wisdom from the Gods of the *West*, prior to a great deluge which covered their continent. The geometry and mathematics of both early Egypt and America (as seen from the Great Pyramids of Ghiza, see Chapter 4) attest to their supreme understanding of our universe. Evidence from the early American calendar stones, as well as from Himalayan scrolls which predate Hinduism, point to an ancient knowledge of the existence of the planets Pluto and Uranus, which we pride ourselves on having discovered within the last century.

On both sides of the Atlantic the ancients attributed the bringing of this wisdom from the opposite side, which feeds the myth of the lost continent of Atlantis which once existed between them.[18]

Among the prognostications made by Edgar Cayce, the late American seer, was that early in the year 1962 the first traces of the sunken continent of Atlantis would re-emerge off the Bahamas. The story goes that, inspired by Cayce's previous success with predictions, the twenty-three-year-old daughter of a New Orleans millionaire chartered a light aeroplane with some friends in January 1962, and spent weeks of careful aerial reconnaissance over the clean Bahamian waters, until they found a regular formation off the north-west tip of Bimini Island. Subsequent diving expeditions to the area – some of them supervised by Dimitri Rebikoff, the pioneer of underwater cinematography – have revealed long, regularly laid walls of rectangular blocks at the edge of the continental shelf. Some of these weigh over 80 tons, and they lie in only 16 to 50 feet of water. Archaeologists can only suggest that they may either be part of a distant Maya outpost, or traces of a hitherto unknown 'Atlantic Civilization'. Here we see an example of how 'myth', enlivened by Cayce's clairvoyance, begins to ground itself in the reality of the material world.

The myths further speak of the antediluvian carrying of Atlantis's wisdom, in the 'arks' of survivors, to the high places of the globe, such as Tibet, Peru and Ethiopia. These places, where the oxygen is rarefied and the boundaries between the two worlds are more blurred, glow with myths, glyphs and architecture which attested to a different order of knowledge. For over a decade now they have been the 'golden fleeces' of the peripatetic hippies, the twentieth-century pilgrims who journey on rough and often dangerous trails in search of the traces of an ancient wisdom; to those high pockets where the waters of life were once distilled, and where some drops still remain. Everywhere about the globe, for those with a nose for today's emergent mythology, there are clues to a Garden of Eden – shattered by some cyclic upheaval – where man once walked as a giant, united with the rhythms of the cosmos.

2. *Star People myths*. Our sense of distance from 'meaning', our shining origins, is projected into the distance of time past, as well as into spatial distance, and Star People myths – which are a different dimension of Garden of Eden myths (and more clothed in the symbolism of our technological orientation) – tell of visitors from outer space who in distant antiquity descended to earth to crossbreed with the early humanoid creatures in order to boost their evolution. Is this perhaps a symbol for the enigmatic process of 'mutation', whereby a species somehow makes a leap – with no 'earthly' precedent – on to a higher cycle of the evolutionary spiral?

The Toradja people of the mountains of Celebes island tell of their royal descendants coming from the constellation of Pleiades, the Seven Sisters, 'following the rainbow's arc, and powered by the lightning's fork'. They still build their homes, great arcs of woven bamboo and rattan, painted with the rhythmic spirals of vibration, to remind them – they say – of the ships which brought their ancestors through space. Now that they have begun to replace their sago roofs with shining corrugated iron (the ubiquitous by-product of Western technology) their 'arcs' even more closely resemble the upward curvature of flying saucers. The Toradja sepulchres are in the same form, and the purpose of their funeral rituals is to send the souls of their dead across the waters of the 'invisible sea' which separates them from the star of their origins.

On Bali, another Indonesian island, the traditional method for calming a child when he cries at night is to take him outside to look up at the stars – at the infinity of light and space which remind the human heart that sorrow is relative.

This 'Star' myth has gathered momentum in the West through the books of Erich von Daniken,[19] which provide evidence that ancient civilizations evolved, or copied from somewhere, a knowledge of space travel. He brings to our mythic, if not rational, attention the existence of electric batteries in Bronze Age Persia, of stone maps in Iceland of the earth from a non-terrestrial viewpoint, of golden 'flying machine' models from Japan, two millennia old, which have been tested in contemporary wind tunnels and found to be as aerodynamically sophisticated as today's supersonic jets. He brings to our attention again the bones of humanoid giants from Java and Northern Europe – giants which appear in our fairy-tales and Nordic myths as Gods, before later degenerating into ogres, and finally into extinction – like God Himself. Everywhere in the remains of our distant antiquity there are clues to a lost knowledge, from the vast and perfectly-fitted monoliths and walls of decaying cities to their inhabitants' knowledge of outer space.

Glistening in this myth are the 'Star Children', the stellar mutants which walk among us, and which we may be ourselves – the pure descendants of the union between terrestrial and galactic beings. Throughout the 'sleeping ages' – those ebbs in the vast rhythms of evolution – the Star Children band together in secret communities, nurturing the inherited wisdom in their blood. But in the times of great change the wisdom flowers through them again; whether bards, leaders or artists, their voices and eyes are clear, like lenses through which a broader dimension shines, and they attend as midwives at the birth of renascent vision.

Man's recent nausea at his surroundings has made him look up at the sky again, and there he sees lights and shining ships, from whose speed and mysterious beauty he knows that he is not alone, but visited by 'signs' attesting perhaps to a greater order and purpose. George Adamski's book *Flying Saucers Have Landed*,[20] published in the mid twenties, was like the Fuegan shaman asserting that there really *was* something to be seen *outside* ourselves. Since that time thousands of sightings have been recorded, scores of books and articles written and societies have blossomed with international networks to correlate the data.

The Condon Report, incorporating twenty years of U.S. Airforce research into UFOs and covering nearly 8,000 sightings, salvaged merely 253 which finished up in the 'unidentified' basket. For the 'saucer seer', these are more than enough; for the cynic, there can never be enough, and even these 253 are explained away via devious rational myths. But already the UFO myth has caught on; scholars look back into the annals of history for UFO sightings, even into the Old Testament, and find them. Wanderers and sailors, when they look at the sky, cannot help but feed the flames of the myth 'whose time has come' by constantly seeing UFOs. But, shackled to rationalism, many of us try to find out what flying saucers *are*, instead of what they *mean*.

It is interesting that the case against UFOs is based on the same logical error which sustained for so long the geocentric cosmology, since it maintains that whatever we see up there, we know what it is. If I do not know, then someone else round here does. The medieval clerics who refused to look through Galileo's telescope were afraid to abandon themselves to the power of a new myth. But Galileo, with the same innocence as the man who has actually watched sky objects moving faster and with more versatility than anything made by man, could only say 'look, and *see*'. For a culture to ignore UFOs, to try to reason them out of existence, is analogous to an individual ignoring a powerful and recurrent dream: its message (if it is real, which this is) cannot be suppressed, and will insistently make itself known in different and more drastic symbolic guises until its meaning *is* recognized. For the collective unconscious is far more powerful than the individual unconscious – it is a living, macrocosmic entity, the invisible, evolving organism of the planet earth, which in its wisdom responds (long before our individual 'conscious' egos) to the moving forces of changing consciousness.

The Star myth asks what creatures watch us, what miracles of civilization – as I sit reading – are at this moment unfolding in the same universe as myself? Where are we now, and where have we been in the past, touched by corporeal gods?

3. *Invisible World myths*. A further strand of myth, which unites and transcends the previous two, includes those which maintain that we are immersed in deeper and different dimensions of reality to those which this culture normally 'sees'. These myths tell of our subtler faculties – either atrophied or barely awakening – which, once alive, can reveal the symbiotic unity of 'unseen' energies which unite the entire physical and metaphysical universe. It is in these areas of altered consciousness – which each of us has at some time glimpsed through dreams, drugs,

waking visions or moments of great danger – that time and space are experienced quite differently.

Despite the space/time discoveries now being made by the biologists and physicists (with reference for instance to the behaviour of photons or electrons) we are still as fearful of freeing ourselves from our habitual concept of space/time as, five hundred years ago, we were of relinquishing the concept of the earth as the centre of the universe. Examining the inseparability of space and time now countenanced by science brings us surprisingly close to the 'One-ness', the spiral circularity of our space/time environment, the existence of which has been maintained for centuries by travellerrs in higher states of consciousness.

Invisible-world myths, then, hover about the knowledge of those peoples, both ancient and contemporary, who were specialists in the deeper reaches of consciousness. It requires no great mental leap to realize that whereas mechanical laws hold true for one level of phenomenal reality – allowing us to construct the labyrinthine edifice of technocracy which now surrounds us – *different* laws maintain in the more rarefied superstrata of existence. This is the area which the secret 'science of religion' deals with – and it is the fragments of this supreme science which lie buried in the giant megaliths of superstition which most of the world's 'great religions' have now become. The scent of invisible-world myths drifts to us from the archetypes of our own radial unconscious which appear (a) in Britain, in the guise of the ancient Druids and the traditions of Celtic magic; (b) in America, in the vanishing wisdom of the Red Indian cultures; and (c) on both sides of the Atlantic in the mystery of the Oriental traditions which seep down from the Himalayas, the plains of Persia and the Javanese jungles into the western mind.

(a) The Druids, along with those other vanished cultures which we mythically remember, are known to have possessed a subtle 'technology' so far in advance of ours that it is difficult for us to imagine even its frame of reference. Our science, for instance, has brought us the motor car so that we can get from *a* to *b* supposedly with less effort than by walking. But the magician's frame of reference precludes the endless need to 'travel' in the lateral dimension – or to 'light' his universe synthetically with electrical power stations, or to commune with his brothers (those participants in his own soul) via the tentacular confusion of a telephone system. All the keys to 'travel', 'light', 'communication', etc., are locked, in the utmost simplicity, in the sleeping soul of man. To be aware of the flux of energies in which being and meaning are cradled, means also that the priorities of our *needs* are unrecognizably altered. Recent measurements and research[21] have shown the megalithic sites such as Stonehenge and Avebury to be built to 'golden mean' proportions which mirror the movements and altering energies of the earth through space. Professor Thom's recent surveys suggest that these sites were measured in megalithic yards, which, like the Egyptian cubit – in contrast to today's arbitrary units of measurement – are a proportion directly in keeping with a unitary cosmic hierarchy; the same proportion as is reflected in musical octaves, variations of colour on the electromagnetic spectrum and the mean distances between stellar bodies – as we shall see in the chapter on 'sacred geometry'. But, like the Egyptian pyramids, or the temples of Chichén Itzá in Mexico, or Machu Pichu in Peru, the 'standing stones' in Europe were much more than astronomical observatories. Druid mythology too, with its alphabet deriving from the trees and their time of blossoming, indicates that these stones mirrored the points of vibrationary change in the electrical or 'plasma' body of the planet. Catching these tides, knowing how to move, feel, plant and reap with them, was the essence of ancient religious science, and its architecture sought literally (as well as symbolically) to unite man with the forces which maintain the biosphere of which he is a part.

Even in legend, the 'Aladdin's lamps where myths tend to wait in hibernation, we sense the resonance of primeval truth. The Druid myths, for instance, link with the legends that Joseph of Aramithea brought the next 'evolutionary step' – Christianity – to the shores of Britain at Glastonbury in the symbolic Holy Grail, a magical chalice which, together with its mysteries, was preserved in the legends of the wizard Merlin and King Arthur. Thus 'Glastonbury' or 'Arthurian' mysticism, so richly revived in recent years, became entwined with the later guardians of the Holy Grail, the Masons, who brought their wisdom of harmony and proportion to the medieval cathedrals, and whose persecuted lodges harboured the first burning crucibles of European alchemy. These myths of the 'western mysteries' tradition have been preserved and nurtured in the arcane and magical groups, and now flow like tributaries into the fermenting humus of cultural belief.

As already mentioned, myths may lie dormant and inert for millennia, like the virus, until the 'chemical' time is right for them to exteriorize into rational fact. An example of this is British Geomancy – the practice of water divining, or dowsing for 'ley lines' – which has sprung into life from the sub-rational power-house of Celtic and Druidical myth. This re-discovery was focused through Charles Watkin's book *The Old Straight Track*,[22] published in 1925, and its resurgence shows again how the intangible – once powerful enough – bears tangible fruit.

Water diviners had often noticed 'rod reactions' which did not indicate either hidden water or other physical geological factors. One of the requirements in learning how to dowse is in fact to ignore those specific reactions which are known to reveal 'nothing'. These reactions (for example the willow branch or dowsing rod leaping *up*, instead of *down* as it would to indicate water) have since been found out to be responding to what geophysicists refer to as 'geodetic force lines', and occultists refer to as 'leys'.

These can be traced across the country by experienced dowsers, and show offshoots from the main stream (or 'whorls') known as 'positive' or 'negative' nodes. Country lore has long known the positive nodes to be favoured by wild animals for giving birth on. Even cows, which prefer to wander along ley lines, will, if possible, branch off to have their calves on positive nodes. It is also over these nodes that insects, such as gnats, hover in summer months, returning to their position when blown away from it by a breeze. Negative nodes, in all cultures (particularly China) which have known of these forces, are recognized as having an unhealthy and disorienting effect on the houses unwittingly built on them. They are also the sites favoured by certain plants – particularly the weeping willow tree. It is interesting that the willow, in Britain and other European countries, has long been known as the 'Sorceress's Tree'[23] and today's magical groups still often begin training the more 'dense' and earthbound of their initiates by introducing them to the sense of vibration apparent under a healthy willow at full moon. What truth, one wonders, lies hidden behind the Lancashire superstition: 'Build your house *between* willows; never uproot them.'

Dowsing for leys has proved a useful archaeological tool, since the points where strong concentrations of leys converge – like the spokes at the hub of a wheel – appear to be where the ancients built their 'magic circles'. Several 'standing stones' and barrows have recently been unearthed in Cumberland by dowsing along leys, finding their strongest point of convergence, and digging. Since a conquering religion usually places its temples over the shrines of the earlier religion, powerful ley convergences also tend to be where the foundations of medieval cathedrals were built. Guy Underwood,[24] a life-long dowser, describes how workmen several years ago were trying to repair the steeple of Canterbury Cathedral – whose apse is built on a powerful hub of leys –

and were repeatedly driven off by a swarm of flying ants which happily buzzed in the 'column of power' surrounding the steeple.

Grace Cooke describes a waking vision she had during a summer evening at Stonehenge when she saw re-enacted the solstice dawn ceremony as it took place before the time of Christ. As the sun rose precisely between the two central monoliths – as it does to this day, except for the slight variation caused by the precession of the equinoxes – the stone was charged with vibration, and turned a translucent rose, like quartz, sending waves of power along the network of leys throughout the country, transforming the columns in its path into tuning-forks of energy.

However 'irrational' their power, these sites yearly draw increasing numbers of pilgrims – particularly at the solstices and equinoxes. The historic Glastonbury Fayre, held over the week of the summer solstice of 1971, was preceded by days of careful dowsing for the placing of the forty-foot pyramid, containing the musicians' platform, which mirrored the geometry of Ghiza (see Chapter 4). The music itself was secondary to what was in fact a religious festival, one which drew thousands of people from all over Britain and the Continent who sensed the power of the emergent myths of the late twentieth century. There was no prior announcement of the festival, the news travelled throughout the esoteric grapevine, like energy along ley-lines, that this was a massive interdenominational witnessing of the quickening of the cosmic energy which regularly floods the aetheric network of Britain. This ritual, within sight of King Arthur's burial-place, was not without its visions in the sky, and will be remembered by many who attended it as one of the truly alive religious celebrations of this century.

Geomancy is but one of the areas where the 'myth' of the existence of subtle forms of energy has begun to precipitate into *facts*, and their rational recognition. These energies, recycled by the seasonal angles between the earth and the stellar bodies, have long been recognized in other cultures, and in China form the basis of 'Feng Shui' or Chinese geomancy, which the anthropologist Maurice Freedman[25] has referred to as 'mystical ecology'. It is here that ecology rings a deeper note; it becomes a 'sacred' undertaking rather than a sudden panic for our survival. The earth is seen as an animal to be husbanded, an organism pulsating in the same cosmic groundswell in which we ourselves swim, and we think again of the early seventeenth-century discussion between Johannes Kepler, one of the fathers of modern astronomy, and the occultist Robert Fludd on the priority of seeing the earth as a living creature, whose 'whale-like respiration', corresponding to sleep and waking, produces the ebb and flow of the tides. Kepler even went on to study this creature's anatomy, its nourishment, its colour, its memory and its imaginative and plastic vigour.[26]

The Chinese also recognized that while the earth is webbed with vital though invisible streams of energy, so too, in a lower key, are animals. In the human body they called it 'Qi', and it also consists of positive and negative currents, which correspond to the nervous system no more than blind springs correspond to ley lines. It is into these 'Qi' streams that the needles of the acupuncturist are placed in order to harmonize the metabolic 'ecology' of a patient.

(b) In America, where the amalgam of different peoples results in a richly varied store-house of racial memories, there has been the recent emergence of the Red Indians as the source of a wisdom still to be discovered; so too with all the primitive peoples of the world who nurture memories of Eden: the Egyptians, the Eskimos, the Incas and others. In the Southern States' deserts, bordering on Mexico, the vision of the Peyote God, brought to vivid life by Carlos Castaneda's description of his odyssey into a different reality under the guidance of Don Juan, the shaman, has helped to shift the poles of consciousness.[27]

Inspired by different shamanistic experiences, people are now attempting to re-learn the capacity of seeing through their dreams – using those neglected areas of consciousness (so denigrated by rationalism) as tools for self-knowledge. Although this practice is widespread it has become semi-institutionalized in the Institute of Dream Research at the Maimonodes Hospital in New York. But the incentive comes from those fading cultures which, in order to survive, developed the faculties which could mesh with, and perceive, the soul of their environment. At the antipodes of the earth we still find the Aborigines training themselves to see with their 'inner eyes', to know precisely where their prey is on the other side of a mountain, to go 'walkabout' and travel directly and alone, for hundreds of miles, to their tribe – homing in on the beacon of their nomadic group soul. In these living myths man catches the scent of omniscience; they gradually become as real as Magellan's ships in Tierra del Fuego. People are returning to the earth, feeding on its vibrations, living in organic communes. No naïve Rousseauean 'divine savages' these, but technological savages. The first outer changes in response to the new myth appeared in America: the sudden growth of hair, like an unchecked emergence from the natural world; the clothes borrowed from the romantic, nomadic peoples – the Apaches, the Afghans, the frontiersmen of Alaska, the almost-naked, beaded Polynesians. They sought to let the body reflect the vision which had touched their hearts, and they questioned how, in a universe reverberating with filtered light, our culture should have worn for so long the clipped costume of greys and blacks; the suit, with a white collar which constricts the organ of speech and song.

(c) For several decades now the great source of mythic vocabulary has come from the East, from the kernels of Tantric and Zen Buddhism, Hindu Yoga and the Sufi enclaves of Islam. Here are reinforced the Western mysteries beliefs in the 'knowable' existence of a hidden world, the capacity for astral projection, the releasing of the body's myopia, the recognition that the 'life force' in food affects the 'life force' of the body which eats it: 'You are what you eat.' Here too is corroboration not only of the existence of the 'subtle body', but of its actual anatomy: the 'chakras', or aetheric power-points in the vibrationary fields which maintain us, and the coloured auras which they emanate (see Chapter 6). The concepts of karma, reincarnation and the transmigration of souls have all crept into the language, blending with the mythopaeic experience which is being shared and distilled.

As the astronomer H. S. Haldane puts it: 'The universe may well be not only queerer than we suppose, but queerer than we *can* suppose.'

Yet the cycles of myths through which we 'suppose' are continually spiralling through the rhythms of inner and outer perception, each time taking some of the previously acquired insights with them. The outer myth of science is giving way to the inner myths of subjective meaning, while still retaining the knowledge acquired through rationalism. As Bryan Wilson remarks, in a society where intellectual criteria dominate 'it may well be that what cannot be intellectually accepted cannot be emotionally reassuring'.[28]

Man is increasingly rejecting the traditional symbols used to articulate the Numinous, in favour of symbols closer to his present experience. Thus congregations are drifting away from the churches not because the essential Mystery is powerless over technological man, but because the symbolic attitude of the age has shifted.

Those who ask how non-objective myths can possibly stand up against the weight of reason must first ask how constant are the myths of fact, and how 'reasonably' we guide our lives. When he who feels the power of inner myth is challenged to provide evidence to justify his belief in distant Golden Ages in which man built temples reflecting invisible worlds, and was visited from outer space, his answers are no less valid than the ephemeral criteria of rationality. First, there is the growing body of esoteric knowledge, large enough to treat statistically, to forge into the kind of theories which actually gestate truth. Secondly, with the upper echelons of science now increasingly open to the 'impossible', facts continually come to light which, though they may threaten a man's reputation, no longer threaten the entire cultural world view in the same way, and are at least filed, rather than rejected and lost. Finally, since even rocks and consequently artifacts decay over several million years, the stream of history remains unbroken only in the chemistry of our own bodies – altered, but not broken – and it is in the genes of racial memory that the great truths are preserved and, once sensed, can be re-awakened.

For this reason the questions of cataclysm and lost horizons of knowledge in our distant past are being answered no longer so much by the 'diggers in the earth' – the palaeontologists and archaeologists – as by the 'diggers in memory' – the anthropologists and psychologists of myth.

The new rhythm of vision we have entered upon is thus a fusion of inner and outer myth. To see through this framework involves turning away from, rather than ignoring, the factual restraints of our inheritance – and again the new world is seen to be alive with energies, with deities and demons, but viewed as altered symbols. For symbols – the stuff both of feeling and of knowledge – rather than being the lenses through which we see reality, are the very *organs* of reality itself. So, with all the symbols at our disposal, let us look up at the stars again.

3   Astral Logic

I saw eternity the other night
Like a great ring of pure and endless light,
All Calm as it was Bright,
And round beneath it, Time; hours, days, years,
Driven by the spheres,
Like a vast shadow moved, in which the world
And all her train were hurled.

HENRY VAUGHAN

'Cosmologies' are the most abstract as well as the most fundamental of a civilization's views of itself. Deriving from the Greek word *kosmos*, meaning 'order', a cosmology refers to a single, holistic system in which the *totality* of our experiences may be encompassed. Despite the disorder which exists among today's conflicting cosmologies, an essential unified pattern is emerging, for instance in contemporary physics' recognition that matter consists simply in its own movement and organization. Mind, too: the process of thought (whether viewed from the outside in, by neurosurgeons, or from the inside out, by psychologists) consists, no less simply, in its own movement and organization.

The realization that both matter and thought ultimately interweave in the same enigmatic matrix of rhythms of movement indicates a fundamental change in our view of 'reality'. This reality consists simply in the vibrationary rhythms of movement, from the most rational and distant discoveries of the giant radio-telescopes to the myths and moods which ripple through the human heart.

We shall begin with the more 'rational' area of this emergent cosmology, and move progressively inwards to our individually experienced cells and psyches.

To become aware of this universe involves seeing as 'real' what to date has culturally been considered invisible. Just as the microscope revealed a real and immediate world which had until then been out of sight and mind, the lens of the electromagnetic spectrum reveals an additional and no less immediate vision. It is this invisible world, with its streams of ionized particles, vibrationary frequencies and magnetic fields, which is now more *real* to the astro- and geophysicist than the visible one. Rather as the X-ray photograph presents us with the solid reality of the skeleton, while the flesh, which is more familiar to us, hangs about it only as a nebulous ghost, the new 'eyes' of science see the sensible world only as an indistinct haze within the lambence of its radiations.

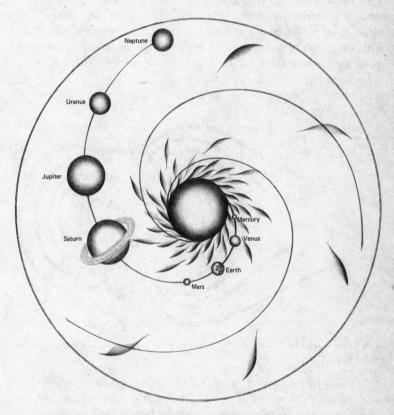

3. From a space/time perspective, a 'head on' view of the solar body, containing its spiralling planetary organs. From a purely 'space' perspective, of course, the planets orbit the sun in ellipses, but when the dimension of 'time' is also considered then – in 2-dimensions – they can be seen as spiralling.

The sun which we see in the sky, for instance, is but the *kernel*, the only visible part of a much larger sun, the sun which envelops the very limits of the solar system with its radiative body. The earth is *within* the sun, plunged in the solar wind, spiralling with its sister planets like organs within the same solar body. I can touch the sun with my face, even in the dark.

This new shape of our earth with its phasing away of solar energies on the night side, its veins of geo-magnetism, the giant, hovering vortices of the Van Allen belts, has a strangely unfamiliar profile – much larger and more fluid than before, glowing with electrical fires. Our own bodies, too, are each but the visible kernel of a broader, invisible self which extends around us, and with which we can feel another's body. The blending of subtle bodies activates an ever-changing chemistry; to sit within four feet of someone for over ten minutes is already to exchange water vapour with them, for we are as much a part of each other as are the planets in the system of the sun.

4. The terrestrial body, swathed in an envelope of force fields, swimming in the Solar Body.

But does it really matter to me that the earth is not flat; would my life be lived any differently if it were? Our children's textbooks still bristle with diagrams of the solar system which, set next to the dimensions now entertained by cosmology, are flat indeed. We still see the sun depicted as the centre of a clockface, with the planets revolving round it like hands of different lengths and speeds. 'Relativity' is ignored, presumably because it is considered too abstract; yet it is an immediate abstraction, one which touches each one of us now.

If I drop an onion, its path traced from my hand to the floor looks like a straight line, but since the earth's surface is moving on its axis at the rate of 1000 m.p.h. at the equator, in space the onion's trajectory is really a *diagonal*, or rather, since the points on the earth's surface are moving *round* its axis, a *curved* diagonal. But the earth arcs round the sun at 66,000 m.p.h. in a different plane to the curved diagonal, so the onion's fall is really a spiral. The relationship of speed, mass and time are here in my hand but to realize this the imagination still waits anxiously to be released from the gravity of a long-outdated cosmology.

If we just eat the onion and forget about its contortions, and turn instead to the solar system, the sun, at the edge of the Milky Way

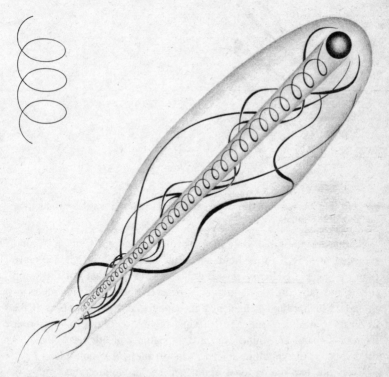

6. The 'long body of the solar system' seen in an eighty-year 'macro-moment' of perception. The 30,000-million-mile-long gossamer seed of energy is spiralling into the void between the constellations of Lyra and Hercules. (After Rodney Colin, *The Theory of Celestial Influence*.)

galaxy, is itself travelling – in order to keep up with it – at 481,000 m.p.h., and the Milky Way in turn circles around a supercluster of galaxies at the rate of 1,350,000 m.p.h. Thus our tiny solar system, like the onion, is really spiralling *behind* the sun; the whole organism, like an incandescent sperm-cell – or the microscopic infusoria which it resembles, is screwdriving through space/time with the planetary orbs in its twisting, golden tail.

7. (Left) The microscopic 'Infusoria', the water organism which resembles the body of any spiralling form.

Spirals are more than the timeless symbols of eternity which we find scrawled or woven throughout our earliest mythology; they are more than the layers of Hieronymus Bosch's 'Tower of Babel', or the spiral mazes and labyrinths of antiquity – or even the spiral hierarchies of thought which awed the ancient philosophers, and such poets as Blake or Yeats. Spirals are the actual 'shape' of fluid energy evolving order from chaos, and are found even in the anatomy of our own biological inheritance – the spiralling nucleic acids in the DNA molecule.

Even the two-dimensional spiral reflects its connections with the higher dimensions of growth. It both begins and ends in infinity; it is a continuum which mirrors the harmonic ebb and flow between the polarities of positive (+) and negative (−), as well as between the polarities of infinite contraction, at the centre, and infinite expansion, at the periphery. In a three-dimensional spiral – the spherical vortex – the opposing infinities dissolve into one another. It is *visibly* infinite; its beginning is joined to its end, it perpetually spirals into and out of its own middle, its centre and its circumference eternally alternating their roles.

More than a symbol, this three-dimensional spiral is the form of the Van Allen belts which hover over the poles of our planet. With its simpler spiral sisters, it is the form of *order* which exists on the very brink of non-existence; the most 'passive' of elements (water, gases, even electrical fields) express themselves in these twisting doughnut-shapes, from a smoke-ring blown from the lips, to a drop of milk released into placid water. The mushrooms which materialize in the field are governed by the same vortical laws as the mushrooms which de-materialized most of Hiroshima and Nagasaki in the summer of 1945.

More familiar spiral forms – showing the harmonic stages of recuperation, repetition and growth in life's ascent from chaos to order – are found in the three primal movements of water (Fig. 9) which in turn govern the forms of many of the higher constellations of order – including ourselves. The spiral's symbolic depth connects us to the sustenance of our invisible source as surely as, in the biological dimension, we were once connected to our mothers by the spiralling umbilical cord; for the spiral is a living thread which can lead us to different dimensions of vision and energy.

Even if we return to a flat representation of the solar system, we tend in our everyday lives to think of the sun and planets as 'way out there', on the other side of the sky. The earliest objections to astrology ask how we can possibly be affected by planetary bodies so exceedingly distant from and peripheral to our onions in the kitchen. Yet the question stems from a myopia which is the twentieth-century equivalent to the geocentric and 'flat earth' theories. Whereas we were once addicted (in our actual thinking) to the focal depth of the linear dimension, to the exclusion of other dimensions, we are now only just emerging from our addiction to 'mass' or matter – a concept which excludes the dimension of *space* or non-mass. The 'space' in an atom, for instance, has been illustrated by comparing its electrons to a few bees buzzing around inside the dome of St Paul's Cathedral – the dome representing the constraints imposed by the orbiting protons and neutrons. Thus the sun and planets are no more *distant* from us than are the electrons in the cells *inside* my hand distant from the electrons in the cells on its surface.

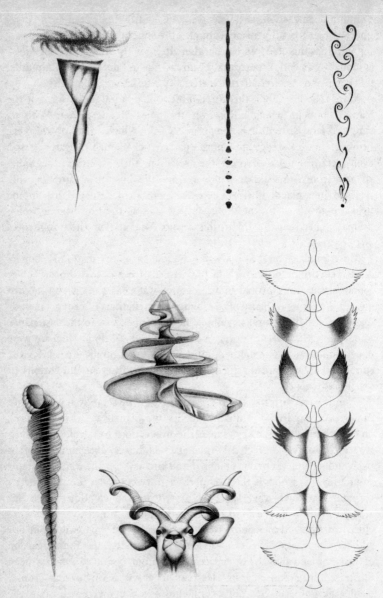

9–13. The three harmonic movements of water: as a current of eddies, as a dropping stream, and as a spiral – or vortical funnel. The vibrationary harmonics which water obeys are the same which condition the growth of bones, shells, antlers, plants and internal organs.

The distances are similarly astronomic, yet I seldom question the integrity of my hand.

It is the recognition of this symbiosis between matter, space and time which is beginning to breed the new science of 'cosmo-rhythmology' – the detection of rhythms or bio-cycles in the unified field of life which mantles the earth, and which Teilhard de Chardin,[1] the Jesuit priest and scientist, termed the 'Bio-sphere'.

The delayed growth of this branch of learning – typical of a science which always seeks to *ground* itself – is largely due to resistance to the belief that the planets can have any mechanical effect on us. Yet the sun and moon, it appears, exert a more empirical influence over us than economics, that powerful fluctuating invention of our own minds which rules our lives.

It has been calculated that the cycles of our moon regularly raise and release the city of Moscow by twenty inches twice a day, as well, of course, as raising millions of tons of water with the tides, which in certain areas reach fifty feet in height – fifty feet of fish, weed and ships. At the purely mechanical level, then, our physical bodies are less dense than land, which is raised twenty inches by the moon alone, and only slightly more dense than water, which is raised fifty feet. But it is at this point that 'mechanics' begins to move into physics, in the way that physiology in medicine has moved into chemistry; for the subtler envelopes round the earth, such as the rarefied gases in the atmosphere, are far more responsive to the planets. At Guanacayo, in Peru, lunar tides of forty miles in amplitude have been measured in the Appleton (F) ionized layer of the stratosphere.

Certainly the moon exerts the most obvious 'mechanical' effect, since it is 385 times closer than the sun, but the sun's mass is twenty-six

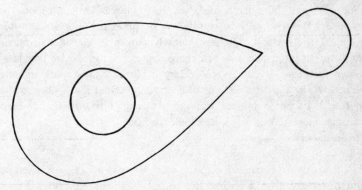

million times larger than the moon, and in the realm of invisible physics its distance is no longer a conceptual barrier to its effect on us – since the Newtonian theory of a mechanical universe has long been superseded by Einstein's photo-electric theory, which demonstrates that the effect of a photon does not diminish with distance.

Above the forty-mile lunar tides in the stratosphere is the ionosphere, a mantle of mainly ultra-violet solar radiations which is subject to vast invisible storms – to the consternation of no one but the radio men who use the mantle to bounce their transmissions round the globe.

No language seems a barrier to the hidden brotherhood of 'hams' and professional radio operators. They sit, all over the world, thousands of miles apart, yet connected by electronics – the only clue to their existence being the prongs of steel emerging discreetly from their attics. This international brotherhood never sleeps, but continually monitors and feeds the thought-forms of the planet: the political upheavals, the new discoveries, the disasters, are all exchanged within moments. Teilhard de Chardin's hypothetical 'Nousphere' – an envelope of 'thought' around the world – is now quite real. It is comforting to know that thousands of human ears constantly hover in the ionosphere, sensitive to the faintest, most isolated Mayday signal, like a pain-detecting nervous-system latticing the globe 200 miles above its surface.

This terrestrial nervous system, the ionosphere, is the source of 'poor' or 'good' radio weather, and there is now ample evidence to link ionospheric disturbance with the movement of the planets. John Nelson, formerly a 'propagation analyst' at RCA Communications, has discovered that these disturbances are associated with the angular relationships between the planets and the sun. If two or more planets are within 15°, or a multiple of 15°, from each other (e.g. 45°, 60°, 90° or 180° – all the traditional 'trines', 'sextiles', 'squares' or 'oppositions' of astrology) then ionospheric storms can be predicted. For still greater accuracy, the particular planets themselves must be considered; maximum interruption results when these angles are formed by two fast-moving planets (Mercury, Venus, Mars or Earth), and one slow-moving planet. Of the 1,460 predictions of bad radio weather that Nelson made in 1967, 93·2 per cent were accurate.[2] It seems fitting that when man becomes more aetherialized, he should also begin to find that he is part of the stars.

The study of our relationship to the cosmos has two faces – an exoteric and an esoteric face. The first, known as 'cosmo-rhythmology', is concerned with *quantifying*, and objectifying, the correlations between astral movements and events on earth; whereas the esoteric face (drawing much of its wealth from ancient wisdom) is concerned with the *qualitative* and subjectively experienced effects which these same correlations have on the human character and psyche. It is this astrology which – *beyond* the area of scientific measurement – unabashedly works with the languages of symbol and metaphor. In its full maturity, when freed from the cobwebs of superstition which invariably accompany the legacy of lost wisdom, this true astrology is as different from the pop astrology of the newspapers or the amateur next door as metallurgy or nuclear physics are from popular mechanics.

We shall begin with the scientific face of astrology – cosmorhythmology – which is as eager as all sciences to disassociate itself from anything smacking of superstition and, as its name implies, relies solely on a statistical approach to rhythms and cycles.

The Foundation for the Study of Cycles, in affiliation with the University of Pittsburg, has for over twenty years been correlating a mass of data which at first appears 'unconnected', but later shows itself to be precisely related through rhythms.[3] The 9·6 year cycle is shared by the incidence of heart disease, barometric pressure highs, salmon and lynx abundance in Canada, tree rings in Java, river overflows in Europe and ozone measurements in the atmosphere of Paris. The 3·86 year cycle is shared by the burst of growth in limber pines in North America and the mass suicides of lemmings in Norway. Stock market crashes go in cycles, people join and leave Churches in cycles, are born, die and commit suicide in cycles, women's skirts go up and down in cycles, bacteria in the human body abound and diminish in cycles, and so on. It is as if many circles are being drawn indiscriminately on a piece of paper. *Connecting* the cycles requires either a traditional unifying symbolism, grounded in newly available statistics, or a scientific reappraisal of the phenomena as a composite whole, rather than as a proliferation of separate parts. Already the two approaches are moving closer together, perhaps led by the powerful polarities of thought symbolized for millennia by the sun and the moon – the male/female, Rational/ Feeling opposites which were so vital a part of the psychologies of our ancestors.

The sun, like the earth, is a mysterious living being. It is culturally assumed that we know roughly what its physical kernel is, but this is far from being the case, and erudite theories are still flying into its enigma, like space-probes, and being consumed. A recent theory, still in flight, maintains that the sun's centre is a 'black hole' – that ultimate joke of physics, where matter is born from and disappears into nothing, independent of cause and effect as we know it. The sphere we see is only one and a half times denser than water, and in 1956 Mr K. Takashi, of the Japanese Meteorological Society, calculated that despite the fact that the sun comprises some 92 per cent of the solar system's matter, it has tidal oscillations which appear to be influenced by Mercury, Earth and Jupiter.[4]

Despite being 'liquid', the sun obeys its own form of hydrodynamics, its equator mysteriously revolving more *slowly* round its axis than its higher and lower latitudes. It is a seething giant of magnetism,* and it periodically exhibits blemishes, or sunspots, some of which could swallow a hundred earths. These spots, which were noted by the Chinese astronomers of antiquity, have a regular average cycle of 11·1 years, and they appear mainly in pairs, one in the northern and one in the southern hemisphere, each oppositely magnetized, as if they were the ends of a vast horseshoe magnet embedded in the sun. With each 11·1 year sunspot cycle, alternating like the yin and yang of Taoism, the polarities of the spots in the northern and southern hemispheres are reversed, spraying billions of differently charged particles throughout the solar system.

The Russian scientist A. L. Cizevskij made a life-long study of the correlations between rhythms of solar activity and the biological processes on earth – mainly 'mass excitability', as he called it, in the history of man from the fifth century B.C. until 1962. His work shows that wars and social unrest appear in about nine cycles per century – each averaging 11·1 years – like sunspots. Continuing his graph we see that the period of 1968 to 1979 promises to be socially tumultuous!

The vulcanologist T. A. Jaggar, who successfully predicted the 1929 and 1945 eruptions of Kilauea on Hawaii, did so by isolating the regular rhythms with which Kilauea and other volcanoes blew their tops. The smallest of these cycles was 11·1 years. The Iron Curtain countries seem to be in the vanguard of Aquarian Physics, and the Russians have recently correlated the 11·1 year sunspot cycle with global flu epidemics.

From Takashi's 'solar tides' it is clear that the sun, despite its size, is affected by the other planets or, as now seems more likely, that the

---

* Magnetism – along with gravity – is the force we know least about; these dual polarities of energy, and their hierarchical interplay, are also reflected in the history of religions and politics.

entire system responds to certain cyclical phases 'outside' it, giving the convenient impression of one unit affecting the other.* From our present perspective the relationship even between earth and moon is almost metaphysically subtle. Professor Frank Brown of Northwestern

15. Graph of the correspondences between sunspots and terrestrial magnetism between 1835 and 1930. The left curve shows magnetic activity, and the right curve shows sunspots over the same periods of time.

University has shown how 'biological clocks', which initiate such cyclical activities as 'been sleep' movement, rat-running, colour-change in Fiddler crabs, etc., are subject to lunar rhythms.[5] The better-known of his experiments involved the placing of oysters in hermetically-sealed and controlled containers, removing them from the shores of Newhaven where they were gathered, to Evanston, Illinois, 200 miles inland. Within a couple of weeks they had adjusted the opening and closing of their shells (their most salient rhythms) to the lunar phases above them, and thus to the lunar tides which would have existed at Evanston had it been on a coast. These small amorphous creatures, however well

* There is a parallel here with the way we know the earth to circle the sun but retain the convenience – for the purposes for instance, of navigation, of assuming that the sun circles the earth. Both views are quite correct within their *own terms* – which brings us back to relativity again.

shielded, continued to respond to the ubiquitous 'magnetism' of the moon.

But is this really so odd? The terrestrial environment is rich in electromagnetic phenomena and their secondary effects – and these in turn are demonstrably related to greater events, of the same nature, in outer space. Since supposedly 'inert' matter is electrical at the atomic level, it is hardly surprising that all life has an electric and therefore a magnetic potential. Dr H. S. Burr of Yale University has kept thousands of records of the regular voltage change in forests. He found that by drilling two holes in the trunk of a living tree, a yard or two apart and one above the other, and inserting the two ends of a wire in these holes, an electrical current can be measured flowing through the wire. This current flows sometimes up and sometimes down, at different voltages, but in regular cycles which are not directly correlatable to the moon. Whatever the nature of the current, it will be shared simultaneously by all the trees within thousands of miles: the electrical rhythm of the forest moves as a single *prahnic* breath.

As we may suspect from Clive Backster's experiments with the feelings of plants (explored in Chapter 5), trees harbour many mysteries. Botanists still puzzle about how sap, a heavy viscous fluid, can, without a pump, defy the laws of gravity and ascend hundreds of feet up the body of a tree. We see later (also in Chapter 5) how matter defies gravity on the vibrating disks of Chladni and Hans Jenny, where particles of sand can stand vertically and dance on one another. To what music do the trees, the plankton of the oceans and the human body dance?

Chemistry is considered, even by many chemists, to be a predictable science, but any serious cook knows that cooking is more than chemistry; that a fine and a poor omelette can result from mixing precisely the same ingredients for the same time over the same temperature.

Magical inconstants are at work at even the simplest level – for the simplest is always, paradoxically, the most mysterious. In the case of chemistry, it is water. Professor Picardi of Florence University, whose experiments have been widely duplicated throughout the world with similar success, showed that the rate at which bismuth oxychloride precipitated in distilled water *varied* from day to day. When shielded with copper, the substance, unlike Brown's oysters at Evanston, precipitated at a constant rate, but unshielded, the fluctuations were rhythmic as a heartbeat. This led Picardi and his colleagues to conclude that the rhythms were extraterrestrial. 'Water,' he wrote, 'is sensitive to extremely delicate influences, and is capable of adapting itself to the most varying circumstances to a degree attained by no other liquid.'[6]

His procedures were applied to other chemical interactions with water, particularly to colloids, with the same results. It need hardly be added that all life takes place in an aqueous and colloidal system, which exhibits, even at the microscopic level, electrical currents and magnetic polarities.

Thus the methods of the astrologers are being surreptitiously adopted by the cosmo-rhythmologists. Work has appeared correlating such phenomena as cyclones, hurricanes and earthquakes with planetary 'aspects', or angles. The German scientist Dr R. Tomaschek,[7] on examining the charts of 134 earthquakes equal or greater than magnitude 7 on the Richter scale, discovered that the position of Uranus was strongly significant – Uranus, incidentally, being the traditional planet of tension, disruption and revolutionary outbursts.

As a child in Mexico City I experienced many earthquakes, and I remember my family remarking on, and then trying to detect beforehand, the extraordinary feeling of apprehension which preceded a major quake. On the night of the great 1958 Mexico earthquake my brother and I were alone in the house. All that evening a kind of madness had been gathering in the air, driving us about the house in pointless games which were never finished. Suddenly, at 2.35 in the morning, all the parrots in the zoo, and most of the wolves, gave chilling tongue. The other creatures gradually took up the cry, the monkeys frantically trying to escape from their cages. This uproar lasted about four minutes, then died to utter silence; a minute later the great quake struck, felling buildings, splitting streets and power-cables, and leaving over 200 people dead in Mexico City alone. Folklore is full of such tales. Edward Dewey[8] describes how millions of birds which normally lodge on the shores of Lake Hegben, twelve miles from Yellowstone Park, began, at noon on 16 August 1959, to take to the sky. Eleven hours later not a bird was to be seen – to the wonder of the locals – and at midnight the first shocks of the terrifying Yellowstone earthquake were felt.

To what do these creatures respond: what qualities are heavy in the air and ourselves, of which we are unconscious?

It is at this point that we find our inquiry moving inwards, towards our own bodies and temperaments – towards the fledgling science of 'bio-rhythmology'. An intriguing series of papers on cosmo- and bio-rhythmology has been published by the Astra Research Foundation in

Nitra, Czechoslovakia. One of these, by Dr Zdenek Vocasek, studies the sun-moon phase angle in the astrological charts of people with Down's syndrome, or mongolism. A study of fourteen mongols' charts showed five with Mercury in Libra; a control sample of twenty healthy siblings to these showed only one case with the same configuration. With the 'aspects' taken into account, namely the angles formed by the planets to each other, seven of the mongols had Mercury opposition (at 180° from Venus) in their charts – the control group showing but one case. Since certain chromosomal distortions in the foetal stages of development are known to cause mongolism, Dr Vocasek went on to suggest that these could well be correlated with specific radiation interference which occurs during 'unfavourable' planetary aspects.

Although 'lunacy' has been recognized in folklore for centuries, only recently has medical opinion admitted that mental disorders may well be affected by slight modulations in the earth's magnetic and electrical fields – which in turn correlate with the moon, and its aspects to more distant planets. Statistically, more babies are born during a waxing than during a waning moon. Haemorrhaging in hospital operations is 82 per cent more likely to occur when the moon is between its first and third quarter. Lunar phases have now been correlated with crime, suicides, epileptic attacks and even car crashes. The bamboo knots at the full moon, and the twenty-eight-day rhythm has even left its pattern in the human sexual cycle, though most people think it is only women who respond to this. The precision of the original rhythmic patterns which

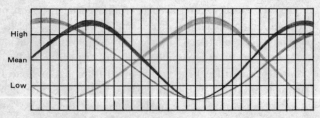

16. A typical bio-rhythm graph for one month – each vertical division representing a day. Beginning from the left, the middle curve represents the 23-day cycle of physical strength, endurance and energy; the lower one the 28-day cycle governing feelings, intuition and mood; and the upper one the 33-day cycle of reasoning power, memory and mental agility. The eleventh and twelfth days of this month, where the three curves are close to crossing each other at the 'mean' point between the high and low extremes, advise caution – since it is statistically the period when the person for whom this chart was made is 7 per cent to 8 per cent more accident-prone.

left their momentum in our bodies can be sensed from the lunar timing of the 'grunion'. This fish lays its eggs in the sand on the beach, to protect them from marine predators for the first twenty-eight days of its development. Being a fish, how does it manage this without getting stranded? It judges not only the highest equinoctial tide of the year, but precisely the highest wave of this tide: its yearly reproductive cycle is gauged to those few seconds in which it can be carried up, deposit its eggs and be carried back to safety again by the same wave.

With the discovery of three distinct bio-rhythmic cycles in man, cosmo-rhythmology begins to dovetail with astrology. The first of these rhythms is a pure physical energy cycle, lasting twenty-three days; the second, a 'feeling' or emotional cycle of twenty-eight days; and the third, an intellectual or cerebral cycle of thirty-three days. Each of these can be discerned merely from the positions, at the moment of our birth, of the sun, the moon and the planet Mercury. From the instant of our first breath, when we left the waters of the womb, the stella metronome was imprinted on our metabolism, and our three main cycles began to flow from peak to trough for the rest of our lives. Although the cycles are the same length for all of us, with each individual they will overlap at different times, or points on a graph, since the angular phases of the Sun, Moon and Mercury – which initiated these rhythms – were different for each of us at the moment of our birth.

Here is an interesting example of being unable to see what we have no *vocabulary* for seeing. Without a bio-rhythm chart, for instance, we can still easily detect when body, feelings and intellect are peaking, or troughing, together, since we know we are generally in an 'up' or 'down' period – where everything 'swings', or nothing seems to work. But with a chart we can actually realize the interplay of the three rhythms, and how they are differently combined at different periods. Linking the unconscious processes to 'awareness' of them at the conscious level is the first step to self-knowledge.

There are times when the emotions are vibrant, though the body and mind are dull, or when the mind's memory and precision far outstrip the emotional sensibilities, or the cramped and liverish condition of the body. These three curves on the graph can be noted to ascend from the 'recuperative' periods of low, up to the 'maximum efficiency' periods of high. The periods of least equilibrium in our systems are when the three curves cross each other at the same point. Statistical work in Switzerland and Germany, where much of the early bio-rhythmic work was carried out, has shown that at the mean point between the highest and lowest curves – that weakest moment just when the body is 'changing gear', as it were* – we are 7 to 8 per cent more accident prone. These discoveries are now increasingly being put to use by hospital and factory managements – particularly in America and Japan – to achieve the maximum efficiency and safety of their personnel.

The Omega Watch company has recently marketed a bio-rhythmic watch which, when set to the wearer's birth time, shows at a glance how his bio-rhythms are functioning for any given day. This is possibly the first technological instrument that enables the thoughtful wearer to order his life with greater awareness: he can begin to treat his body with the understanding that is any animal's right, contrary to the way we usually treat our bodies, driving them on like tanks over thick and thin, without the smallest clue as to the subtle integrity through which they work. With knowledge of our bio-rhythms we can face any important appointment, physical, mental or aesthetic, at the time when the corresponding faculties are at their peak: the boxer's big fight, the academic's exam, or the lover's tryst.

In the way that bio-rhythmology opens a new dimension to metabolism, astrology opens a new dimension to character itself. Using the same graph of stellar rhythms and angles, though with far greater complexity, it shows *why*, in the first place, a person is professionally predisposed to boxing, researching or loving. It describes the influences – as do the three bio-cycles – *behind* those of heredity and environment, which make us what we are. Our universities still teach us, in the social sciences, that to find out what a man is he must be studied in the 'social mass'. Sociology seeks to find out what we are by scrutinizing the 'social forces' – and if *one* man is looked at it is only to place him as a statistic in the context of these hypothetical forces, for it is in these – the creations of our own minds – that the answers to the question Who am I? – are assumed to lie.

Astrology begins from the other end, with the realization (obvious to any parent, though ignored by sociologists) that four children of the same family, brought up in the same way and at the same schools, will from earliest childhood be quite different sorts of people. Whereas the bio-rhythmic chart concerns itself with only three planets, astrology recognizes all ten of them and sees the solar system as a ten-stringed

* In the *I Ching*, the Chinese Book of Changes, as we shall see later, the weakest point is also that between the two extremes – although we are conditioned to think that this is logically the point of most equilibrium.

instrument, emanating the ten primary vibrational themes which oscillate their integral harmonies down from the cosmos into the broader 'characters' of an age or culture, down to the individuals within it, and to the cells within the individuals.*

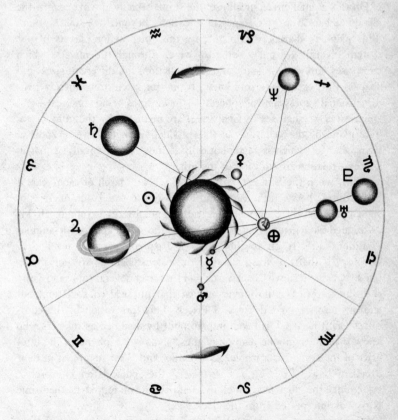

17. The 'Plane of the Ecliptic' as seen from above, with the relationship of the planets to one another for a given moment in time as seen (from the earth) against the zodiacal constellations. The Sun (☉) is in Aries (♈), Pluto (♇) in Scorpio (♏), and Venus (♀) in Aquarius (♒), etc.

* Despite our culture taking the credit for the very recent discoveries of Uranus, Neptune and Pluto, there is evidence that these were already accounted for in ancient Mayan and Egyptian astrology – although detectable only by those trained in both astrology and in the relevant hieroglyphics. In spite of these 'new' planets which astronomers held up as the final refutation of the Pythagorean and Cabbalistic decanate on which it is partially based, the decanate in fact remains intact – the Sun and Moon, plus the eight planets as seen from the earth.

To discern these 'chords', or primal vibrations, we must look again at the space/time continuum of our universe, but with an eye to the *symbolism* of relationships. The earth wheels about the Sun in what is called the 'plane of the ecliptic'.

On this annual circle, or ellipse, the sun is seen as moving against the changing backdrop of distant constellations beyond our solar system. This plane is shared, within 18°, by the other major planets of our system, creating a 'band' – some 18° wide – through the universe which comprises millions of stars and constellations of different sizes and shapes. But, as the ancients knew, bands (or circles) are merely two-dimensional expressions of spheres* – the Cosmos being spherical – and spheres (as we shall see in Chapter 4) are mediated by the number 12. The plane of the ecliptic was thus divided into just twelve zodiacal signs, each of which is metaphorically (if not astronomically) equal in size and relationship to each of the others.

Thus, when the Sun enters Aries, around 21 March of each year, it lies precisely between the earth and the distant constellation of Aries in such a way that the Sun (metaphorically, if not always astronomically) is positioned as a magnifying lens focusing the Aries energy (or angular vibration) directly on to the earth. A frequent criticism levelled at astrology is that the 'fixed stars' of these constellations are not always fixed, but move slowly 'backwards', so that over several thousand years the 'sun in Aries' is no longer against that physical constellation, but shifting into the first degrees of Pisces. This 'precession of the equinoxes', as it is called, is taken into account by qualified astrologers who know that the symbolic naming of these signs is peripheral to the integrity of the system as a whole. As Toonder and West suggested in their excellent book, *The Case for Astrology*,[9] the zodiac is an interpretive system like the clock face which in itself need be no more true than time is true as interpreted from the clock face.

The basic grid of this astrological clock face is thus combined from (1) the decad of stellar bodies beyond the earth, (2) their angular aspects to one another and (3) their placing in the duo-decad of zodiacal constellations against which they appear. This grid is like a sheet of music, with spaces for all the possible combinations of keys and notes – meaningless to the unmusical, but to the musician of cosmic frequencies (the

---

* As 'straight lines' are merely two-dimensional expressions of circles – since, as Einstein showed, all lines are eventually constrained to turn back on themselves and form a circle. Thus 'lines' – the edge of a table, or a telephone pole – are only the 'partially seen' fabric of gigantic space/time spheres.

accomplished astrologer) it offers a picture of an individual character as precisely as, to the trained composer, a written sonata describes the living totality of its individual components.

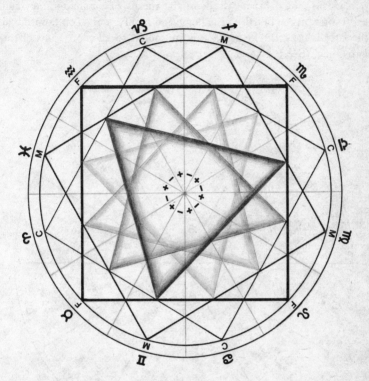

18. The zodiacal mandala, before any of the planets have been added, shows the geometrical integrity of a chart. The 'modes' of the Fixed, Cardinal and Mutable signs are related through the squares; the triplicities of the Four Elements (Earth, Air, Fire and Water), through the triangles. The horizon is represented by the horizontal line, above which (on the left) Aries (♈) is beginning to rise, which it does at the start of the year. The six polarities of 'Positive' and 'Negative' signs alternate throughout the zodiac.

For those who are interested in pursuing astrology more closely there is now a plethora of excellent books on the subject (see Bibliography) but we shall now have a brief look at the strands of colour which make it so complex.

Each zodiacal sign is interrelated, yet separate (as are numbers or rhythms), and the twelve 'houses' in an individual's chart correspond to these signs, mirroring the different spheres of a man's life. Beginning with Aries, or the first house, they move outwards – like the planets from the sun – from the 'ego' of the self to, in the second house, the possessions, then, in the third, to the means of communication and expression, in the fourth to the home and family, and so on towards, in the later houses, the highest ideals and outer, social expressions of the individual. (See Fig 19.)

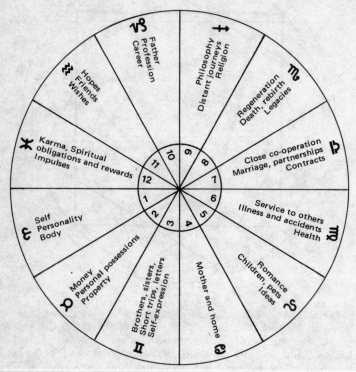

19. The houses in a zodiac, as they resonate to the archetypes behind each of the astrological signs.

The Sun is the creative and essential power-giving principle which stamps the *self*, the life-spark of the ego, and it rules the sign of the noble and extrovert Leo. The 'ascendant', or zodiacal sign rising over the horizon at the time of birth, adds the quality of 'personality' – as distinct from ego – the medium through which the sun-self operates. We each tend physically and expressively to resemble our rising signs more than our sun signs, for the 'persona' is only the mask, or vehicle, which carries the self. Sun and ascendant (or 'rising') signs in our charts may be very complementary and mutually harmonious or the reverse. A sun in Leo, with an Aries ascendant, will find his 'self' working happily through a brave and impulsive vehicle – though with a tendency to too much fire, which can reduce depth and stability. A sun in Pisces, the watery, receptive and sensitive sign, will be less comfortable with an Aries ascendant, because the 'fire' and 'water' clash – but whether constructively or antithetically will depend on the 'aspects' in the chart, or the wisdom of the individual *behind* his astrologically determined character.

The Moon is the feminine pole, ruling Cancer; it is instinctive, magnetic, accommodating, and its position in each chart conditions the way the Sun-ego, in the vehicle of the ascendant, 'responds' to the circumstances of life. The placing of the Moon in our chart indicates the way that we *feel* ourselves, and our connection to all that surrounds us, to be, and for this reason the relationship between Sun and Moon in two people's charts, particularly if they are of opposite sexes, can bind them closely together. Statistical work has shown, for instance, that a couple with, say, the man's Sun in Gemini and his Moon in Libra, and the woman's Sun in Libra and her Moon in Gemini, is more likely to form a lasting relationship – unless there are specifically disruptive aspects in their comparative charts.

Mercury is the planet of the nervous system, of cerebral functions, communication and dexterity, ruling the signs of Gemini and Virgo. Here the qualities of mixture begin to appear, since each sign is ruled by both a planet and an element (earth, air, fire or water). Whereas Gemini is both an air sign and ruled by the airy planet Mercury, Virgo is an earth sign, but ruled by the same planet, so the quality of Mercury in earth is more *grounded*, more practical and diligent in Virgo than it is in Gemini. Thus the complexities multiply, and it is clear that the Sun sign alone – which is the only planet referred to in newspaper horoscopes – is usually a poor indication of character, since the other components of the chart may well influence it out of salience.

That each planet has individual electro-magnetic 'tones' is no balk to plasma physics, and even astronomy can be seen to mirror the powerful symbolism of astrology. For instance, since the earth wheels round the Sun, and the Sun itself is travelling at great speed in order to keep its place in the spiralling Milky Way, there are times when the earth is 'ahead' of the sun, and times when it is 'behind'. In early spring when the sun is in Aries (seen from the earth against the constellation of Aries) – the fire sign of adventure and initiation – the earth has swept up from behind the sun to its side, and is beginning to forge ahead of it into a part of the Universe never before broached. Three months later, it is fully ahead of the sun – and the sun is in Cancer, the sign of feeling, retention and security – and we look back down the entire train which the solar system has travelled, into the million light-year history of our past, but wrapped in the total, nurturing moment of the present. Six months later, at the end of the year, the sun is seen against Capricorn (the earth sign of fixity of purpose), and the earth is now *behind* the sun, nestling in its train, fixed in matter, appraising, preparing to forge ahead and achieve a new cycle in the evolutionary spiral, and the earth arcs again towards the impulsive fire-sign of Aries. Similar associations can be discerned for each of the earth's positions relative to the constellations in the space/time spiral of the 'long body' of the sun.

It is precisely the complexity of accurate astrology which makes it as difficult to treat scientifically as any other 'art', but some intriguing headway has been achieved by Michel Gauquelin of France and John Addey of England.

Gauquelin, trained as a statistician at the Sorbonne, was affronted by the use to which statistics were being put by a Parisian astrologer named Leon Lasson, and he set out to discredit Lasson's work as an example of the obvious misuse of statistics.[10] Gauquelin began by taking a group of 508 eminent doctors to establish whether or not their charts had Mars and Saturn (the planets traditionally known to influence these professions) significantly aspecting their 'ascendants' – the sign rising over the horizon at the time of birth. He found that they had, and against the odds of 10,000,000 to 1. Embarrassed, but still sceptical, he doggedly began to collect data from throughout France, where, unlike Britain or America, the time of birth is recorded on the birth certificate; and he continued to apply them to the planetary aspects in the charts of soldiers, actors, scientists and doctors most eminent in their professions. The results, to Gauquelin's consternation, supported what astrologers had maintained for centuries, namely that soldiers and athletes are strongly aspected by Mars, scientists by Saturn and actors and clerics by Jupiter – all statistically well over a million to one against the odds.

Gauquelin mentions that he only became really addicted to this pursuit once he discovered that if sample subjects were taken from those who were not at the top of their professions, they yielded progressively more chance and random results. This implies that the relatively few people who in astrological terms of temperament and capacity, as predicted from the moment of birth, are thoroughly well-suited to do what they are doing, are also those who are invariably successful. It makes us wonder if it is not simply a lack of self-knowledge which allows us to fall too soon into a given profession. How many of us, after many years in the same job, begin to chafe with the feeling that we were always intrinsically better suited to something else?

Gauquelin's work, however, merely scratches the surface of the complex mysteries of true astrology. From the rational viewpoint, if we

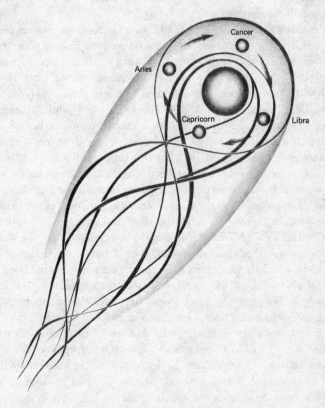

20. The graphic symbolism of the earth's position in the 'long body of the sun' as related to the zodiacal constellations against which the core of the sun is seen.

wished to determine what characteristics, if any, are produced by Mars in Scorpio, it would seem enough to take a random sample of cases born when Mars was transiting the constellation of Scorpio and to isolate what, in terms of temperament, aptitude and life-style, they had in common. The astrologer knows, however, that much of the significance lies in the many 'aspects' (trines, squares and so on) formed by this Mars in Scorpio in relation to all the other planets and their houses in the chart. Gauquelin, not being an astrologer, used only one or two of these 'aspects' in his analysis.

John Addey, President of the Astrological Association of Great Britain, began at the opposite end from Gauquelin, by knowing that astrology *does* make sense, and proceeded to apply to his data the kind of statistical methods used by the Foundation for the Study of Cycles in their search for rhythms.

In Addey's first tests he sought to isolate connections between people who had lived to over ninety, and also between victims of polio. Longevity is traditionally associated with Saturn – which rules the sign of Capricorn – and since polio victims are usually bright, nervous and intelligent, Mercury could be expected to figure prominently in their charts. Being an astrologer, Addey knew there was a subtle connection, in this case through antithesis,* between these two groups. But what he discovered was not that more Capricorns were long-lived, nor that more Geminis and Virgos (ruled by Mercury) contracted polio, but that if their data were superimposed on the 360° zodiacal ecliptic, then a wave motion could be discerned moving regularly through the degrees, 'peaking' at those points when the nonagenarians or the polio victims tended to be born. In the case of polio, the wave peaks every three degrees – meaning that throughout the year, defined as a circle of 360°, the wave is vibrating at the 120th harmonic – and a child born on this degree is 37 per cent more likely to contract polio than if born at any other time. We immediately think of the foetal radiation disturbances suggested by Vocasek in his study on mongolism, but Addey went on to isolate certain harmonics characteristic of specific professions as well.

Being trained in symbolism, Addey had a wide spectrum with which to interpret, as well as to programme, his statistical findings. He chose doctors and clergymen because he knew that in the esoteric tradition they are connected: both are concerned with different levels of 'making man whole' – one caring for the body, the other for the inner self.

* Not that polio victims are short-lived, but that airy Mercury is the antithesis of earthy Saturn.

Addey's work, which has been successfully repeated by others, shows that the significant harmonics of doctors and clerics are 5, or the factors of 5 – that is, the 5th, 25th and 125th harmonics, or 5, 5^2, 5^3. Such patterns, or harmonics, which occur throughout all the occult systems, point not so much to the 'influence' of the planets on man as to a subtle but incontrovertible harmony which pervades the entire universe, and perhaps to which we as well as the planets themselves respond.

In this respect the patterns in mystical symbolism tend to be confirmed by the nascent science of cosmo-rhythmology. And astrology, together with the other mantic arts, which have suffered dark centuries of misunderstanding, is being purified of its accumulated dross of superstition, and is beginning to emerge as lambent with forgotten meaning.

If we go to the amateurs or the mass media for astrology, our negative suspicions may well be confirmed, for as an art it is largely in the same position as medicine in its early days, before a centralized code of ethics and competence was established. It is wiser to refer to the teaching institutions, or to those who have been rigorously trained in them and are aware of the subtleties, traps and frailties of the various systems.

For five years my brother and I shared a London flat with two identical twins. Born twenty minutes apart, they both had Sun in Virgo and Leo in the ascendant, as well of course as many other slower moving planets in common. So alike are they that our friends have difficulty in telling them apart, and even we mistake them occasionally, particularly their voices on the telephone or their laughter in the next room. They had their charts done by an expert astrologer who received only their times and places of birth. Despite neither meeting them nor hearing a word about them, she sent back two analyses which were so uncannily accurate that we wondered why we had been blind to their character variations before. Their subtle differences, their balances of shyness and extroversion, of calculation and imagination, which we had only instinctively responded to before, and could not easily have described, were suddenly articulated: territory which was merely sensed, by being mapped became totally real.

Astrology is foolishness only to those who think that such subtleties do not matter and who do not care to look through the 'Galileo's telescope' of experience. But the subtle and superfluous concerns of one age become the dominant themes of another, for the self, and consequently society (rather than the other way round) are moulded by hidden powers. For more than a decade, in streets and in communes, people unable to wait for a statistical corroboration of astrology have recognized it as a vibrant language for understanding others and themselves. Its symbolism appears on book jackets and record sleeves as a powerful biographical code; friends feel their way into each other's charts, for it is a medium of great intimacy, which quite transcends the superficial categories of class, sex and profession, and throws light on the hidden workings of the self. On first meeting, many people now ask each other the placing of their Sun, ascendant and Moon in their charts, rather than asking what they do for a living, for this is now the short-hand of a 'cognitive minority', a clue to genuine rather than cliché communication.

In the brief history of psychology at least one great mind has freed itself from trying to interpret the psyche in mechanistic terms. This was Carl Jung, whose capacity to follow the clues of his own soul, totally alone and in the face of ridicule, opened him to the full treasury of esoteric symbolism. Through this he articulated a great and coherent vision of the psyche which – as we shall see in the decades to come – will serve as a framework for responding to the Aquarian age. An increasing number of psychologists are, like Jung, realizing that astrological data offer a deeper and more accurate language for describing character and motive than many offered by the psychological schools. There are at least three London psychotherapists, and considerably more in America, Holland and Germany, who, just as a doctor first runs laboratory tests on a new patient, begin by examining their patients' natal charts. In this way the psychotherapist learns how his own character combines, constructively, or otherwise, with that of the person he is seeking to help; for the healing profession is learning that it does not heal others from the 'outside', but rather that the doctor 'interacts' with his patient, committing himself to the creative chemistry of 'making whole', rather as lovers do.

Parents too are realizing that chart comparisons between themselves and their children give a new dimension to the way in which the whole family functions, revealing the points of contact and of friction, how one child needs more gentleness, another more freedom, and how the parents' own needs conflict with these. Most of us content ourselves with a merely instinctive knowledge of even our lovers and our children; but there is now enough evidence to warrant a closer look at astrology as a tool for adding colour, dimension and wisdom to our relationships.

Many shy away from astrology not because they do not believe in it, but because they fear they will find through it that their fate is unalterably fixed. But our chart mirrors only some of what we are, only the cards we have been dealt to play out in an eighty-year hand of poker: it is always the self which plays the hand, and only by learning the cards do we learn of the self behind them, the self which is free to play them well or badly. For astrology treats only of the patterns which mould our character (and thus how we are *likely* to respond to certain circumstances, now or in the future), but the character is only the vehicle for the higher human self, which exists as a different 'mode of energy'. To argue otherwise is to suggest that we *are* our bio-rhythms, or even more absurdly – and prevalently – that we *are* our bodies. Thus if it is the laws of 'circumstance' which places us in a difficult character harness – say one which attracts troubles and makes the world look cruel and pointless – we are free to live under these in perpetuity; but we are also free to discern who we *are* beneath these laws, and to respond to a different spectrum of influence.

There is now an increasing interest in esoteric astrology, which provides a more sophisticated grid for perceiving our deeper individual drives or 'soul purposes'. The greatest classical exponent of this is still the prolific Alice Bailey,[12] but enormous creative insights have been added to the field by the profound and lucid books of Dane Rudyar,[13] the grand old man of American astrology.

In this new science all the old questions of good and evil, free will and determinism, raise their thorny heads, and show themselves to be not so venomous as was first believed. The idea that some laws are 'good' and come from God, and others are 'bad' and come from the Devil, is still ingrained in our superstitious hearts. C. S. Lewis seemed nearer the truth when he wrote that all laws are God's laws,* and it matters only which laws we have the dignity to align ourselves with! 'If a man walking along a slippery pavement neglects the laws of prudence, then he comes under the laws of gravity.'

Since astrology treats a given mode of energy which is not yet that of the Self *behind* the character, the art has always been considered – by the truly esoteric groups – as belonging more to the profane end of the metaphysical spectrum. But to us, who have never seen the Sun, the candle is indeed a bright light, and its dimness can only be perceived when the first rays of what it leads to are discerned. The links between psychology, biology, rhythms and the cosmos are beginning to reflect

* Or, for the agnostic, issue from the same Cosmic Generator that behaves the way God would behave if He existed.

those rays, and to reveal that everything, visible and invisible, distant and immediate, is part of the same pulsating body.

The medium of this body is the symbiotic spiral, the double helix, of space/time – 'Tace', as we may call it. At the Jodrell Bank observatory radio-waves from quasars have been monitored which left their source 1000 million years before the earth came into existence. This instant we can see, with our eyes, the infinite past – or is it the infinite future? The quasar 3c273 – millions of stars packed together somewhat more closely than a galaxy – is seven light years in diameter, yet all its stars occlude and brighten in unison. Though separated by billions of miles from one another they pulse at a constant rate, like the equally mysterious Malayan fire-flies which ignite and darken the trees in synchrony. Bacteria in the body of mankind as a whole, as Dewey has shown, pulse through scarcity and abundance. The electromagnetic pulse of our individual bodies can even tell us the most convenient time for having a hair cut!

We are enveloped and penetrated with a tidal power which functions with total precision, from the galactic to the subatomic, and the precision is only at fault in the still-developing human understanding. But we begin to sense, even in this darkness, that our own individual feelings are part of the musical movements of the cosmos, and that we are one and the same breathing Leviathan of Life.[14]

4 Number and Form

Hast thou entered into the treasures of the snow?
Asked God of Job. And Job was silent.

JOHN STEWART COLLIS

We have hinted at the extent to which rhythms suffuse the universe, but how do we understand volume repetition and connections – which are the stuff of rhythm – if not through the basic grammar of number and form? Whereas language has been described as 'fantastic logic', mathematics is generally assumed to be pure logic, stripped of fantasy, and thus the most stable of intellectual tools. But the higher mathematician frequently deals with 'imaginary numbers' – the converse of 'real numbers' – which, even within the framework of rationalism, branch into mysterious realms of hypothetical reality. It is here that numbers, quite distinct from their empirical use, become a language as full of metaphor and dimension as poetry.

The ancients recognized mathematics and geometry as both 'rational' and 'super-rational' tools which could provide a key to the more rarefied system of order underlying the purely quantitative universe. To see numbers and forms holistically, as tools both for the 'feelings' which require meaning, and for the intellect which requires reason, we must view them as the ancients viewed them – in the context of myth and symbol. For whereas 'dia-bolism' – that which 'throws apart' – splits our vision, 'sym-bolism' is that which brings it together. The timeless traditions of numerology and sacred geometry – numbers and forms as 'bringers-together' – are the unifying threads behind all the diverse systems of occult science. For this reason the religious leaders of the past were also the scientists and mathematicians, which suggests that there was a time when neither we, nor the gods we created, were so schizophrenic as to maintain that the world of matter and reason was *distinct* from the world of spirit and the awareness of God.

If we can feel our way into the symbolism of numbers and geometry (an unfamiliar exercise for our modern minds) we can detect the primal grammar on which our perception, and the evolution of our consciousness, is founded. As awakening babies the first thing we are conscious of is movement; this is followed by the awareness of forms, the things that move: and finally we distinguish quantity, or how *many* things are moving. Following this order in the process of awakening consciousness, we shall begin with the symbolism of forms and then move to the symbolism of the numbers which delineate them.

In all the cultures versed in the use of supernatural metaphor the square (for reasons which we shall explore later) symbolizes the 'earth' of matter and rationalism, while the circle, as its shape suggests, symbolizes the encompassing world of spirit, heart and feeling. It is this

21. *The Pythagorean Tetraktys* – the integral decad of touching spheres, each containing the crystal forms of numerical unfolding. From the centre – which from our standpoint is the pentagram of microcosmic man – springs a parabolic spiral, passing through all the spheres, and moving on to encompass infinity.

duality which each of us tries to reconcile in his own life; we seek to harness our ideals to our practical necessities, to balance the demands of logic with the demands of the heart. Thus the 'squaring of the circle' was the architectural as well as the philosophical pursuit of the ancient sciences of religion.

The geometrical squaring of a circle requires the measuring out of a square whose perimeter is exactly the same length as the circle's, so that the two figures are 'harmonized' by containing precisely the same area. The reverse, of course, is the case for 'circling the square' – which symbolically would be required of the person whose 'square' of rationalism is greater than his 'circle' of inner feeling. We can see this symbolism in the recent cultural revolution of the Western world where the spherical 'fantasy' world of the perennial children has begun to encompass the 'squares'. Like many other problems of particular interest to the sacred geometrician, the squaring of the circle cannot be achieved by measurement alone, but only with a compass and a straightedge through *relationship* with the first-drawn figure. But as John Michell has remarked, this curious problem is daily solved in nature with the relative dimensions of the earth to the moon.

If, for instance, we take the circle of the earth – which we know to have a diameter of 7920 miles (twice the radius of 3960) – and 'box' it within a square, each of the four sides of this square will measure the same as the earth's diameter, so that the perimeter of this square is four times 7920, or 31,680 miles. Circling this terrestrial square involves finding a *circle* whose circumference is also 31,680 miles. Against all the odds of chance, this is achieved through the relative proportions of the moon to the earth. Since the moon has a diameter of 2160 miles (twice its radius of 1080), its enclosing square (which we place tangent to the square containing the earth) is four times 2160 or 8640 miles.

Taking Pi as $^{22}/_7$ the combined radii of the earth and the moon (3960 plus 1080) are precisely the radius of the circle which circles the earth's square. In other words, the circle with its centre at the centre of the earth, traced through the centre of the adjacent moon, has a circumference just equal to the perimeter of the square containing the earth.[1]

This figure also marks out the 3,4,5 triangle which is formed by joining the corner of the terrestrial square to the corner of the lunar square. It was from just such proportions that the 'sacred canon of numbers' was derived, since they reflect the ratios of the universe's actual distribution, rather than the arbitrary measurements invented by cultures which never look beyond the terrestrial dimension – even when examining outer space. It is this canon of largely irrational proportions which the symbolist sees as the key to a natural harmony so subtle that it often escapes our intellect, though it is not beyond the grasp of our intuition.

Sacred geometry thus concerns itself with the 'order in space' whereby 'existence' unfolds with minimum effort and maximum harmony through successive modes of energy – the ideal paradigm, in fact, for the growth of the soul. Since our earliest perceptions involve the ordering of forms in space, all human discussion of religious and supernatural experience abounds with the term 'dimensions'; sacred geometry graphs how 'dimensions of vision' unfold, either in the natural universe or in our own psyches. Its basis is the sphere, or circle, whose shape, both as infinity and totality – nothing and the basis of all beginning – resonates life.

Each of us begins as a single-celled sphere, we live on a sphere, nurtured by a flaming sphere, in a spherical cosmos; for the straightness of lines (or the path of light) is only 'relatively' straight and in the end is constrained – like the self-devouring snake – to turn back on itself. Thus the Pythagoreans sought, with their 'geo-metry', to *place* themselves in the very real sphere of the infinite whole; for whereas the scientist seeks to catalogue the contents of the universe, the occultist seeks to realize his relationship to it.

Once a circle, or 'sphere-point', has moved at least one radius distant from itself, it produces an archetypal symbol: the vagina-shaped 'vesica piscis' – the feminine principle of generation from which spring all other geometrical forms, such as the triangles, squares and 'golden mean' rectangles which abound in sacred architecture. (See Fig. 26.)

The fusion of any two soap bubbles of equal size produces a three-dimensional vesica piscis, which in turn generates all the crystalline three-dimensional forms, such as the Pythagorean 'sacred solids' of which we shall hear more later. Form and number, as they change 'modes', bring something from quite outside themselves. Two circles, for instance, produce only one vesica, but three circles give *three* vesicae.

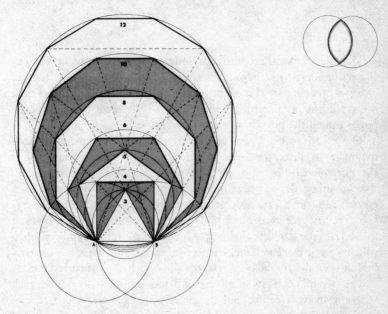

26. All the degrees of generation of the basic regular polygons from the fusion of but two circles: forming the vesica piscis. The dotted lines show the relationships of concord between them all.

By adding one circle we have gained two vesicae. From what dimension, the occultist asks, have these two vesicae sprung?

The circle is full of logical improprieties, while yet being the mother of all flat geometry. It is mathematically irrational in that Pi – the relationship of its radius to its circumference – can only be expressed as an imperfect fraction: $^{22}/_7$. Expressed in decimal fractions, this proportion goes gibbering on for an infinite number of decimal places, but we usually settle for four of these with the formula 3·1428. A circle's radius just 'won't go' into its circumference precisely; it is a mathematical incompatibility which is resolved only with visual geometry, which overleaps the constraints of the intellect, for precisely six (the symbolic number of beauty, harmony and mediation) of a circle's radii go round the inside of its circumference.

Thus the irrational proportion is 'ordered' in a dimension of relationships which exist just beyond the reach of pure mathematics. It is an order so predominant that of the billions of snowflakes which swirl from the sky during a blizzard, all, though each is different from the other, hover around the hexagonal geometry of sixness.

The nature of this order can again be discerned in the man-made mountain at Ghiza, the Great Pyramid, which housed the mummy of the Pharaoh Cheops who ruled Egypt in the third millennium B.C. Recent carbon dating suggests that the pyramid itself may have been erected as many as 73,000 years ago. For generations of number symbolists it has been recognized to be permeated with rhythmic waves of numerical ratios, which also supply a canon of 'sacred numbers' upon which a later, more profane, science was to be built. Here we can only hint at the full symphony of relationships which the structure hides.

The pyramid consists of 2,600,000 blocks of limestone granite, each weighing an average of 50 tons and cut to within a tolerance of 1/1000 of an inch. It has been calculated that if ten of these blocks were fitted together with precision each day – some 500 tons a day – the pyramid would have taken 664 years to complete. It has five vertices (or points); five faces; a square base; and four triangular sides which angle up at 51°.51 of slope. The apex of the pyramid, although now missing, is strongly suggested by the mathematical currents in the structure to have been a further pyramid of five cubic inches in volume – for the 56th part sliced from the top of a pyramid of these dimensions is itself a tiny and exact replica of the angles and proportions of the whole.

---

29. (Right) Snowflakes, from the massive collection of the late W. A. Bentley, the 'ultimate snow-flake freak', who at the beginning of this century spent nearly fifty years photographing water crystals under a microscope.

The pyramid's height of 275 Royal Egyptian cubits* (minus the missing apex) is proportional to the perimeter of its square base in the same ratio as Pi's; that same irrational though miraculous ratio between a circle's circumference and its radius. By circling the square of the pyramid's base, the resultant circle has a radius identical to the height of the pyramid. The structure thus ingeniously manages to square the circle in three dimensions. Once the circle is squared, a Pandora's box of correspondences is unleashed. For anyone with a pocket adding machine and a developed sense of the coincidental, the height of the pyramid can quickly be calculated to be precisely one thousand millionth part of the mean distance between the earth and the sun, and its weight as being one thousand billionth part of the weight of the earth. So what? one may ask.

The pyramid is oriented precisely north/south to the magnetic pole, and rests on the latitude 30°N. (exactly one third of the way between the equator and the pole), as well as on longitude 30°E. – which is odd in view of how recently Greenwich was established as the zero meridian. But the meridian of 30°E., passing as it does from Finland to S. Africa and traversing only the Caspian and the Aegean seas, is the longest land-covering meridian on earth. Piazzi Smyth has calculated that, 'On carefully summing up all the dry land habitable by man the wide world over, the centre of the whole falls within the Great Pyramid's territory of Lower Egypt.'[2]

30. The location of the Great Pyramid at Ghiza on a flat projection of the globe.

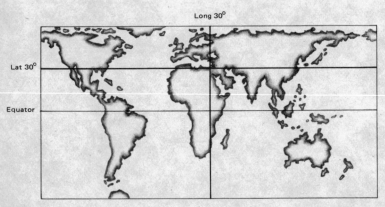

Long 30°

Lat 30°

Equator

---

* One Royal Egyptian cubit is equal to 2·96 feet.

It has long been reasoned by pyramidologists, and recently supported by more of John Michell's intriguing calculations, that whereas the tiny apex at the top of the pyramid – of five cubic inches – mirrors the proportions of the whole by being a 56th part of it, the visible pyramid on the desert is in turn but the apex of a successive series of ever-increasing and invisible pyramids. While the five-cubic-inch apex expands to 56^2 (56 multiplied by itself) of its volume to achieve the Great Pyramid which we *see*, if expanded further, to 56^3, the base of this subsequent pyramid would cover 64 square miles, the area of the plateau on which the pyramid stands. If expanded to 56^4, the pyramid thus formed would have base edges measuring 448 square miles, and thus cover 200,700 square miles – exactly the area of the whole country of Lower Egypt. Finally, 56^5 of the fist-sized apex produces a pyramid with base edges measuring 25,088 miles – a vast square which 'squares the circle' of the earth's equator, the distance of the pyramid's apex above the north pole being precisely the same as the radius of the moon. And so the harmonics of the system escalate into the cosmos, encompassing the motions and phases of the planetary bodies.[3]

We are reminded of Professor Eddington's comment that the stellar bodies appear to be strung out from the sun in specific 'mean' distances from one another, suggesting that when the gases constellated into planets they did so at points of harmonic constriction – like musical scales – in obeyance to (as yet undetermined) laws of hierarchical order.

It is increasingly apparent that such shapes, determined by numbers, actually trap, resonate and amplify specific modes of vibration – and thus that sacred geometry and numerology are much more than purely 'symbolic'. The resonance of the pyramid shape was only re-discovered this century by a Frenchman named Bovis. He was visiting the King's Chamber – situated on the centre line of the Great Pyramid, and one third of the way up its height – when he was struck by the fact that a dead cat, together with various other organic matter in a rubbish bin in the chamber, gave off no smell of decay. They were in fact as well preserved as the body of the Pharaoh Cheops at the time of its removal from the same chamber several decades earlier. Wondering whether the pyramid's geometry was perhaps related to the anti-decaying process,

Bovis carried out a series of experiments, placing organic matter within small, precisely scaled replicas of the pyramid's shape. He noticed that if these replicas were oriented with their sides to the magnetic north (as is the Great Pyramid), and if the matter – egg, meat or vegetables – was placed inside, just one third of the distance up the pyramid's central axis, then it decayed – under identical conditions of barometric pressure and temperature – appreciably slower than if placed anywhere else.

32. The 'form' of the Great Pyramid – a square base and 4 triangular faces which angle up at 51° .51 of slope. The point marked one third of the way up the vertical is that area in the form with the greatest concentration of those electro-magnetic properties presently being explored by science.

Bovis's work was continued by a Czechoslovak radio engineer, Karel Drbal, who after successfully repeating Bovis's experiments suggested that the correct orientation of a pyramid shape completely altered the electromagnetic qualities of the space contained within it. Knowing that folkloric superstitions not infrequently harbour germs of very practical truth, he first thought of the old saying current in Prague, his home town, that a razor blade became blunt when left in the light of a full moon. He also knew from personal experience, as well as scientific knowledge, that this is a fact; for the simple reason that moonlight, being *reflected* light from the sun, consists of particles which are polarized, and therefore vibrating, in primarily one direction. Thus if the crystals – often merely one layer thick at the edge of a razor blade – are exposed to uni-directional molecular vibrations, they are 'pushed over' in that direction, blunting the blade. He therefore replaced Bovis's organic matter with razor blades, and found that when placed in the pyramid shape at the right spot they not only remained sharper for greatly extended periods of use, but actually reconstituted their crystal-line edges in a matter of hours.

The experiments of Bovis and Drbal have since led to the widespread marketing of pyramid shapes. Companies in Italy and France are mar-keting milk, yoghourt and other perishables in pyramid forms because (we are still not sure *why*) they withstand much longer periods without refrigeration. Two companies are now selling small polystyrofoam pyramids which fit on the bathroom shelf, for preserving razor blades.

In America and Canada tent-sized pyramids are available as enclosures for sleeping or meditating in. Maximum results are obtained from orienting them along the north/south magnetic axis of the earth, where they exert a revitalizing effect not only on 'inert' matter but on the living tissues of the mind and body.

That shape and vibration are crucially, though mysteriously, connected is known to any musician, from the designer of violins to the singer trying to shatter a vase with her voice. The fact that certain harmonic shapes resonate to cosmic frequencies too fine to be recorded on the electromagnetic spectrum, but which are nonetheless powerful, emerges from the *understanding* of the forms and numbers which the ancients sought to follow in building their temples – those granite organs designed to resonate the life-sustaining powers of the universe. So let us look more closely at the grammar of sacred geometry and numerology, which were the principles from which sprang our present profane manipulation of numbers and forms.

Geometry begins with the 'point', which is circular or, in three dimensions, spherical. It exists only as the intersection of two or more

The point

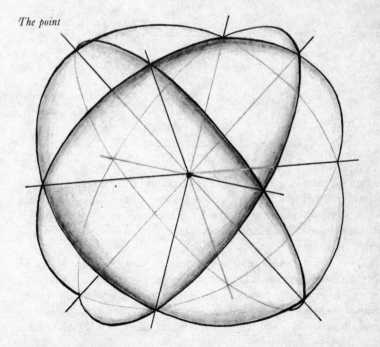

lines, being purely abstract, while yet the only empirical beginning – and end. Thus all our geometry, whether sacred or profane, springs from 'nothing', as evidenced by the fact that the 'point' doesn't even qualify as a dimension. The first dimension begins with a line – the point that has 'smeared' itself through space, like the 'red shift' photographs of distant galaxies. This line is the shortest path between two infinities, or 'points'. From *one*, the duality of *two* lines is born. Our rational lives are associated with this *first* dimension, the line which travels at its own pace between the void before birth and the void after death.

But no 'closed' or stable figure appears until there are *three* lines, or rather until the first line has 'smeared' itself again – like a windscreen wiper – into a plane, the second dimension. The simplest possible planar expression is the equilateral triangle, symbol of the fiery trinity of active creation.

This 'trinity' sheds its vibration even into the practicality of chemistry and mechanics. If three needles are placed in three corks, and the corks floated in a bowl of water with a magnet beneath them, they arrange themselves as the corners of a constant equilateral triangle. A stool, in order to stand, needs a minimum of three legs. White light

38. Vesica piscis. In the symbolism of sacred geometry, the $\sqrt{3}$ rectangle contains the 'fish' form of early Christianity.

remains undifferentiated into colours until it is passed through a triangular prism. And three spheres of equal size provide the basis for a fourth to rest upon them in a higher 'mode' of form.

Brahmanic scripture speaks of two 'fires' – the spiritual energy which descends from heaven, and the 'earthly' aetheric energy which ascends from matter.* In the ancient traditions we find these concepts mirrored

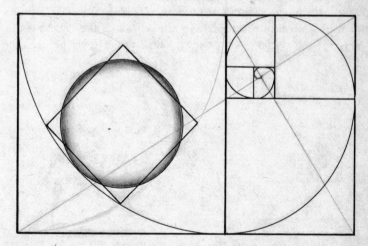

39. The $\sqrt{3}$ rectangle – the sacred proportional mean borne from the square, and generating ever-increasing, squares and rectangles in the same proportion. This is referred to as 'the figure of the whirling squares', and it obeys the same laws which govern the growth of many natural forms, such as the Nautilus shell. the largest square contains two equal vesicae piscis – at 90° to each other – showing how the 'squared circle' is contained within them.

* This is the 'kundalini' energy which, as we see later in Chapter 6, enters the body at the base of the spine, the point which the yogi or fakir connects to the earth prior to his meditation.

in the triangle which is based in matter, its point aspiring upwards, and the triangle which is rooted in the invisible heavens and despires downwards. Their union, the union of polarities, is spirit wedded to matter – the macrocosmic man, in his complete and feminine sensitivity to the Divine. It is the Star of David, each point – as with every true symbol – touching the edge of an invisible circle of totality.

Geometry and myth can be closely intertwined, as we can see from the fusion of two circles to form one vesica piscis. This figure (Fig. 38) produces both triangles, squares and the $\sqrt{3}$ rectangle – the mean proportion which occurs in sacred architecture as constantly as it does in the growth of spiralling shells or galaxies.*

In Gnostic Christianity the symbol for this generative proportion (the tuning-fork for the soul's growth) was the fish, the fish's 'eye' being the intersection of the diagonal of the larger $\sqrt{3}$ rectangle with that of the smaller, proportional $\sqrt{3}$ rectangle within it. These rectangles generate each other, in proportion, from macro- to microcosm, together with their squares, as we see in Fig. 39. From this mean ratio of the vesica piscis – which underlies the architecture of Gothic cathedrals – springs the 'fish' symbolism which pervades the religion of the Piscean Age – the now waning aeon of Christianity: Christ as the 'fisher of men', the

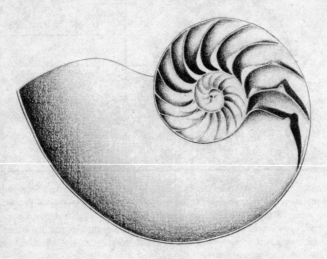

40. Nautilus shell.

* Ancient religious architecture, both western and oriental – as we see from the research of Michell, Critchlow and Thom, is transparent with these sacred 'ratios'.

fish-shaped mitres worn by bishops and the Pope, the 'piscina' or baptismal font, and so on. The two circles producing the vesica piscis in Fig. 38 are also precisely contained within a larger 'mother' vesica, from two circles contained within a yet greater one, and so on.

It is the circle, or sphere, which we try never to lose from sight in sacred geometry, for within them is contained the duality of the human predicament. From the fusion of *three* circles (Fig. 41) producing three vesicae, we have generated – without changing the compasses – both the macrocosmic, feminine hexagram, and, beneath it, the microcosmic masculine pentagram. In the middle of the figure we see the central equilateral triangle of creativity which fires the fusion between these two worlds of matter and spirit. The hexagon, the six-sided figure of beauty whose edges are equal to the radius of the circle encompassing it, abounds in nature, in plankton, snowflakes and the faces of flowers. It is the shape formed by circles when they wish to nestle together with the most economy of space – as we see from crystals and honey-combs.

41. Three vesicae producing the macrocosmic hexagram, and the microcosmic inverted pentagram.

42. The hexagonal 'close packing' of circles found in honey-comb cells, or the eyes of a fly.

It is this strange 'inside-outness' of circles which means that six equal-sized circles, themselves arranged in a circle (Fig. 43), will touch each other to leave room for a seventh 'invisible' circle of the same size in their midst. Both seven and thirteen have long been considered singularly 'supernatural' numbers, symbolizing either heaven or hell. For the geometrician they represent the movement into a new mode of energy, which can be good or bad 'luck' depending on one's capacity to handle it. For whereas six is the number of harmonic totality in two dimensions, in three dimensions it is twelve. For instance if we take twelve spheres (rather than circles), such as sticky ping-pong balls, they cluster around each other just leaving space for an 'invisible' thirteenth sphere of the same size in their midst. Osiris, Christ, Mohammed and King Arthur were but some of the transcendent centres of twelve retainers, or sub-cells. This is further evidence that the crystalline unfolding of geometrical order is mirrored not only in the human mind, with the growth of myth and symbol, but also at the rarefied levels of 'supernatural' order which appear to condition the physical universe.

The hexagram and the pentagram have long symbolized the two natures of man: the spiritual and the physical self. Like all dualities, these can be either 'positive' or 'negative'. The pentagonal star, or pentagram, for instance, can either be upright like the Leonardo da Vinci figure, or else inverted (as it appears in contradistinction to the

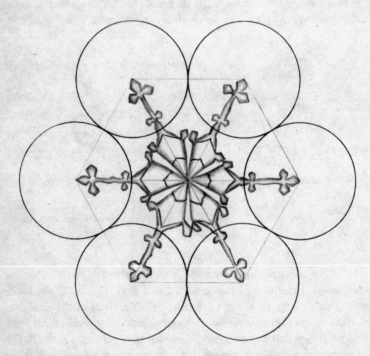

43. Six equal touching circles, themselves arranged in a circle, exactly contain an invisible, just touching, seventh. Thus the polarities of the visible and invisible worlds generate the multitudes of hexagonal beauty found so abundantly in nature.

spiritual hexagram of Fig. 41). In the latter case it resembles – as its symbol implies – the horned and bearded goat of the underworld.

The fusion of hexagon and pentagon, which we see in Fig. 41, has the same shape and proportions as the nucleic connections of the DNA molecule which carries the genetic code. The chemical model for these proteins consists of two-dimensional platelets of two fused pairs of hexagons and pentagons (Fig. 45) joined by a 'golden mean' rectangle, which rise upon each other in a three-dimensional spiral (Fig. 46).

45. The flat hexagon/pentagon components of the DNA spiral.

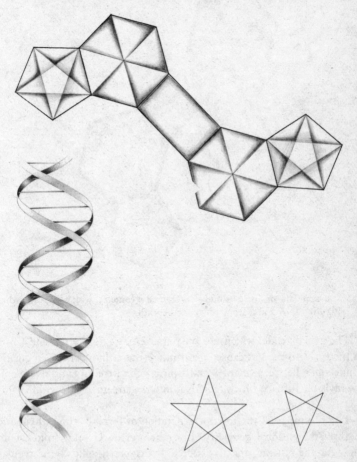

46. The spiral connections of the nucleic acids comprising the DNA molecule.

When viewed from the top we see a 'mandala' (Fig. 47), the form which the Tantric priests also saw as a flat representation of a spiral, a crystalline map of the potential energies of human consciousness.

47. The mandala or 'rose window' of sacred geometry which appears when viewing the DNA spiral from above, or beneath.

The genetic code, which was only cracked by Drs Watson and Crick in the early 1950s, has caused great interest as it hints at the enigmatic connections between 'matter' and 'spirit' – between organic tissue and the invisible furnace which moulds it into the stream of biological evolution.

The full range of the interior generation of forms becomes hypnotic in three-dimensional geometry. Long before the Greeks, from whom they got their name, the five sacred Pythagorean solids – or regular polyhedra – were recognized as a primal grammar of perception, and as the ciphers for 'points of rest' in an infinite variety of harmonic relationships mirrored both within and without us.

Keith Critchlow, lecturer at the British Architectural Association,[4] has pointed out that the easiest way of tracing the growth of the five sacred solids is by observing the *simplest* way in which spheres – like

48. Tetrahedron emerging from tracing the lines between the centres of but four touching spheres.

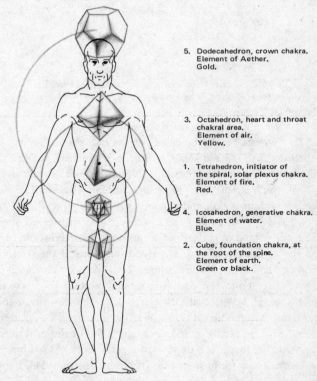

5. Dodecahedron, crown chakra.
   Element of Aether.
   Gold.

3. Octahedron, heart and throat
   chakral area.
   Element of air.
   Yellow.

1. Tetrahedron, initiator of
   the spiral, solar plexus chakra.
   Element of fire.
   Red.

4. Icosahedron, generative chakra.
   Element of water.
   Blue.

2. Cube, foundation chakra, at
   the root of the spine.
   Element of earth.
   Green or black.

49. The five sacred solids, as symbols of the different vibrationary sources in the 'subtle' or 'aetheric' body of man.

developing cells – unfold from one another, and then drawing the lines traced between their centres.

Bearing in mind this primal economy of movement we see that these forms are the *only* five polyhedra (yet known to human consciousness) which have equal angles, equal faces, and whose points (or vertices) touch the edge of an invisible, enveloping sphere. Since spheres are 'totalities' or 'universes', and the five polyhedra contain spheres, they can be seen to mediate an infinity of cosmic relationships, both physical and cerebral. Symbolically, each of the five is associated with one of the five elements of alchemy (Earth, Air, Fire, Water and Aether), the five aetheric 'power points', or chakral 'tones' of the human body,* the five 'Akashic' or aetheric colours, and so on. We shall briefly explore these five forms in the order of their unfolding from one another.

50 and 51. Two views of the tetrahedron, one pointing up from Earth, the other pointing down from Heaven. The tetrahedron has four points, or vertices, and four equilateral triangle faces.

1. *The Tetrahedron.* Since 'threeness', or the triangle, is the first stable unit, the first of the sacred solids is a three-dimensional triangle (Figs. 50 and 51). It is the simplest possible three-dimensional form, except for the sphere which is both everything and nothing. It is the first 'fire of creation', its colour is red, and it points towards 'fourness', or four, of which it has both points and faces. When made with glued sticks or threaded straws (and to make these forms oneself is a powerful meditation on the perception of both inner and outer space) the tetrahedron sits firmly on its base and aspires upwards – as does man. Since it is the fire of primal creation – the 'omphalus mundi' – it corresponds to man's centre, his navel or solar plexus area, where the downward-coming energies of spirit combine with the upward-going energies of matter (the kundalini force). In early exoteric Christianity this duality was unreconciled in the belief that man's upper half was the work of God but below the navel was the work of the devil. In the hidden tradition, however,

* These chakral areas are not to be confused with the chakras themselves, which are discussed in Chapter 6.

these opposing energies are 'symbiotic', and their fusion – or 'alchemical wedding' – is understood to exteriorize as a human being by way of a spiral whose point of beginning (as we see in Fig. 49) is at the tetrahedral fire-navel of man. Indeed, from the earliest amorphous stage of an embryo we see that it is connected at its centre, by a spiralling umbilical chord, to its mother's sustenance.

The tetrahedron is the form containing the *least* volume for its surface area, and thus withstands the greatest amount of external pressure. This is why milk and other liquids are frequently marketed in *tetrahedral containers*. The reverse is true for the sphere, which contains *maximum* volume for minimum surface area and can consequently – as we see from bubbles or spherical gas-storage tanks – withstand maximum *internal* pressure. Whereas a tetrahedron touches its enveloping, invisible sphere at only four points, each subsequent polyhedron touches its enveloping sphere at progressively more points – meaning that they become both more complex, by having more points and faces, and more like spheres themselves, which, paradoxically, are of both the utmost simplicity and the utmost complexity.

Like the two flat triangles constituting the Star of David, in the three-dimensional mode of energy there are also two tetrahedra – one based in matter and aspiring upwards towards spirit, the other based in spirit and despiring downwards towards matter (Figs. 50 and 51).

2. *The Cube.* Once these two tetrahedra are interpenetrated we have a structure which, in Fig. 53, rests on its side. This is the three-dimensional eight-pointed star (sacred to the Western Mysteries tradition) which *delineates* the cube. Since it combines the upward-going and the downward-coming vibrationary powers it is the four-square earth of our universe, our world or our own bodies. The cube has six faces and eight points, its colour is black or dark green, and its chakra is at the root of the spine, where the spiral power has curved from the 'fire navel' down to *ground* itself in the kundalini vibration of matter which enters the body at that point (Fig. 49). It is the spine, of course, which is the

53. Two interpenetrated tetrahedra – or eight-pointed star – lie on their side, forming the 'skeleton' of the cube – the next of the sacred polyhedra – the 'walls' of which have been folded down to show the Cross of the Christian Gnostic tradition. For this reason the eight-pointed star, which hangs on the cross, is also referred to as 'the crown of thorns'. Many of the early Gothic cathedrals, built by the Masons (whose canon in life and deed was the pursuit of sacred proportions), reflect the structure of this figure.

'tree of life' in the physical frame, the trellis upon which man rises upright from the biological world to walk erect in the direction of consciousness. The foundation of the spine, symbolized by the cube, is thus our solid point of departure towards the higher modes of energy.

Because the Egyptians and other ancient peoples represented the earth as a square, our two-dimensional minds have assumed that they thought the earth *was* square – something patently false in view of the obvious sophistication of their astronomy. Sacred geometricians have pointed out that the square is the glyph of the cube – the inner meaning of which is the 'sphere' of the earth of matter. The cube too, of course, like the other sacred solids, is surrounded by an invisible sphere whose surface precisely touches its eight points.

Whereas the two fused tetrahedra form the skeleton of this subsequent solid, the cube (whose faces are unfolded in Fig. 53), it is within the cube that birth is already being given to the next solid, the octahedron, whose profile emerges traced between the points where the diagonals cross on the faces of the cube (Fig. 54).

54. Different view of the two interpenetrated tetrahedra, contained within the as yet unfolded cube. The tetrahedra's edges, forming as they do the diagonals on the square faces of the cube, are the points of generation for the third of the sacred solids, the octahedron.

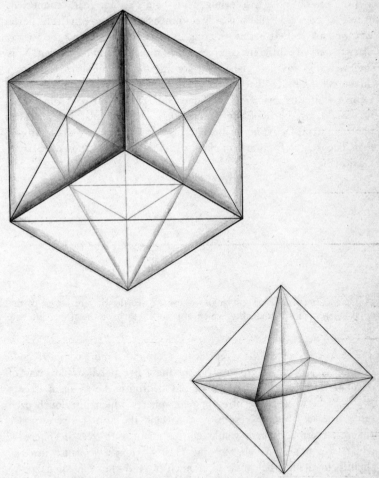

55. The octahedron, third of the sacred solids, has eight triangular faces, but only six points. It is in fact simply three flat squares interpenetrating in three different planes. Note the three-dimensional cross contained by the figure.

3. *The Octahedron*. Born from the womb of the cube of matter – the eight-pointed star – is the octahedron, which is simply three flat squares fused together in three different planes (see Fig. 55). In symbolism, by being the child of fire and matter (three-ness and four-ness) it is matter released into mobility, which is rarefied earth, or the alchemical element of Air. Its colour is yellow, and it corresponds to the chakral area of the throat and heart, where the complexities of the universe are given *voice* and the echo of reflective feeling. If its points are internally connected, as in Fig. 55, we see that it is a three-dimensional cross, equal whichever way we look at it. It is this ordering in space which gives us the vocabulary to perceive different complexities of direction and dimension. This interior cross in the octahedron, for instance, symbolizes the seven directions of Chinese Taoism: North, South, East, West, Up, Down and Centre – all the primary coordinates for *placing* ourselves in directionless chaos. Each of the octahedron's six triangular faces has its opposing twin, facing up or down, on the opposite side of the figure, so that if looked at from any of three different planes it shows a Star of David (Fig. 56).

56. Octahedron from different angle, where we see the Star of David of the opposing triangles – a duality which appears in each of the three different planes.

4. *The Icosahedron* (Fig. 57) represents a leap into a more complex mode of energy. If we trace the growth of these five polyhedra by way of developing spheres, then while the tetrahedron is the result of tracing the lines between the centres of *four* spheres which just touch each other, the icosahedron results from tracing the lines between *twelve* spheres. Normally these would cluster about a thirteenth sphere of equal size, but in its absence the cluster tends to collapse inwards slightly to define the icosahedral nucleus, and the miraculous polyhedron of twenty triangle faces. The faces are in ten different planes (two to a plane) so that each triangle (like the octahedron) has its inverse twin facing it on the opposite side of the figure.

From the △ and the □, from which the first three solids spring, in the icosahedron we have moved to the higher mode of the ⬠, or the quality of five-ness, the symbol for microcosmic man – the five-limbed creature of God. Despite the icosahedron having triangular faces, the pentagon, with the quality of five-ness, already lies hidden within it. We can see this by discerning the twelve points of the icosahedron, from each of which slant down five edges to delineate the twelve interior pentagons which nestle within the figure. These twelve interior symbols of man are still knitted together – like the petals in an unopened bud – and are in six different planes, two to a plane, each also having its inverse twin facing it. All these can be discerned in Fig. 57, beginning with the horizontal plane.

The icosahedron symbolizes the element of water, and resonates to the sexual chakra in man. Its colour is blue, for endless regeneration – like the sea.* If we build these for ourselves, the icosahedron, above all, appears as a vibrant optical illusion of different modes of harmony,

57. The Icosahedron, the fourth of the sacred solids, has twenty triangle faces and twelve points, from each of which issue five rays, or edges. Just as there are two opposing triangles, forming the Star of David, on either side of the figure (like the octahedron) but in ten different planes, so too – on the *inside* of the figure – there are six polarities of opposing pentagons. Two of these can most easily be seen on the horizontal plane.

* Whereas the octahedron is simply three flat squares penetrating each other in three different planes, the icosahedron is simply three 'golden mean' rectangles (that irrational proportion of perfection) interpenetrated in three different planes.

containing as it does the growth of the previous three solids, and the latent form of the final and fifth one. It is also the shape of certain bacteria. These smallest of known organisms, on the border of life and non-life, can lie as inert matter for thousands of years before the right chemical conditions surround and resurrect them. As they are too small to see or photograph, they are blasted from the side with light, which utterly destroys them; but their elongated shadows can then be caught by the microscope and reassembled to reveal an invisible universe of perfect icosahedra. Theirs is also the form which has inspired the genius of Buckminster Fuller, the architect of the twenty-first century, who has evolved, among other things, the geodesic dome, of which we shall hear more shortly.

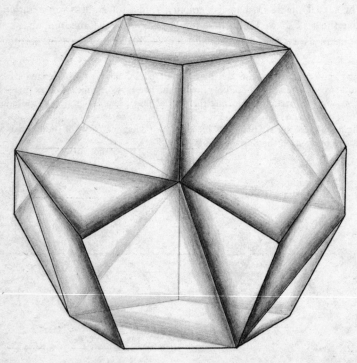

60. The Dodecahedron, fifth and final of the sacred solids, has twelve pentagonal faces and twenty points – the inverse of the Icosahedron, which has twenty faces and twelve points. This crystal is in fact simply five interpenetrating cubes – one of which is picked out for the eye, though all of them, with a little patience, can be discerned.

5. *The Dodecahedron.* With this fifth and final sacred form, the five-ness of the twelve pentagons in the womb of the icosahedron has flowered outwards and become its twelve pentagonal faces (Fig. 60). This resonates to the fifth element of alchemy, Aether, the subtle substance which unites all the material elements in organic symbiosis. Our culture, in its preoccupation with matter (four-ness) has recognized only four elements, forgetting this last one which is only now being broached again by the subtle sciences of vibration. The dodecahedron's colour is gold – for sunlight – and the arcing spiral in man's aetheric body sweeps from the generative chakra of the loins (in the previous 'mode') up to the brow, where all the rhythms of his being are consciously reconciled.

At either end of the five solids (excluding the first of fire) are the cube of matter and the dodecahedron of aether: the former is kundalini 'earth' energy, the latter, solar and transcendent energy; and they are barely in the 'physical' world at all, as is illustrated by the fact – in the spiral of the human body – that the cube's vibration extends *beneath* the coccyx of man, and the dodecahedron's *beyond* the crown of his head. This paradox is mirrored even in their geometry, since they are the only two solids which are physically and structurally unstable. In model form, unless their connections are rigid, they collapse. They are thus generally built in 'skeletal' form – structures which *ground* their aetherial properties. The skeleton of the cube (as we saw in Figs. 53 and 54) is the two fused tetrahedra of fire, while the skeleton of the dodecahedron is twelve pentagonal stars, or pentagrams, which fill the twelve five-edged faces (Fig. 61).

These pentagrams are the classic symbol of man, his five limbs touching the circle of totality – but in three dimensions the totality is twelve. It thus takes just twelve men to form a group which functions at all levels, responding to the full hierarchy of vibrations. This totality is implicit in the twelve apostles, the twelve members of the jury, the months of the year, the signs of the zodiac and so on.*

In the 'skeletal' dodecahedron (or penta-dodecahedron, as it is called) the most immediate of numerous visual paradoxes is that whereas it is

---

* John Michell raised an eloquent plea for the retention of Britain's now vanished duodecimal monetary system, on the grounds that it was the world's last link with the hierarchical modes of *meaning* behind money. With its fall to the merely decimal mode of energy, it appears that money acquires yet greater power in *dis*proportion to the real rhythms which permeate society.

simply twelve pentagon stars joined tip to tip, it is also five large inter-penetrating cubes, and no stars at all! (Fig. 60 – and 61, if you have the patience.)

A specific mind-quietening technique prior to meditation, which is still practised by certain esoteric groups, is to sit before a pentadodecahedron and to distinguish, without moving the eyes, first each of the stars, and their six planes, and then, shifting only one's focal depth, each of the cubes, and their planes.

Each of the five Pythagorean forms contains the other four harmonically within it. For instance, internally connecting with wires each of the points of the dodecahedron would produce, in the 'golden mean' proportion to its size, a perfect icosahedron inside it. And internally connecting each of this new figure's points to each other would generate a tiny dodecahedron again, and so on; like the pyramid and the vesica piscis, the chain extends from micro- to macrocosm.

61. Penta-dodecahedron, or pentagon star dodecahedron. This is the 'skeletal' version of the above figure, and the only form in which it is structurally stable. It can be made simply by connecting twelve pentagon stars, or pentagrams, point to point.

All these sacred forms are found in nature, for all existence (including chemistry) exteriorizes itself through harmonic economy – each 'step' or 'mean' delineating a given mode of energy – to which primal energies resonate. At a time when gemstones were known to give out vibrations, each according to its colour and density, they were cut in the forms of the sacred polyhedra – or their variations – in order to amplify that resonance. The enormous sapphire in the crown of the Maharaj of Jaipur, dating back to 1300 B.C., is cut to a precise icosahedron – the actual 'shape' of blue water and radiant regeneration. The history of the Hope Diamond is one of continual tragedy – its many owners meeting with sudden death and misfortune – and the esotericists of gem-cutting affirm that this great African diamond demonstrates the danger of ignoring crystal vibrations when cutting a really potent gem.

It is interesting to note that the animal world builds its nests, cocoons and shelters with an almost crystalline economy of form which in many respects mirrors the quality of the creature itself, or rather its adaptation to the materials and 'ordering' principles at its disposal. Researchers testing the effects of LSD on animals at the lower end of the evolutionary spectrum have remarked that few of them exhibit much change except for certain species of spider. When 'tripping', these creatures tend to build extraordinarily complex webs – still performing their basic structural function, but with baroque decorative variations on the basic theme which would ordinarily have been their sole preoccupation. Man too, as his chemistry or consciousness expands, tends to build his shelters, and particularly his places of worship, in inspired variations of 'sacred order'.

It is this recent expansion of awareness which is already giving rise to the architecture of the future, to homes and temples in a 'new dimension' of light and simplicity. Where there is enough freedom from the square and uniform restrictions of 'civilization's' planning permission, buildings are appearing which tend to be circular, or elliptic, their forms hovering again around the proportions of sacred geometry.

Many of the societies which still live in close proximity to their inner environment tend to dwell in circular homes – the igloos of the Eskimos, the wigwams of the Indians, the kraals of African tribes and the round houses of the Celtic tribes in Britain. 'Rational' man, however, is still living largely in square blocks and rooms, inspired by the hundreds of years of war and mistrust which characterize the over-emphasis on reason, when square fortresses and houses are built for defence and the intellect is caged in cubes. But the sphere, like the flower, is open on all sides, and is as vulnerable as the feelings. The geodesic dome, developed by Buckminster Fuller (see Fig. 62), is an extension of the icosahedron which, like the other sacred polyhedra, has powerful qualities that far exceed its purely structural singularity. On the practical level, once the underlying geometry of geodesics is understood, domes are far cheaper than ordinary houses and can be built by a single, barely trained person with little more than a saw, several trees and lots of glass.

Fig. 62.

To live in spheres quickens our awareness of the celestial environment; the sun rising each day in a different place, the lunar phases, solstices and equinoxes, all become as 'real' against the wheeling constellations as they were for our ancestral magicians. The inhabitants of domes become sensitized again to the sphericality of the globe and the sphericality of the fluid universe in which it swims. One of the natural arcs in a geodesic dome, for instance (Fig. 63), can be replaced with twelve facets of differently tinted glass so that as the year progresses, we can see from the colour of the morning's rays (if the dome is correctly oriented) what sign of the zodiac the sun is rising in, and are thus constantly aware – without reference to an astrological ephemeris – of the changing resonances of inner time. People have already responded to the future with premonitionary dreams of a green earth mushroomed with the gem-like homes of Aquarian man – as crystalline as the microorganisms which wheel in the rhythms of the sea.

63. Geodesic dome with tinted glass facets so as to see whether the sun is rising in Aries, Taurus, Gemini, etc.

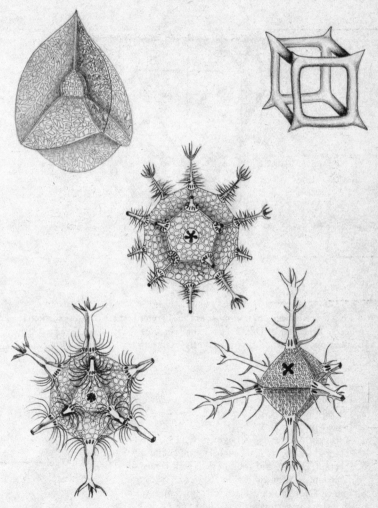

64. The five sacred solids as found in the skeletons of radiolaria, a species of plankton.

65. The Seventh circle, in the midst of the surrounding six of equal diameter, as the heart of the Star of David, from which blooms the Cabbalistic Tree of Life. Observe how the shapes of our presently-used numbers are traced on the Tree.

1: The path traced from Sephiroth 1 to 9 – or down to 10.
2: Traced through B,A,C,8,7.
3: Traced through B,A,2,H,4,7,9,F.
4: A straight to 9, and A straight to D,H,E.
5: C straight to B, to 1, through H, and round 4,7,9 and 8.
6: A round, B,D,F, and round circle with centre 6.
7: B straight to C and down to 8.
8: Traced through the two circles with centres 1 and 6.
9: Round circle with centre 1, round C,E,G, to F.
10: The '1' plus the 'cosmic egg' containing the three circles with centres 1, H and 6.

It is the unfolding of primal forms which gives birth to numbers. Fig. 65 shows the skeleton of the Cabbalistic 'Tree of Life', of which we shall see more in the chapter on 'Maps of Self-Discovery'. It is based entirely on touching circles or, in three dimensions, spheres. The 'cosmic egg' covers the centre of the Star of David, whose six points terminate at the centre of six touching circles. This figure *delineates* all the numbers of the 'sacred decanate', 1 to 10, as well as the twenty-two vibrationary paths between them – equivalent to the twenty-two letters of the Ancient Hebrew alphabet. The actual shapes of the numbers themselves can also be discerned on the tree. The progression of numbers on the Tree of Life, beginning with the Godhead of One and working down to the ultimate diversification of matter at Ten, takes the numerologist to the core of our minds, as well as of the physical world.

Just as water, the basis of all chemistry, has almost no chemistry itself, and yet is the catalyst for many unions, so numbers – unlike words – have almost no intrinsic meaning. Yet their vibration has an integral grammar, which is reproduced in the unfolding symbolism of forms in space. To grasp their 'quality' means also to hold in abeyance our habitual 'quantitative' association with numbers, as in the digits on a bank statement or in a telephone book. Whereas mathematics uses numbers as two-dimensional tools, the numerologist uses them as multi-dimensional symbols. It is this perspective which, although unfamiliar to our early twentieth-century minds, we shall try to grasp.

The order of numbers, like the world of everyday experience, *mediates* between 'odd' and 'even', the 'rational' and the 'sensed' – and it is through the 'sense' that the numerologist awakens a neglected faculty, one with which he teaches himself to count again. To see anew means always to return to the beginning, to where nothing exists, and the story of the genesis of numbers, which for the symbolist parallels the development of the human consciousness, unfolds as follows:

1 Our beginning is already our most distant and abstract of numbers, as well as our first and simplest. It is the digit which borders on the ineluctable 'O', the Nothing, called by the Cabbalists 'The Infinite Light of Chaos' – the place too bright even for numbers to exist. 1 stands up like a phallus; it is the vertical 'I am' to which *everything* attests, the chord between the abyss and the heavens of non-existence on which the pearl of Being is threaded. But for 1 to question, to become conscious of itself, there are:

2   The mirror-image of 'I am'; the 'I know that I am'. The 'I am' and the 'I know'* woo and war and mate with each other throughout the panoply of creation. In Christianity God and the Devil are at war: sin and sanctity are irreconcilable. In Taoism the Yin and the Yang are symbiotic opposites, where the masculine/feminine, light/dark, centrifugal/centripetal polarities are fused in the same protean womb of creation.† Our smallest particles are either positively or negatively charged, but they are mediated by the fickle neutron, which is neither both nor one nor the other – but nevertheless it is:

3   For 3 is harmonious stability, and stability is now conscious movement, and movement is function – in the case of man, understanding. From the (1) I am, and the (2) I know that I am, comes the (3), the putting into practice of that wisdom; it is Zeno's 'point from which to move the earth', and the fiery tripod towards one's destiny. With awareness of the kinetic prodigality of 3, comes:

4   The stocktaking, the measuring and cataloguing of the gift of life. It stands 4-square at the corners of the earth and surveys its vast potential; and seeing the cornucopia of its inheritance it is forced to 'Be' anew in:

5   Which judges now what it has conserved in memory and experience. It represents Law – the Law of the lower worlds of which we are partly made – and is the master of the intricacies of chemistry and mechanics.‡ It is universally the number of Man, the 5-limbed microcosm strung between two worlds – being at the middle of 10, the Pythagorean decad – between the 'o' before 1, and the 'o' after 1, or 10: thus 5 is the 'I' at last between the absolute above and the absolute below, the self which can use the Promethean power for himself – and

* We are reminded of Descartes' famous 'cogito ergo sum', the logic of which was later tarnished by the wits' 'cogito cogito ergo cogito sum' – perhaps a more accurate dictum in the face of the new scientific dissolution of any solid point on which to stand.

† Decade by decade the pendulum of modern cosmology has swung between an 'expanding' and a 'contracting' universe. 'Entropy' maintains that the pole of disintegration is winning and the universe is winding down; whereas the 'expanding' concept holds the opposite, that from out of the o of nowhere, energy leaks into existence. The 'steady state' theorists are playing it safe, despite knowing that all is in constant flux.

‡ The Pentagon in Washington became a symbol of unyielding human law. During the peace demonstrations of 1968, the flower children tried to levitate it three feet above the ground with mantras. The guards were not amused by the flowers placed in their gunbarrels nor, it would seem, did they believe that the power of 5 could be raised to 6.

be cast from the Garden of Harmony which he has broached – or else look up further, to the laws he does not manage but of which he is also a part, to:

6 And see that there is a lambent order in the world of matter, that the laws he has discovered as 'his own' are open also to the influences of symmetry and style. 6 is the triad of dualities, the venusian mediator between invisible and visible worlds; the goddess of beauty and love, for the ripples on the surface of natural law attest to a heavenly influence, from:

7 Where the focal depth is changed again, into a world of Victory and Magnitude, associated with safety and delight. It is sacred and mysterious, like the veils of initiation, or the seals of Solomon; as barren yet as fruitful as the Virgin – being neither the product nor the factor of any other number in the decad, and the highest one divisible only by itself. The heptagram alone (bottom left of Tetraktys – Fig. 21) is confusing to the eye while still being symmetrical, for it reflects a world different from the one of our normal understanding. In Hebrew the words for 'seven' and an oath are closely related, for the number rings with the knowledge that just out of sight is profound and magical security, and 'the Oath of Seven' was to resonate **trust** into the temporal world. The long list of deities, sections and pillars which come in sevens (the colours of the rainbow, the musical notes, etc.) represent the sacred triumph which cannot be empirically grasped. God rested on the seventh day, and the week was ended and begun, like a king's reign at his death, thus:

8 Brings awareness of heavenly rhythms, that each point of rest is a point of beginning. 8 is the vertical sign of infinity, the only number other than zero which can be endlessly traced with the same rhythmic stroke. It rings of flux and reflux, of involution and evolution, of the enantiomorphic process of space and time. It involves the duality of 2 (of which it is a product – being 2 touching zeros), but in a higher 'octave'. In 'gematria', the magical application of number power where numbers are ascribed to specific letters, 8 is the digit value of 'IHVH', the Hebrew term for Jehova – as it is for the Greek 'IEOSUS'. 8 was also the 'Dominical Number' for the Egyptians' Thoth, the Assyrians' Nebo, the Greeks' Hermes and the Romans' Mercury; it was the quicksilver principle between the spheres, and hinted of:

9 Which, like 1, borders again on the ineluctable zero. It is the end of a macrocosmic and spiritual attainment, the goal of endeavour, called in the kabbala the Basis or Foundation, for its scope is so broad that it is immutable, while still, to the adept, being knowable. Whereas 3 was the first tripetal, fiery departure, 9 is a tripod of 3s, corresponding to 'pure intelligence' of all the vibrationary worlds to which man is potentially heir. And with:

10 We return to 1, the self as a conscious microcosm again. The 'spirit puts on flesh' and returns again to this world. 10 is the Kingdom of God on earth – the bricks and the pains and the flowers of my own life, but now transformed by the evolutionary journey through numbers, for no amount of spiritual attainment has purpose unless it is ultimately grounded in matter, in who and where I am. It is the number 10, the highest of numbers, because uniting the infinite with the here-and-now, that it occupies the most menial place at the bottom of the kabbalistic Tree of Life (Fig. 89). This wisdom of 10 does not exhort the adept to leave the material world and enter the world of spirit, for it recognizes that ultimately we are the stewards of divine power on *this earth*, and that to live an aetherialized consciousness alone is as unbalanced as to be absorbed by materialism alone.

The essential polarities of thought and feeling run through numbers in the alternations of odd and even, as we can see in the great 'magic squares', once recognized as mirroring the vibrationary qualities of the seven major planets. The simplest is the magic square of Mercury – the planet closest to the sun.

We start with a grid of squares – the '4-square' framework of matter – which we divide equally with 2 vertical lines to attract the upper fires, and 2 horizontal lines to attract the lateral or worldly fires. These 4 lines, in the strange generative nature of numbers, produce 5 columns, giving us 9 microcosmic squares for placing all the numbers in the decade between the zeros.

The sum of these numbers 1 to 9, added consecutively ($1 + 2 = 3$, $3 + 4 = 7$, etc.), is 45 – the gematric equivalent of ADM, or ADAM,* the first and last man. Since the system of numerology requires reading numbers from right to left, with number 45 we find the 5 – the sign of

---

* Transposed from their Greek gematric equivalents.

Man – is backed with the strength and stability of 4 – and their sum is again equal to 9, for it is a cycle in itself. To place these numbers in the squares we start with our *own* point of inquiry, so the number of Man, 5, goes in the centre. As we are surrounded by the Infinite, the subtle, feminine cosmos, the even or feminine numbers are places in a circle around us, in the 4 outer corners of our large square.[5]

It remains to fill in the 4 'male' numbers. The primal '1', which emerges from the abyss of nothing, is beneath me, and the '9', moving up into the zero of transcendence, is above. And since our square is only a mirror of the god in ourselves, we see the god looking back at us in reverse, and the heavenly number of 7 sits at his right hand (our left), and the 3, the Holy Ghost of creative power, at his left.

67. 'Lightning bolt' from the smallest magic square of Mercury.

The 5 of Mankind is the centre of both the feminine, lunar circle, and of the masculine, solar, straight-angled cross.* The integrity is maintained, for the sum of the 3 numbers in any one of Adam's 'ribs', whether vertical or horizontal, is always 15 (Man's 5, and his beginning, 1, which must include woman), and the sum of these are 6, the harmony of polarities, the venusian number of beauty and love.

The sum of all the male numbers, 1, 3, 5, 7 and 9, is 25, and of the female numbers, which includes mankind's 5 as the centre of the square and the circle (since man and woman are part of each other): 2, 4, 6, 8 and 5, is also 25. 5 and 2 are the creative polarities in mankind, and with

---

* We see the 2 represented still as an integral symbiosis in the Bishop's orb ☒. Alternatively, we find it with the female polarity dominating, but with the male always present, in the zodiacal symbol for Venus ♀.

them enters the heavenly transcendent number of 7, which is their sum. Thus in this square of Mercury the sum of both the male and female numbers is 25, or 5^2 – alternatively their combined sum is 50 – which numerologically is also 5, or mankind linked to the infinite.

Tracing merely the sequence of the numbers produces the 'lightning bolts' distinctive of each of the planetary magic squares, long believed to mirror the vibrationary nature of their particular integrity. In W. S. Andrew's book,[6] Paul Carus traces the relationship between such lightning bolts and the Chladni figures (discussed in the following chapter) produced on a disk vibrated at certain frequencies.

'Frequency', which is how *often* something occurs, makes up the immeasurable stuff of diversity. All that you have so far read are the frequency patterns of just twenty-six letters. Science has to date isolated merely 106 elements which constitute the entire physical universe – their essential differences (rather than being 'shape' which distinguishes letters from one another) are determined only by the *number* of electrons which orbit the nucleus. We also know, in the words of Columbia University physicist Dr Rabi, that: 'Atoms can act like little radio transmitters broadcasting on ultra short-waves.'

These 'waves' are again determined by frequency or number, but just what these frequencies *are* – like the pyramid, or the potential range of our own vision – is still an enigma. But the clues are here now; for geometry is the heart of shape, and number the heart of geometry, and even language (our own thoughts) is both the *shape* of letters, and the *numbers* of their repetition.

The symbolic power of numbers opens chamber after chamber of secret order merely waiting to be released. For this reason 'mathematics' derives from 'mathesis' – reminiscence – from the Pythagoreans' recognition that all wisdom is but the bringing out of laws already latent within us.

We pride ourselves on having taken up the torch of Rationalism from the Ancient Greeks – but have we misunderstood them? For 'ratio' means harmony, which surely entails harmonizing the 'intellect' with the 'feeling'; and our 'rationalism' of today is quite out of harmony with the 'meaning' of the hidden power beneath things. Even in the profane sphere the naked logic of numbers has led to miracles of technology, but to what mysteries do they lead in the sphere of the sacred?

The rational manipulation of numbers has its limits, and we are now being forced to transcend them and to move into deeper, symbolic layers of order. The limits of mathematical logic, and yet also the music it leads to, are illustrated in the remarkable Fibonacci series, which, although expressed in far more ancient antiquity, is named after the twelfth-century visionary mathematician. Both the Pi proportion (that of a circle's circumference to its radius) and the Phi, or 'golden mean' proportion are harmonies which are visually and aesthetically obvious, but logically and mathematically imprecise. They are numerically expressible only in irrational fractions and decimal places. The simplest visual expression of the golden mean proportion is:

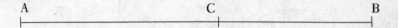

where CB is in the Phi proportion (or 1·618 etc. etc.) of AB's length. In 'space' this proportion is an intrinsic part of the grammar of growth. All the arms of the pentagram cut each other in this proportion, the golden mean rectangles in the icosahedron are 1·618 of a square, the icosahedron generated inside the dodecahedron (or the reverse) is in the same golden mean proportion to the larger one's size, the points depressed along a violin string, producing the octaves, are factors and sums of the

same proportion, and so on. The Fibonacci series makes a valiant attempt to trap this proportion in numbers, and the patterns of its pursuit – like an entomologist after a butterfly – are oddly alluring. Every number in the series, after zero, is followed by the sum of the two preceding numbers: i.e. 0, 1, 1, 2, 3, 5, 8, 13, etc. If any of these terms is divided by its predecessor, we get increasingly close to Phi, but it is always just ahead of us. As the terms in the series ascend they reach: 21, 34, 55, **89**. Once 89 is divided by its predecessor: 89/55, or 1·61818, the series has settled at least into the regular 0·618 after the decimal point – though there are constantly shifting numbers beyond those three places. The precise 'golden mean' is numerically achieved by this series only somewhere near' where its sequence spirals into infinity. Thus the hidden order which surrounds us cannot be perceived by 'logic' alone, and we must pass over to the ships of symbolism to ride through the waters of the soul.

Sacred geometry and numerology are now being used as tools not only for self-knowledge, but to uncover the science and philosophy of

69. The generative properties contained by the twelve-pointed star, or Dodecagon, which give rise to the 'diminishing' or 'expanding' squares in the 'golden mean' proportions. The numerical relationships in the figure parallel the 'Fibonacci Series' – and are to be found on the centres of daisies, sunflowers and other plants. In this figure, the geometry of the sunflower is superimposed over the ground plan of the Lady Chapel at Glastonbury Cathedral.

our distant ancestors; for these patterns are reflected in the pyramids, the temples of the Hindus, the observatories of the Incas and the Aztecs, the mosques and tiles of the Muslims and even in the proportions of certain Gothic cathedrals. The stars we see on the conical hats of fairy-tale wizards derive from the sacred polyhedra once worn by gnostic magicians; and the 'lightning bolts' in their cloth and seal rings were but the sequence tracings in the numbers of magic squares. The flowers and shells which figure as temple symbols or as the insignia of masonic guilds, reflect in their 5- and 6-fold symmetries the clues to a lost knowledge of cosmic equilibrium (see Fig. 41).

The central place occupied by music in the education of the Greeks was due to the recognition that the harmonics of sound unlocked in the student an awareness of the interplay of invisible relationships. Novalis, in his *Fragments*, comments that:

'Sound seems to be nothing but broken movement in the sense that colour is broken light.'

That form, light and sound 'break' and change mode at specific points is the pursuit of occult symbolism, and we learn to see the truth in Alberti's statement that:

'The numbers by means of which the agreement of sounds affects our ears with delight, are the very same which please our eyes and our minds.'

The fact that certain shapes, determined by numbers, actually vibrate – have power – is being put to practical use by architects in Britain, for instance, who are applying the angles and forms of Pythagorean geometry to the design of hospital wards and school-rooms (and ordinary living spaces) so as to enhance the psychological attitude, as well as

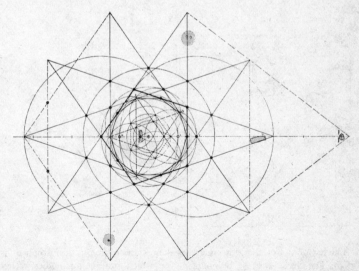

70. The geometry of two opposing pentagrams – as found on the opposing faces of the Dodecahedron – superimposed over the groundplan of Stonehenge.

the actual physiology, of the inhabitants. It has been established that the walls of a room slanting inwards towards the ceiling at specific angles: / \ tend to psychologically 'ground' and practicalize the occupant, whereas the reverse: \ / lightens his mood, altering his entire mental attitude and predisposing him towards inner experience, reverie and creative imagination. The forms of the pyramids, as we have seen, are being marketed for their unequivocal – though still immeasurable – vibrationary qualities. The laws of mechanics, the working of pulleys, the moving parts in engines, reflect the same economy and 'points of rest' determined by the ratios and proportions of the lost science. But it is now that the tangible forms of arcane symbolism are beginning to appear and breathe again. Perhaps 'aestheticism' of form as well as of thought, of music as well as of colour, is as vital a part of our preservation – and survival – as the air we breathe and the water we drink.

The proportional ratios mirrored in the sacred solids may still appear merely curious, until they are also seen to determine the unfolding of shells and ferns, the curvature of the cochlea in the ear, the spiralling of water, antlers, human bones and the Crab Nebula in Ursus Major. The human foetus also develops to the constant music of these proportions – as does the explorative human soul: for the universal laws operating in the gravitational field do not originate *in* it, they are not found *within* the

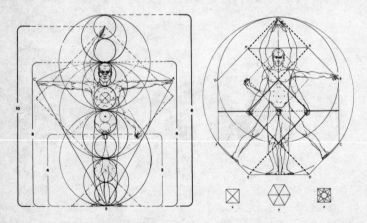

71. The harmonics of sacred geometry as they relate to the physical proportions of man. The circles suggest 'points of power' which underlie our bodies, rather as the 'points of power' in a parabolic spiral determine the morphology of a Nautilus shell (see Fig 40).

minute particles of matter – these particles merely respond to what originates 'beyond', at the periphery of infinity, which is nonetheless always immediate.

Olive Whicker, in her amazing book on projective geometry, writes:

Tradition has always been overcome by courage . . . An equally courageous step is required by the biologist: to realize and admit that *a living body is alive precisely when it is not functioning solely according to the known laws of physics and chemistry*, but is under the influence of laws which save it from the fate it would undergo if it were – laws which actually counteract the disintegrating processes of the lifeless realm.[7]

That the physical world ebbs and flows against a hidden and vital order is brought to light in the following chapter, where matter and experience – in our most immediate realm – are seen to exhibit patterns of connection which attest to an underlying energy of great beauty.

5 Vibration

Experiences having the same rate of vibration will fuse.

SUSAN HILLER (Painter)

A curious inconsistency remaining from the early and literal days of rationalism is that what we cannot see, touch and hear, is not real. Although science may have engendered a 'cold cosmology of determinism', its basic concern is now with energy, or 'vibration' – a word deriving from *vibrare*, to shake or move, and giving the root of many European languages' terms for 'life'.

The process of 'life' – the constant flux and regeneration of everything, from nebulae to pebbles on the beach – is as invisible, and yet as real, as the deities and spirits which fell out of favour *because* they could no longer be seen. Yet through the illusion of 'vision' on our electronic screens and amplifiers, the invisible frequencies of the electromagnetic spectrum have become pivotal realities, although at a different level (like the world of spirits) from that which can be directly experienced by the five senses.

At the lower end of the vibrationary spectrum, television and radio frequencies constantly penetrate our walls and ourselves, and our culture nightly sits transfixed to their dancing signals. Tapes and records are also essential parts of our environment, and for hours we envelop ourselves in the shifting fabric of their amplified vibration. But what other vibrationary frequencies permeate us?

Chromatics

Light, heat and colour do not exist on their own. Energy of many different wave-lengths streams from the sun and other sources, but very little of it makes itself perceptible to the human senses by reflecting off, or interacting with, matter. Heat is the tangible result of the disturbed oscillation of atomic particles; light, in the case of sunshine, is the visible reflection off the particles in the atmosphere; and the colours we see are simply the vibrationary rebound of the frequencies which a 'coloured' object has refused to absorb. A black cat absorbs all the colour rays, and gives back none; a white one rejects them all and gives them all back; while the morpho butterfly has absorbed all except that which we interpret as blue. In a total vacuum there can be neither heat, light nor colour – merely that insensible energy which streams from outer space and so mysteriously maintains the quick as well as the inert world.

John Stewart Collis writes:

Just as heat waves are incompetent to excite vision, so also there are waves which, though feeble as regards heat and powerless as regards light, are yet of the highest importance on account of their capacity to produce chemical action. In fact they feed us. The whole vegetable world may be considered as a vast mill receiving its motorpower from the sun. This is so much more than a mere figure of speech that some scientists speak of organic phenomena as altered or differentiated sunshine.[1]

Whereas most of us can name – and therefore distinguish – perhaps twelve or fifteen different colours, there are professional dyers and painters who have a colour vocabulary of several thousand shades. This range of vision causes them to *see* a coloured universe which is as different from the average man's as a fifteen-word language is different in its scope and dimension from one of two thousand words. With depth of vision come the dimensions of quality and mood. This flat schema of the presently-known electromagnetic spectrum, the minute range detectable by our physical senses, gives no hint of the deeper dimensions in which the vibrations of light alone (at the infra- and ultra-visual levels) loom the universe with life. We tend to forget that the profusion throughout the centuries of our painted art, which commands such immense value both philosophically, in the 'ordering of our cosmos', and monetarily, in the markets of the world, springs from that tiny, two-dimensional wave-band marked 'colour' on the chart.

But at Hygeia Studios in Gloucestershire, under the direction of Theo Gimbel, the energies of the deeper dimensions of colour, shape and sound are being explored. It is one of the increasing number of organizations now providing statistical credence for the chromatic visions pursued by such pioneers as Goethe and Rudolph Steiner. It is here also that the work of Lüscher, who correlated colour preferences with human temperament, is being explored in finer detail. Rather than merely exciting emotional 'mood', specific shades are revealed to have a measurable physiological effect on the body. A precise shade of red has been isolated which increases the pulse rate, blood pressure and respiration; and another, of blue, which correspondingly reduces them. High concentrations of a certain shade of yellow are being used in the alleviation of migraines and asthma, and of green to 'settle' victims of shock.

Much of Gimbel's work at Hygeia Studios also correlates colours with shapes – particularly the five sacred solids and other organic forms. The 'quality' of certain shades is mysteriously amplified by specific forms: certain combinations of shape and colour have either a destructive or a regenerative effect on living organisms. The British National Health Service has commissioned Gimbel to design various hospitals and sanatoria incorporating combinations of shape and colour known to benefit certain ailments. Colours known to sustain weak patients are being used for lighting in post-operative wards. Other shades are put on the walls of psychiatric wards to soothe those suffering from hypertension. Colour is now being used in various schools for handicapped children – most notably in the Sunfield Children's home in Worcestershire – where considerable success is reported in the treatment of what are described as 'chronic personality deficiencies'.

Chromotherapy, the practice of healing with colour, has long been a part of occult medicine. With the physiological, as well as psychic, effect which certain shades are known to have on us, we look anew at the use of colour in religious traditions: the powerful cochineal blue of the Western Mystery's priestesses, the black habits of nuns, which absorb all the sun's rays and give back none; the use of stained glass in cathedrals, or of gems cut to those forms which amplify their colour vibration for specific rituals.

Colour itself appears as a tenuous film over the world of matter, and its differentiation reflects qualitative differences which exist at invisible levels, for colour itself is perceptible not only to the visual sense. Since the time when the first Westerners arrived in Samoa and discovered blind people who could describe the colour of objects merely by holding their hands over them, there have been pockets of research into 'eyeless sight' or 'dermochromatics'. One of the more recent and remarkable possessors of this faculty is the Russian housewife Rosa Kuleshova. Though not blind herself, she was brought up in a family of blind people, and as well as learning many of the sensory techniques of location and orientation normally only used by the deaf or the blind, she also taught herself to distinguish colours simply by holding her hands over them. Various neurologists and psychiatrists, under the auspices of the Soviet Academy of Sciences, have thoroughly tested Rosa and found that she can not only distinguish colours, but also read newsprint and sheet music under glass, all through her fingertips!

One of the researchers, Professor Novomeisky, extended his tests to other blind people, and now has a class teaching eyeless sight to over eighty students. Some find their tongues, earlobes or the tips of their noses more sensitive to colour than their fingers.* Novomeisky has shown that by one or other of these methods, one in six people can be taught to distinguish between two primary colours after merely a few hours' training. Some of his students can describe colours which are shielded with copper plate – 'seeing' what is invisible to the sighted. Many people practising dermochromatics note that colours produce specific sensations which – since colour is radiated – can be felt from up to a foot above the coloured object. A loose scale of these sensations was evolved by the Soviet students: 'Red burns, orange warms, yellow barely warms. Green is neutral, and violet cools while simultaneously pinching.'[2]

Apart from sensations of hot and cold, students also reported that colours: '. . . stung, bit, hit, pressed, pinched and, it seems, blew on their hands' (ibid.).

This has led to a strong interest, particularly among the fringe and occult circles of the West, in the capacity to experience colour with a miraculous new intensity – to say nothing of the fringe benefit of reading in the dark! Dermochromatics is an intriguing example of an avenue of vision awakened by the blind.

When in recent years Newtonian mechanics began to give way to physics, and to the study of energy in its more rarefied forms, even light, matter and sound revealed themselves to be merely differences in the frequency of vibration. Now each of these manifestations is found to have reverberations which extend beyond the empirical spectrum, and, though long accessible to our mediumistic faculties, they are only just beginning to be pursued by the 'subtle sciences'.

* Erotic literature (which like all suppressed media is alive with archetypal symbols and thus with clues to our invisible environment) often refers to the penis and the vagina as being able to perceive both 'taste' and 'colour'. These most sensitive of organs – at times of transcendent lovemaking (as described in certain Tantric texts) – may experience the 'deep blue' or 'radiant yellow' of their lover's counterpart.

Cymatics

One of the first people in our time to render vibration into visible forms was the eighteenth-century German physicist Ernst Chladni, who began by scattering sand on steel disks and observing the changing patterns produced by playing various notes on a violin. These 'Chladni figures', which have so inspired artists and symbolists, result from the fact that the disk resonates to the violin only in certain places – shifting the sand to those areas which are inert.

Chladni's work inspired the late Hans Jenny of Zurich to spend ten years duplicating and expanding his experiments with sophisticated equipment, and he named the pursuit Cymatics – the study of the interrelationship of wave-forms with matter.[3]

Since the circle seems to *mediate* harmonic patterns as no other shape will do, Jenny also used disks, and scattered them with liquids, plastics,

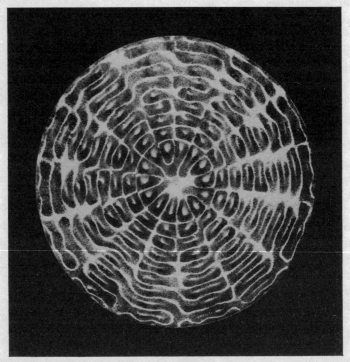

72. Chladni figure, resulting from vibrating sand particles at given sound frequencies.

metal filings and powders. He then vibrated the disks through the controlled medium of a crystal, observing that as the pitch ascended the musical scale, the harmonic patterns on the disks also changed, many of them to organic shapes: the vanishing spirals of jelly-fish turrets, the concentric rings in plant growth, the patterns of tortoise-shell or zebra stripes, the pentagonal stars of sea-urchins, the hexagonal cells of the honey-comb, etc.

All these, of course, are the same geometrical and vortical forms which the sacred geometrian discerns underlying both the ordering of physical matter and the ordering of human consciousness into deeper dimensions of vision. With Chladni figures, as well as with the crystals of sacred geometry, we see how symbols are not merely abstract ideas, but actual ciphers to the vibrationary music which knits us all together. To him whose feelings are alive to depth, the forms of snow crystals, the mandala faces of flowers, actually resonate to the awakening harmony within him. It is only to the culture – or individual – which sees merely in three dimensions, that the universe is an existential fluke of chemistry with no rhyme or purpose.

The intriguing point about cymatics is that *inorganic* matter vibrated simply with sound produces '*organic*' shapes, both moving and static. Jenny's remarkable film *Cymatics* shows that raising the pitch of sound causes a static pattern to invert itself into a moving one; by raising it again, a static, though different, pattern is produced once more, and so on. Thus, with the rising of the musical scale – which in all cases is 'fluid' vibration – its formalized expression on the disks alternates between static and fluid.* With any one of these patterns, whether fluid or static, we have a visual expression of the yin/yang concept of duality, having always two patterns on the disk: the one formed by sand, and the background which is free of sand. The runnels of sand which we *see* are simply where it has collected at the 'dead' areas of the disk, whereas the 'life' of the pattern is vibrating in the background behind, or *between* the runnels, where invisible energy is causing chaos to coalesce into form. The paradox is that the *visible* expression of energy is the inverse of the actual vibrationary pattern, which is *invisible*. After centuries of concentrating only on what it can see and touch, science is now beginning to

* We see a parallel here with the evolution of civilizations, which consolidate into giant patterns of static form, crumble into phases of movement and creative vitality, and gell again into periods of conservatism. Like the altering Chladni figures, their points of change – or 'metanoia' – are marked by a return to chaos, to a lack of any coherent pattern, before the society begins to respond once more to the new vibrationary frequency, or perhaps to the same harmonic, but in a different key.

look *between* these runnels, into the background of metaphysical order. We are reminded again of the Gnostic's assertions that the physical world is but a pale shadow – the mirror image or outermost shell, of a supreme ordering energy which exists in another dimension.

These formal 'exteriorizations' of vibration on a disk are not confined to two dimensions: certain frequencies cause all the matter to collect in the middle of the disk, raising it into a vase-shaped column of curves and flutings, reminiscent of tubular sponges. Another frequency observable in Jenny's film raises particles of iron into an army of tall vertical soldiers which march menacingly across the disk in defiance of gravity. Some of these experiments may be practised with sand, or sugar, on a drum. I have tried it on the inside of a tambourine, where the wooden surround prevents the material from escaping.

Jenny went still further and built a 'tonoscope' which transforms sounds uttered into a microphone into their visual representation on a screen. The sacred Hindu syllable 'Om', when correctly uttered into the tonoscope, apparently produces the circle 'O', which is then filled in with concentric squares and triangles, finally producing, when the last traces of the 'm' have died away, a 'yantra' – the formal geometrical expression of sacred vibration which is found in many of the world's religions (Fig. 73). The 'squaring of the circle', symbolizing the harmonic marriage between matter and spirit, also appears in the tonoscope in response merely to notes struck, or uttered, at the correct pitch.

73. A Tantric Buddhist 'Yantra', or meditational mandala, showing the frequency patterns of diminishing harmonics.

Here too is the first evidence to suggest that the script – where it remains – of sacred, liturgical languages (such as High Javanese or Hebrew) bears a much closer resemblance to its forms in the tonoscope than do the commonly spoken languages of today. If confirmed, this supports the theory that liturgical language and music supplied not only a special vocabulary through which the ancient priest classes could speak of different realities, but a vocabulary which itself resonated to the vibrations it described.

The chaotic forms which appear in the tonoscope in response to the profane languages of everyday use perhaps reflect how far we have fallen from the hidden 'Eden' of subtle vibration. Legends of the Navajo Indians – famous for their sand paintings – speak of the time when their shamans produced pictures in the sand by merely 'speaking' to it.

The 'genesis' legends, or 'cosmogonies', of Ethiopia tell of the origins of language, of how the first men could only sing – like the birds, or the wind in the reeds – but how gradually they forgot the tune and had eventually to make do simply with the speaking of words. The vibration of music, such a primal part of primitive expression, hints at a forgotten awareness of the rhythms and tones which actually keep us alive. It has always amazed Western anthropologists that so-called primitive peoples, with their 'childlike' minds, have such a sophisticated grasp of rhythm and pattern. 'Magic knots' and weaves, of extreme complexity and balance, are found even among the 'stone-age' peoples of New Guinea. Until recently, the Melanesian mariners took to sea with them as navigational aids spherical baskets woven with the rhythmical vortices which mirrored the patterns of wind and current in the South Pacific. Whether such tapping of vibration is purely instinctive, or the shards of a forgotten science, we should not be blind to the crystalline mandals in both sacred music and art which can lead technologically-biased man out of the strait-jacket of two-dimensional thought.

Is magic so distant when we can now produce a known shape in a disk of sand merely by striking the right pitch? If magic is the knowledge of invisible laws, then we are hot on its trail, and with its rediscovery comes the taste of what religion might have been – a technology of the laws of macrocosmic equilibrium, which had little use for our gross mechanical toys. Cymatics is showing that form and movement, like light and colour, are simply a matter of 'sound' or vibrationary frequency. It has even been suggested that the primal 'Word of God' so enigmatically mentioned in Genesis refers to the note which causes man, composed of but a few of the 106 known elements, to stand up and walk on the earth.

Resonance

Chladni discovered that his sand particles formed shapes in response to a violin played even in the *next room*. Any musician knows that in an auditorium full of middle C tuning forks (designed to vibrate at precisely 256 cycles per second), only one of them need be struck for all the rest to resonate in sympathy.

It was only recently established that a good violin continually murmurs to itself as it resonates to the many frequencies which permeate its environment.* Resonance is not contingent on volume but on pitch: to resonate in sympathy, the density, shape and proportions of an object must be 'similar' to those of the radiating object – but the 'similarity' is not always readily discernible.

A French engineer, Professor Gavraud, nearly quit his job at the top of a Marseilles office block due to perpetual illness until he discovered that because of its particular proportions and materials, his office was resonating at an inaudible frequency to an air-conditioning plant in a neighbouring building. The frequency was making him sick, but he was able to cure himself simply by recovering his walls with a less resonant material. Gavraud became fascinated by sound and, intrigued by the whole range of low frequencies produced by the French police whistle with a pea in it, he built a giant six-foot version of it powered by compressed air. The unfortunate technician who first tested this whistle died instantly, a post mortem revealed that his internal organs had been thoroughly scrambled by the sound. One is left wondering whether the good professor might have done better simply to change his office in the first place, instead of getting caught up in the magic of resonance.

But if resonance is not contingent on volume so much as on pitch, it is the dimensions and proportions in frequency which remind us again of the occult traditions. In both Mexico and Peru there is a legend which tells that the ancient peoples were scientists of 'sound', with which skill they had no need of technological impedimenta. They could split massive stone slabs along precise harmonic lines with sound alone, and then 'resonate' them into position. Thus the vast and precisely laid

* At a different level, only detectable by very subtle instruments, or the human psyche, certain crystals also continually murmur to themselves.

temples of Uxmal and Machu Pichu were raised and patterned – according to this legend – in symphonies of sound. Their religion recognized each individual as having a particular note and pitch. With the 'sound knowledge', a man could be 'purified' and raised by vibrationary mantras or, conversely, slain by a single note. An echo of this is found in the 'kiai' of the Samurai warriors in medieval Japan. The biologist Dr Lyall Watson suggests that when uttered at the correct pitch the kiai '. . . produces partial paralysis by a reaction that suddenly lowers the arterial blood pressure'.[4]

If sound can kill, then it can also quicken. Are the chants and liturgical rhythms of the Church merely the shadow of a long-vanished science in the West also? Many religions still change the names of novitiates in recognition of the fact that each time they are called by their new name they are being struck with a new vibrationary pitch, one which resonates to the inner palate they are trying to awaken. Name-changing too emerges not only as symbolic, but as the actual re-tuning of an individual's 'resonance' to one more in harmony with his present axis of growth. Even in the profane area of show-business we see what power can accompany a change of name.

Plato, in his *Cratylus*, remarked: 'When anyone knows the nature of a thing – and its nature *is* that of the thing – he will know the thing also, since it is like the name, and the science of all things which are like each other are one and the same.'[5]

There is a universal fear of revealing one's 'secret' name, which ranges from the arcane groups of the West to the islanders of Bali. This fear perhaps echoes the memory that our inner name – its precise note and pitch – could once be used by the black magicians of frequencies to kill or enslave. Even children, the guardians of the wisdom in racial memory, jealously preserve their self-given secret names, or else have 'familiars', invisible companions, whose real names they often keep to themselves.

Radiesthesia

The recent realization that all objects, whether alive or dead, have 'magnetic' polarity and emanate energy, is the basis of radiesthesia – the detection and interpretation of irradiations. Natural dowsing is an ancient art, as we can see from the pendulums and divining rods held by the carved figures in Mayan and Egyptian reliefs. An instrument recently produced in Germany called a proton magnetometer is a crude form of dowsing rod, and can detect magnetic deviations in the earth's field caused by underground streams, pipes and cables with from 50 to 90 per cent accuracy.[6] Professional human dowsers, however, not only have a higher rate of accuracy in this respect, but can also detect subtler emanations, such as ley lines, or the frequency changes in the human aura. But let us examine the basis of this line of inquiry, approaching it from the point of view of 'sound'.

Objects would not resonate to a sound if they had no 'sound' of their own, a 'sound palate' on which to pick up the resonance. An analogy is found here with people: we are often unaware of ourselves, of our own energy, until we are 'in love', when we begin *resonating* to another, at which time the resonance may so fill us that to everyone around us we hum with an unexpected radiance.

The seventeenth-century English physicist Robert Hooke was one of the first people to question resonance. He watched doctors using percussion as a diagnostic aid and wondered why, when a healthy organ was percussed, it produced a different note from an unhealthy one which was nevertheless of the same density, weight and viscosity. There was clearly some qualitative, rather than formal, difference between the two.

Indeed it is in this awakening science of subtle vibration that formal distinctions begin to merge into distinctions merely of 'quality' or 'relationship'. By what rational or formal means, we ask ourselves, do we *measure* the difference between the rhythms of a Volkswagen engine and the rhythms of the Voodoo drummers of Brazil; between a photograph of Van Gogh's chair and his painting of that chair? Are not these qualitative distinctions the stuff of life – while yet immeasurable in purely rational terms? Proportion and harmony hover between the runnels of rational detection as intangibly as 'vibration' hovers between the sand patterns of a Chladni figure. In music, for instance, a sequence of tones harmonically related are named by such letters as C, D and E, each bearing (in rational terms) a numerical *relation* of periodic motions in time to the fundamental tones from which they start. In any C major scale, it will be C, for instance, but a tone C does not mean the *quantity* of periodic motions in a unit of time, as there are several Cs on a keyboard, each with a different frequency. The C harmonic represents *relationships* to other tones which are not purely quantitative, nor evaluative in physical terms – while yet detectable subjectively in the psycho-intuitive make-up of the listener.

A friend of mine recently attended a meeting of eminent astrophysicists where one of their members was propounding a new theory of quantum physics as it applied to quasars. Several blackboards were covered with complex formulae and the speaker's eyes glinted as he wove his loom of abstruse equations to a triumphant conclusion. At the end of it there was a puzzled hush from his audience, but they had caught his elation. My friend asked a neighbouring scientist if he had understood the train of thought, to which he replied that the reasoning was difficult and in places, he thought, erroneous, but that there was a 'right feeling' about it, an *aesthetic elegance* which was so often the compass-bearing to truth. It is this aestheticism, then, a kind of harmonic resonance, which commands more power than we might suspect, even in our 'rational' undertakings. We think of Galileo's discovery of the relative sizes of the orbits of the sun and the earth, when his pages of mathematics contained errors which, in the final equation, rectified themselves exactly through another unwitting error, concluding that the diameter of the earth's orbit is – as has since been verified – nearly 220 times that of the diameter of the Sun.

It is the harmonics of proportion and relationship which give rise to beauty in every field of perception, for they mediate chaos with order. They recur repeatedly throughout the occult milieu, in number, colour, form and sound. If physical health is the suffusion of the body with unimpeded harmonic 'sound', then disharmony within it can actually be heard – as Robert Hooke discovered – from the altered resonances of its organs. It is the harmonic proportions of a building, as well as a melody, which can inexplicably jar, or uplift, the soul – an enigma which has long caused man to associate architectural form with music.

In Britain a Polish physicist, the late Andrew Glazewski, who was also a Jesuit priest, was recently exploring both the formal and qualitative distinctions in vibration. His speciality was crystallography and plant growth – and their relationships to sound. Musical proportions have long been with us in the gnostic tradition, traces of which we see even in Kepler's *Harmonice Mundi* and in Swedenborg's *Arcana Coelestia*, where the frequencies of music are seen as extending beyond the range of our physical senses. Father Glazewski pursued musical harmonics into the ultra- as well as infra-sonic frequencies, the human ear being sensitive only to the narrow range of approximately 2500 c/sec. He began with atoms, which make crystals, and then moved to crystals, which make plants.

'Atoms are known to be harmonic oscillators,' he wrote; 'the nuclei being the oscillators themselves, the electrons and their orbits being seen as the reverberations and echoes of the periodic harmonic motions of the nucleus.'[7]

In Glazewski's terms this is 'music' on the atomic scale, and the music analogy is well preserved: crystals accrete as a lattice of atoms and molecules which coordinate themselves according to their specific axes, producing the physical shape of the crystal, so that the sub-atomic harmonic ratios are reflected in the larger, visible dimension of the crystal itself. Over a hundred years ago the Berlin crystallographer C. H. Weiss showed that the angles in crystals and the proportions between their sides and planes could be represented as musical relationships. This was taken further by Victor Goldschmidt, another German scientist, who isolated specific matrices, the exact measurements of which showed that the principles of musical harmony are fundamental to crystalline growth. In the 1940s specific crystals were isolated which follow precise tonalities – such as E sharp major, or E flat minor – and show along their coordinate axes different motives for polyphony and counterpoint. These came to be called the 'crystal tuning forks'.

Since all organic matter is composed of crystals or fluids, Glazewski showed how plants composed of specific crystals followed the same harmonics as the crystals themselves, extending offshoots from their stems proportionate to the same musical phases and tonalities. That this harmony is actually 'sonic' rather than merely symbolic of sound, Glazewski has shown by using highly sensitive sound-registration devices which eliminate factors of temperature and barometric pressure.* The sonic field which emanates from the human body is particularly strong, and differs with each individual as radically as fingerprints.

Thus, although minerals appear to our senses to be dead and inert, we know them to be alive with the vibrations which render them visible; but with living things even our senses can detect them swaying and dancing around the invisible and harmonic origins which *subtend* them. Crystals, plants and human beings can now be seen as music which has taken on form.

The substances which are raised into vertical forms by certain tones on Jenny's vibrating disks, defying gravity and exhibiting flutings and protuberances at specific ratios, now take on a new meaning. There is strong evidence that they reflect the same ratios in the swelling and narrowing of growing plant stems, as well as the flutings on the columns

---

* Glazewski's devices were adapted from those evolved by F. Savart and J. Tyndall, and include sensitive jets of gas, flame and liquid which, incidentally, when exposed to instrumental music respond with dramatic visual harmonics.

of Gothic cathedrals such as Chartres. This implies that the gnostic masons were building temples which mirrored the fluid world of vibration, and we are reminded of Goethe's statement that, ideally, architecture is 'frozen music'.

This music is both *within* and *beyond* the objects or living things which it maintains, and it now appears that this mysterious 'music' can also be photographed.

74. Rising smoke in a vacuum responding to musical notes.

Well bowed violin Badly bowed violin Flute French Horn

Research carried out in Russia for over thirty-five years by Semyon and Valentina Kirlian has finally blossomed into six institutes under the aegis of the Academy of Sciences, exploring an extraordinary avenue into 'visible' vibration. This began when Semyon was repairing an instrument used in electrotherapy at a university laboratory near the Black Sea. He noticed that when patients received treatment from the machine there was a tiny flash of light between the electrodes. Seeking to take a photograph with this light he inserted a photographic plate directly between the spark and his hand: to discover that the developed plate revealed a lambent, psychedelic ghost of his outstretched fingers.

When he built his own machine, generating high frequency electrical fields of up to 200,000 oscillations per/sec., and connected it up to a screen, he could observe a new dimension to living objects placed between the electrodes: 'An unseen world opened before my eyes,' he writes, 'whole luminescent labyrinths, flashing, twinkling, flaring. Some of the sparks were motionless, some wandered against a dark background. Over these fantastic galaxies of ghostly lights there were bright multi-coloured flares and dim clouds.'[8]

The highly charged electrical field throws into relief an otherwise invisible 'electrical' or 'plasma' body which emanates from all living things. Kirlian describes how his incipient, as well as his actual, state of health and vitality were rendered dramatically visible: low ebbs reflected a dull and chaotic image on the screen, while high ones produced a coherent matrix of kaleidoscopic fire, shooting off beams of light, like sun-flares, from specific energy points on the skin. This is how he describes the plasma body of a freshly-cut leaf: 'Like summer lightning . . . "craters" erupted – not fiery lava, but radiance like the aurora borealis.'[9]

A procession of eminent men came to the Kirlians' laboratory to observe the plasma bodies of their own hands, or of leaves or bacteria, before the Academy of Sciences would support them further with their research.

This plasma body parallels the 'aura' long claimed to be visible by seers and sages, for the aura too alters in colour and density according to health and vitality; it extends beyond the physical body, and exhibits certain eruptive areas. We are reminded of Paracelsus, the early Greek philosopher, who held the doctrine that the flesh mirrors a semi-corporeal 'star body' which inhabits and maintains it.

A 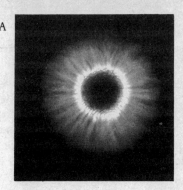 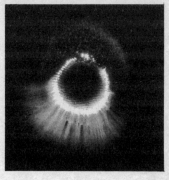 B

75. Kirlian photographs of the 'plasma field' or 'auras' round human fingertips.

a. An even, circular emanation round the finger of a healthy person in a 'calm' state.

b. The aura round the finger of a person in a state of anger. The thick, mottled cloud is raspberry red – a colour characteristic of states of emotional change.

Kirlian has further established that up to a third of a newly-picked leaf can be stripped away, and the entire plasma body remains intact for several hours, exactly mirroring the outline of the leaf before it was mutilated. We think of the amputees who still feel their lost limbs, and of the many creatures, such as lizards, certain insects and octopi, which if not too badly damaged completely reproduce the limbs torn from them by accident – to the continuing puzzlement of biologists. But today's vanguard of zoological research is fully aware of a mysterious ordering force underlying the chemistry of nature. To leave aside for the moment the extraordinary forces at work in the development of the human embryo, which – contrary to prevalent superstition – is not *explained* by the chemistry of the nucleic acids in the DNA spiral, we see a simpler example in certain species of sponges, which grow up to two feet in diameter. Dr Lyall Watson writes of them: '. . . if you cut them up and squeeze the pieces through silk cloth to separate every cell from its neighbour, this gruel soon gets together and organizes itself – and the complete sponge reappears like a phoenix to go back into business again'.[10]

After Mikhail Gaikin, a leading surgeon from Leningrad, had noticed that the flare-points he observed on the skin of his hands under the Kirlian apparatus in no way corresponded to the nerve endings, he was reminded of Chinese acupuncture. He sent the Kirlians an acupuncture chart showing the traditional power-points in the 'Qi' body, and after several months of carefully matching this to the photographed flare-points emerging from the human plasma body, the Kirlians confirmed that the points were identical. This brings us back to 'seeing' again.

The existence of auras is usually denied on the same grounds as was the existence of gorillas until the nineteenth century: namely, that not *enough* people could see them. But auric vision is here to stay, and like a musical sense – or the capacity to detect colour with one's fingers – it is a trainable faculty. With some concentrated practice most of us can develop the capacity to distinguish human auras. In fact the primary barrier to this vision is the cultural conditioning that auras do not exist: but if our culture is in any way swayed by science, then that barrier can now dissolve.

There is already a growing body of people, not necessarily involved in esoteric groups, who specialize in awakening this faculty. At least three general practitioners in the London area now use the shape, density and colour of a patient's aura as a key to diagnosis. Whether this is purely an ocular faculty or one of a subtler nature is still not certain. Personal and shared experience has shown the favourable conditions for seeing auras to be, first, a certain quietness of mood, and secondly, the right lighting

76. That we were once more sensitive to plasma fields and 'auric vision' is suggested by the early depiction of saintly haloes.

conditions, referably a dull background. It is better to look at the whole body *indirectly*, loosening the focus of the eyes, and quieting the self until the senses can be felt as a direct extension of one's consciousness.

Experiments with a practised group of people, each individually drawing the shape and colour of the others' auras, produce intriguingly coherent results. I remember an occasion when four of us individually drew an identical bell-shaped distortion emerging from the side of a disturbed friend's aura. I have attended several esoteric conferences in Britain where, when the speaker becomes too boring (a not uncommon occurrence) the delegates amuse themselves (if the background to the podium is not overlit) by comparing notes on the colour and shape of the speaker's aura. For the more experienced – generally professional mediums or practitioners of fringe medicine – the incidence of agreement is so high that the game ceases to be amusing, and they turn instead to comparing notes on the finer shades of diagnostic and character interpretation.

One of the elder members of the Spiritualist Association of Great Britain, who can see auras under most conditions, relates how once she was on the top floor of a London department store, hurrying to enter a crowded lift. A certain dullness in the lift made her hesitate, and only after the doors had closed in front of her did she realize that her uneasy feeling was because none of the passengers had auras. A moment later the lift-cable broke, and the lift and its occupants plunged to destruction. In the history of occultism there are many other cases which suggest that the aura, that emanation of the 'life force', leaves the body moments *before* death: even in circumstances which (from our narrow perspective) we would term 'accidental'.

But what is it in us that distinguishes perspectives, which even at the coarser levels of vibration allows us to 'experience' anything at all?

Rhythms of the Mind

Whereas mood and thought can both be personally experienced from within, they can now also be partially monitored from without – though appearing to the 'objective' self merely as wave-patterns on a graph. To have had a 'brainwave' is still a quaint expression from the early days of cerebral monitoring; but the body, and the mind in particular, is a hive of electrical and magnetic frequencies. Each thought, as the eminent neurologist Sir John Eccles wrote, initiates '. . . a river of a million sparkling synapses – like a golden loom perpetually weaving and re-weaving its way to a conclusion'.[11]

These eighteen ounces of barely-set jelly – some 98 per cent water – that we nurse in our craniums are suffused with rhythms which are never at rest. Some reverberate to the multiple autonomic processes in the body which are constantly monitored and harmonized; others respond to both external and self-generated impulses in multi-dimensional 'Chladni figures' of thought and vision.

These interlocking rhythms are now being explored with EEG machines and bio-feedback devices (of which we shall see more in the following chapter), and are found to be the very patterns which denote our 'feelings', our 'dreams' and our 'experience'.

Of the vibrationary rhythms which permeate us and which *are* us, some so small that they must be measured in tiny fractions of a cycle per second, the longest – and most recently discovered – traverse the abyss of outer space, originating beyond our galaxy, and have a frequency of millions of miles between troughs. They are very weak and of low frequency, but they are almost indistinguishable from the patterns recorded in the human brain.

It is in this symphony of rarefied order which Aquarian science is beginning to disclose that we find ourselves confronting again the age-old formulae of religious and supernatural science. We wonder if it is perhaps through the laws of harmonics that we can detect the constant order in this invisible web? As John Eccles has remarked, by scrutinizing the mechanics of the brain down to the finest physical detail we still do not find what lives *within* it; and behind the vast chemical machinery of the universe there remains the mystery of the *self which experiences*. It is at this new frontier, broached by the 'twentieth-century alchemists', that the distinctions between 'objective' and 'subjective' knowledge are dissolving, for whereas rational science has hitherto been riveted to the objective approach, in the dimension of subtle vibration (of which we ourselves are made) we are constrained to recognize and monitor our own subjectivity.

There are those who argue that Aquarian science merely expands our *rational* knowledge – revealing the universe to be more complex than we had imagined, but no less 'deterministic'. If this were the case we could conceive of a future sophisticated technology of vibration which, although using the rhythms of nature, is still alienated from their *meaning* – from the realization of their *unity* in a single organic system. But this argument springs from a two-dimensional projection into a three-dimensional framework. The alienation of today's rational technology springs from its addiction to only the unconnected two-dimensional shapes (of Fig. 77), whereas Aquarian science involves the leap into another dimension which shows them all to be facets of a single cosmic form.

At these deeper levels of vibration we detect the first signs of a universal 'homeostasis', a dynamic equilibrium in which we are all integral cells: to 'interfere' with this at any point is literally to harm one's self. For, as the Cabbalists maintained, 'knowledge is power', but in the transcendent scheme of things there is no greater power than being one's *self*. If it is a false power, disconnected from one's essence, then all that we touch, as in the King Midas myth, turns to meaningless gold, as empty of sustenance as our technological toys. It is this direction of Aquarian science, as we see clearly in Clive Backster's work with plants, which brings us sharply back to the meaning of human morality.

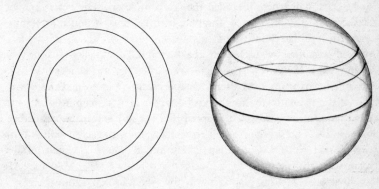

77. These apparently unconnected circles resolve themselves into a single figure – a sphere – once they are seen in the context of a deeper dimension.

Backster Research Foundation

Clive Backster is a forty-eight-year-old former interrogation specialist with the Central Intelligence Agency who until recently was operating a New York training school for police officers in the use of the polygraph, or 'lie detector'. In 1966 he decided to try to measure the rate at which water rose from the roots of a plant to its leaves. He attached the electrodes of a psychogalvanic reflex meter (PGR), a device for measuring electrical skin resistance in human beings, to the leaves of a *Draena*

Massageana plant and, contrary to expectation, discovered that rather than measuring a moisture change, the PGR began tracing a reaction pattern typical of a human subject suffering a brief emotional stimulation. In Backster's words:

I decided to try to apply some equivalent to the threat-to-well-being principle, a well-established method of triggering emotionality in humans. I first tried to arouse the plant by immersing a plant leaf in hot coffee, but there was no measurable response. After a nine-minute interim, I decided to obtain a match and burn the plant leaf. At the instant of this decision, at 13 minutes and 45 seconds of chart time, there was a dramatic change in the PGR tracing pattern in the form of an abrupt and prolonged upward sweep of the recording pen. I had not moved, or touched the plant, so the time of the PGR pen activity suggested to me that the tracing might have been triggered by the mere thought of the harm I intended to inflict upon the plant. This occurrence, if repeatable, would tend to indicate the possible existence of some undefined perception in the plant.[12]

The occurrence *was* repeatable, and led to a wide series of experiments, many of which excluded the 'human factor'. The better known of these was the automated dumping of live brine-shrimp into boiling water at pre-determined intervals within range of the plants. They reacted 'emotionally' each time the massacre took place. On one occasion one of Backster's assistants – whose identity was kept secret from the rest of his team until after the experiment – was elected to destroy one of the plants in the presence of another. The remaining plant was connected to the now 'plant-adapted' PGR, and the team was called in one by one. The surviving plant remained calm with each member until the 'murderer' arrived, at which it went into a 'faint' or, as the Backster team also call it, a 'tizzy'.

Thus not only do plants, until now thought too rudimentary to possess nervous systems, respond as if they did, but they also exhibit a capacity for memory. More strangely still, they appear to be able to communicate, or 'resonate' their shocked or pleasurable experiences to one another. Backster describes how he has attempted to block whatever signals are being passed between the plants with a variety of complex screens and containers. But they continue to communicate, presumably via signals which do not fall within our electrodynamic spectrum.

Backster's discovery of the 'perception' and 'memory' of plants has already been put to practical use – perhaps rather ominously – in various New York criminal investigations.

In one case, when a potted plant had been on the windowsill of an apartment block room where a young woman was murdered, Backster was called in to measure the plant's responses to each of the suspects in the building. It remained calm for all of them, arousing criticism of the use of Backster's technique at such an early stage of its development, until it was later discovered that the murderer was not among the preliminary suspects.

Backster describes how he once kept his dog in the ante-chamber to his laboratory. Before the doorbell rang – which was strident enough to be heard wherever he was working, and greatly disturbed the dog – a faint click could be heard from the bell-mechanism in the ante-chamber, and the dog would immediately creep as far out of earshot as possible. Within his laboratory Backster always knew when his bell was about to ring, because the plants responded dramatically to the apprehensive feeling of the dog next door when it heard the pre-bell click.

This faculty in plants of what Backster calls 'primary perception' seems to be instantaneous. Experiments performed with his colleagues 'attuned' to their particular plants shows that the plants respond to strong 'thought forms' sent by the 'attunee' at the very moment they are transmitted – and despite a separation of hundreds of miles!*

With specially adapted PGRs 'emotional' reactions have also been monitored from amoebas, blood-samples and cell-cultures, and Backster shows that there is a direct inbuilt 'cellular awareness' of life-cycles – of their enhancement or destruction – throughout the biosphere, from man right down to single-celled organisms.† Experimenting with fertilized eggs he found that when an egg was broken, the others in the batch responded with 'shock' even from the next room – an idea which makes us think with apprehension of the suffering caused each time we make an omelette! All life, within its own terms, reveals itself to be just as sensitive to 'suffering' and thus to 'threats-to-well-being' as we are. Vegetarians may now require other reasons for their dietary habits – and there are many others – than the belief that animals suffer and plants do not. Recognition of the 'emotional' or vibrationary states of plants and animals – as well, of course, as humans – at the time of their death, has long been reflected in such religious practices as the Kosher 'quietening' rituals prior to the sacrifice of animals for food, or in the 'blessing' of crops before they are harvested.

* This 'sympathy' or resonance between certain plants and their attunees reminds us of the occult references to 'familiars' in the plant and animal kingdom. This is particularly found among those primitive peoples who are still closely attuned to their hidden environment.
† Indeed, of all the creatures, it appears that man is the least responsive to this underlying harmony.

Backster's first paper,[13] published in 1967, together with subsequent more popular reports in the American press, elicited over 7000 letters from scientists throughout the world requesting reports on his original research; and some twenty-five to thirty universities are now duplicating his major experiments. These researchers, like Backster and 'meta-scientists' in other fields, are finding that unless they carefully monitor their own moods and emotional states, the plants will pick them up, reflecting them on the graph, and confuse the results. We are faced with the paradox that to be truly 'objective' we must first be aware of *ourselves*.

But what is 'mood' or 'emotionality' to the intellect but the changes in frequency on a graph? Music itself is a web of similar patterns and, in turn, evokes mood and emotion. But music, as Glazewski has shown, is more than a paradigm of the forces behind nature. For millennia people have sung and played music to their crops, their lovers and their children. Does this singing perhaps resonate the harmonic ratios in which life itself can flourish? People with naturally 'green fingers' know that no audible song is required, but merely what can only be described as a 'feeling of love'. But research is already being conducted, particularly in America, on the effect which orchestral music has on plants. Dr Lyall Watson writes:

It has been discovered that geraniums grow faster and taller to the accompaniment of Bach's Brandenberg Concertos. If the dominant frequencies in these pieces of music are broadcast to the plants they have some effect, but growth is more marked if the frequencies occur in the spatial relationship so carefully designed by the composer. Bacteria are affected in the same way, multiplying under some frequencies and dying when subject to others.[14]

Certain farming communes in America have already taken to broadcasting music, mainly the slower cadences of the classics, to their wheat and alfalfa crops.

Although 'vibration' is merely an incorporeal symbol, it still leads us to the realization that we are part of a universe far more intangible and tangible, and that we are for the most part like those water-fleas which skate on the surface of the sea in a two-dimensional world – the life beneath them, or above, in the sky or the forests of the land, quite beyond their grasp. If ghosts and angels have become invisible during the two-hundred-year plague of objective rationalism, then with our growing awareness of a transcendent continent we observe the first outlines of the same powers and entities under a different name. The once burning question as to whether such forces are inside or outside us, begins to recede. Religious and occult traditions have enjoined man to turn inwards if he seeks to understand the universe – 'know thyself' – and now science, broaching the subtle environment, finds that it, too, is forced to turn inwards, to know the self which experiences.

6 The Subtle Anatomy of Man

Human egos are multi-concentric halo-systems.

BUCKMINSTER FULLER

With the astrophysicist's realization that the electromagnetic bodies of the sun and planets extend greatly beyond their 'visible' kernels, blending into a vast solar organism, we see the links with the ancient myths of astrology which for centuries have also declared the universe to be a single blend of subtle, though incontrovertible, energies. In this chapter we shall further explore the links between 'myth' and 'science', but now between the myths (once too preposterous to contemplate) of what *we* are, and the facts emerging from contemporary medicine which corroborate them.

In so far as all order, whether in matter or thought, evolves from chaos through rhythms, and rhythms themselves can be seen to reverberate through different dimensions of manifestation, we can look at what we take to be *ourselves* in a more expansive light. Today's physics teaches us that human flesh is not solid, but a lattice of force-fields which is not dissimilar to the lattice of thoughts and feelings which move through our minds. Furthermore, we are not physical 'islands unto ourselves', but simply 'vapours' – as Shakespeare said – which are actually chemically altered by sitting for a few minutes within a yard of another person.

Rather as the lines traced between the centres of four touching spheres form a tetrahedron, a physical body – whether crystal or human – can be seen as simply the *cross-section* of lines of force traced between invisible poles of energy. Our bodies now emerge as diaphanous webs of pulsating form, in constant flux, which change and fall apart as soon as their underlying energies are distorted or withdrawn.

A personal knowledge of the energies underlying our own bodies is being pursued keenly by the more alive and imaginative. To learn and experiment with our own acupuncture points, for instance, is like being shown a globe of the earth for the first time; but in this case the earth is our most intimate companion – the flesh which we walk around in. Awareness of these forces brings a new immediacy to the term 'ecology',

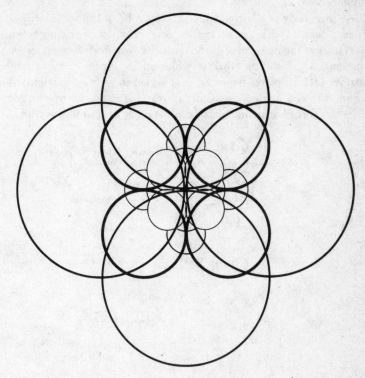

78. The connecting, cellular spheres producing the primary patterns of order in space.

as we learn of the natural language of equilibrium through which the body speaks its needs to us. The localized shooting pains, for instance, which we all periodically suffer and ignore, are instantly seen as signals from specific energy centres, and we can now consciously respond to them before our body – our dearest and closest of animals – is forced to bring its needs to our attention in more drastic ways. So conditioned are we to look *out* of the body that we have forgotten the subtle music through which it inwardly communicates its needs to us. Lost is the integrated sensitivity to the sacred vehicle which houses us and of which we are the temporary stewards, and we are amazed at how supremely this function still operates in wild animals. 'Love your body' is the cry which has moved through the culture recently, 'feel it, watch it and know it: it is beautiful, and it responds to love – like all lovers – with illumination!'

A 'love body' or 'astral body' has long been known to religious science, which speaks not only of an 'auric field' which extends beyond us (rather as the more 'meaningful' radiative solar body extends beyond the sun), but also of the 'chakras' which are the organs of man's subtle anatomy. These power-points are understood to be in harmonic equilibrium with one another, producing a 'weave' of resonance which at one level exteriorizes as an individual, while at other levels it blends with the

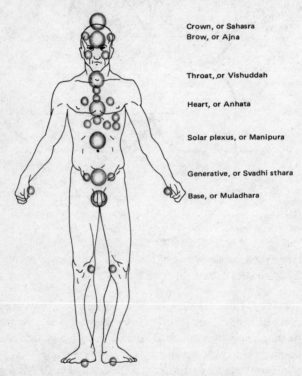

Crown, or Sahasra
Brow, or Ajna

Throat, or Vishuddah

Heart, or Anhata

Solar plexus, or Manipura

Generative, or Svadhi sthara

Base, or Muladhara

79. The predominantly accepted seven major and twenty-one minor chakras in the subtle anatomy of man. As in Fig. 49 a spiral can be imagined as beginning at the navel, and curving outwards through the centres of each of the chakras, finishing at the 'crown' at the top of the head. The six lowermost minor chakras are on the palms, behind the knees, and on the soles of the feet.

entire rarefied fabric of our vibrationary environment. Thus to really *know* our bodies is to know ourselves in *depth*, and by so doing we can know much of the meaning of this cosmic flux of creativity in which we find ourselves.

Oriental scripture speaks of the entire universe as a giant mandala, or spiralling wheel, containing myriad microcosmic wheels. 'Chakra' derives from the Sanskrit word meaning a 'wheel', and those who are trained to distinguish them describe them as vortices of shifting colours, 'sounds' and densities, rather like liquid convolvulus flowers, or the surface shape of water spiralling out of the bath – but in this case spiralling *into* our subtle anatomies. Physics, fringe medicine and 'experiential' religion (e.g. meditational techniques) are between them reconstructing a coherent knowledge of the chakras, but until the map is complete there remain conflicting theories as to their precise location and significance. Fig. 79 shows the predominantly accepted points of the seven major and the twenty-one minor chakras.[1]

Each of the seven chakras 'externalizes' itself in the seven major physiological glands of the body whose endocrinal functions dovetail with one another in a manner still mysterious to anatomical science.

1. *The Base or Muladhara Chakra* is also referred to as the 'root' chakra, and has its physical counterpart in the adrenal glands at the base of the spine which govern the endocrine extension of the autonomic nervous system. The Hindu yogi prepares for meditation by crossing his legs and anchoring himself with his root chakra next to the earth, which connects him directly to the terrestrial 'kundalini' energy. Oriental massage techniques often begin with the pressing gently of a finger up and behind the tail bone, which tends to release a revitalizing charge, like an electric current, all the way up and inside of the body, loosening the subject in preparation for deep relaxation. By an untrained person this can only be experienced once or twice at a time, rather as the knee fails to respond to successive blows with a reflex hammer. But with the practice of experiential religions such as yoga, when the Chakras become storage batteries for very considerable power, the sudden release of kundalini energy (without sufficient training or knowledge) can sear up the spine, severely shocking, or even 'shorting' the other organs in the subtle anatomy.

Indian seers describe this chakra as anchoring the body to the physical plane, providing a channel for the 'will to be' to assert itself. At the physiological level, of course, it is the adrenal glands which in moments of great danger pump adrenalin through the body, throwing it into a chemical overdrive of survival reflexes. Orthodox medicine is aware that an adrenalectomy, for no very clear physiological reasons, is quickly followed by death.

It is the kundalini, or 'matter force', which is associated with the unconscious energies of nature, the elemental forces of the mineral, vegetable and animal levels which we fear and seek to coordinate since they form so large a part of ourselves. The old wisdom speaks of kundalini as a dual serpent, with 'male' and 'female' channels, or polarities, which spiral up around the spine. The nerve-endings of the adrenals in fact migrate up the spine in the same pattern as the double-helix spiral found in the DNA molecule – the basis of life's stable continuity. These snakes intertwined around the caduces of the spine are still the overt – though rarely understood – symbol of the twentieth-century medical profession. The kundalini 'serpent power' has its parallel in terrestrial ley lines, which in Europe were called 'serpent trails' by the medieval gnostics, and in China are to this day called 'dragon paths' by the geomancers. Rites of initiation often involved serpents since it was believed that unless we had mastered this primal power in ourselves, then snakes – the writhing, poisonous energies with their bellies to the earth – were a great threat which could only be conquered through conscious knowledge.

Significantly, the base chakra is the very root of the spine, that most dense and weighty trellis of our anatomy which is the physical lynch-pin (so important to fringe medicines) upon which the fabric of our bodies is hung. The base chakra, by being the seed from which the spine grows upwards to awareness, is thus our 'foundation' in a very real sense.

2. *The Generative or Svadhisthana Chakra* is exteriorized in the sexual glands, an area which many students of occultism find is the first to respond to spiritual energy. The sexuality released through conscious meditation can become a dangerously disorienting source of magnetism, one which literally draws the opposite sex. Many gurus and spiritual leaders are irresistibly physically attractive, particularly to their pupils, not so much for the shape of their bodies or profiles, or even for their aloof unsusceptibility, but for the power of their 'generative' emanation – which is most discernible in the eyes. Their disciples, conditioned like most of us to experience this energy through the cliché of 'love-and-sex', constantly have their consciences plagued with dreams of erotic union with their spiritual mentors. In the Church, this tendency has been

channelled into the symbolism of a nun, for instance, actually becoming the 'Bride of Christ'.

It is this miraculous energy of 're-creation' which can be deflected into creativity other than physical sex, although of course if taken to extremes this too can be a limitation rather than a freedom and versatility brought by the 'knowledge'. What began in early Christianity as a holding in abeyance of our usual unconscious sexuality so as to channel it into more conscious levels of creativity, became in time a complete suppression of the art and philosophy of physical love-making, so that it withered in our culture like an unused hand. The other extreme is found in certain periods of Tantrism, where such full reign was given to the cult of the generative chakra alone that the culture consumed itself in the conflagration of sexual diversity which this power alone can ignite.

Whereas the Greeks actually had a deity of physical love, Eros, our culture has lost its sense of discrimination between the different domains of love, and files them all under the amorphous heading of a single God. Without sub-headings, which our churches are now inadequate to provide, the different manifestations of love are combined in a castrated deity who frowns at genitals uncovered by fig leaves. But despite our 'shame' our Svadhisthana chakras are alive (albeit dormant) and well, and the creative power which nestles in the genitals of us all occasionally leaps in happy resonance to the most 'inappropriate' stimuli. Opera singers report this sometimes happening when they sing, poets when they think, surfers when they are riding a high wave: and conversely, the same chimes in the private parts are experienced by those who merely hear or watch a work of art unfolding in supernal style.

The magical strength of the Svadhisthana chakra was once well known, but with the loss of occult knowledge only the warning of its power remained behind, and the chakra became largely 'closed down' during the long cycle of religious asceticism. In the West, however, after centuries of suppression, its power has recently burst its bounds again and reverberates through the culture in energy without knowledge – a destructive combination were it not accompanied by the shift inwards towards spiritual training and understanding.

3. *The Solar Plexus or Manipura Chakra* is exteriorized in the glandular system of the pancreas, the 'heart' of the intestinal tract – that miraculous network by which the ingestion and transmutation of physical matter provides the vehicle for human consciousness. Being precisely at

our centre, this 'navel' chakra more than symbolically marks the point of fusion between the upward-going and the downward-coming energies, that duality of matter and spirit which not only stimulates all human philosophies, but actually causes us to *live*. Rather as the task of our digestive system is to discriminate between the myriad chemical substances which we ingest, choosing and rejecting so as to retain only that which keeps our bodies in equilibrium, so the Solar Plexus chakra is credited with the power of emotional discrimination, being the centre of our instinctive 'feeling'.

In that chakras respond to stimuli more quickly than the body, sudden fear can be felt like a blow in the diaphragm, where the Manipura chakra has reacted even before the brain has grasped what is happening. It is this balancer of 'feeling' between the upper and lower energies which responds to sudden tragedy or revulsion by 'sounding' so strongly that we instantaneously throw up the contents of our stomachs. The blanket medical explanation that this is simply 'shock', prevents us from looking any deeper into its meaning, from inquiring why, for instance, we each have very different shock thresholds, despite being in the same physical condition of good health. The 'will to live', the 'inherent vitality' of a patient, are terms often used by the medical profession; but they are not qualities which can be discerned by it at first glance, as they can through certain 'fringe' and occult techniques. Are susceptibilities to certain emotional and environmental stimuli perhaps contingent on differing proportional strengths and weaknesses of our aetheric bodies? How is it, for instance, that certain people can still die from a 'broken heart' when it isn't the physical heart which breaks?

4. *The Heart or Anhata Chakra* is exteriorized as the thymus gland, which, though somewhat of a physiological mystery, is known to govern the highly complex system of immunization, for which task it seems to possess (independently of the brain) both memory and discrimination. By belonging with the upper, more 'aetherialized' half of man, the heart chakra has moved from the sphere of mere self-interest and maintenance to encompass awareness, *beyond* the self, of the needs of the broader organism of life in which we have our being. Occultism sees this chakra as the centre of detached and unselfish love, the energy source for handling individuals, or groups of people, beyond the ego. David Tansley, in his excellent book on radionics,[2] suggests that heart diseases are more common among executives and doctors, for instance, both of whom constantly work with groups 'giving' energy to others, often

straining their Anhata chakras in disproportion to the rest of their aetheric anatomies. In the evolutionary spiral relating the five sacred solids to the chakral areas of the body, the heart chakra, in accordance with tradition, can be seen as directly connected to the generative chakra; for the sympathies of the 'heart' are tied inseparably to the actions of the genitals, the 'sensitive' man and woman being unable to function sexually unless their 'heart' (in a very real sense) is also to some degree committed – even if only to the ends of giving and receiving pleasure.

5. *The Throat or Vishuddah Chakra* is exteriorized in the thyroid gland, which governs the endocrine systems of oxidation and metabolism. Esoterically, it is related to the higher forms of expression and communication, the timbre and quality of voice (which can be as commanding as the eyes) being an indication of the degree to which this chakra is developed.

Different religious systems appear initially to stimulate different chakral areas, usually the generative, heart or throat centres. Practitioners of certain types of meditation, for instance, complain of a dry metallic feeling in the throat during and after their exercises. Medicine is often puzzled by the fact that an appreciable number of patients with goitre and other hyper-thyroid complaints (caused ostensibly by 'iodine deficiency') already have a more than average iodine intake. But it now seems that if the throat chakra is overstimulated, the thyroid gland – which is this chakra's physical exteriorization – causes a tremendous hunger for iodine. If this is satisfied (by, say, eating plenty of shellfish) the interior energies can be harmonized and the curing of physical disease is seen as a mere by-product of the miraculous growth and equilibrium which is taking place at the aetheric level. It is at points like these that we see the integral connections between matter and spirit, chemistry and consciousness.

6. *The Brow or Ajna Chakra* is the lower of the two head chakras, exteriorized in the pituitary gland, between the eyes and within the head, which is the master control of the entire endocrine system and harmonizes the hormone secretions of the adrenals, the gonads, the pancreas and the thyroid. The Ajna chakra is considered by Indian seers to be the centre of conscious integration, and people with this area well-developed are said to be both powerful and versatile in their achievements. With practice, this chakra can be sensed in our own bodies,

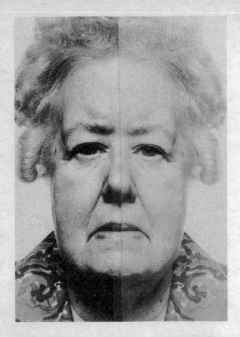

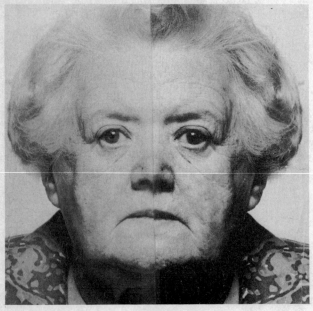

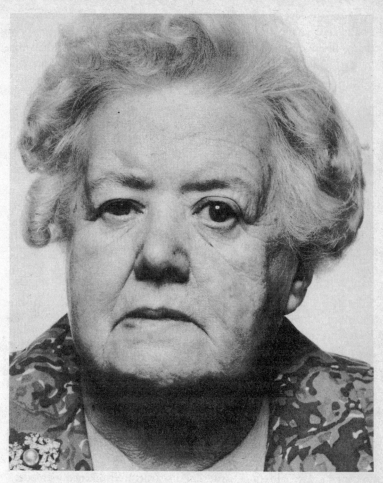

80. The divided face of Rose Macauly, an experienced medium of the Spiritualist Association of Great Britain. Each of our faces are to some degree asymmetrical, a tendency which at times is very pronounced with mediums, occultists, schizophrenics, or any evolving person during specific periods of his growth. The asymmetry between the eyes is very clear in certain portraits of Madame Blavatsky, Rudolph Steiner, G. I. Gurdjieff and other esoteric figures. To dramatize the 'solar' and 'lunar' sides of our faces we can observe our reflection in two angled mirrors, such that they reflect first one half of the face (and its mirror-image) and then the other. In the above photographs this has been done simply by dividing and reversing the negative from the same identical print. One reflects the lunar, aetheric nature of the medium, the other her 'outer' earthly self.

by closing the eyes (preferably masking them from any light penetration at all) and having someone else bring either their index finger, or a sharp, preferably metal, instrument slowly to just above and between the eyes. A localized effervescence, which can be sensed first on the skin, can then be felt to move within the skull, awakening a virtually visible vibrationary sensation. With practice, the finger or instrument can be felt from further than a foot away. Hallucinatory visions are believed to be formed at this chakra, and although it may be activated quite spontaneously, it can become very precisely localized with the aid of meditation.

7. *The Crown or Sahasrara Chakra* is exteriorized in the pineal gland in the upper half of the brain. Little is known about its physiological function, other than that it appears to stop working at about the age of seven when it joins that dormant three fifths of the brain which has no apparent function. Both the Indian and the Greek mystery traditions (the latter probably being derived from the Egyptian) see the Crown chakra as the 'seat of the soul' – both the most 'material' portion of the spirit as well as the most 'spiritual' portion of the body. Descartes, who theorized at length about the pineal gland, saw it as the link between the body and, in his terminology, the 'rational mind'. In Hinduism this chakra is believed to be a microcosm of all the remaining chakras in the body: that with its development the adept lives and experiences through this area alone, projecting his awareness in 'astral travel' beyond the confines of his physical senses.

There is some debate as to whether the 'third eye' can properly be attributed to the Brow or to the Crown chakra; it is perhaps a somewhat academic point but I personally favour the Crown as being its most likely location. The corresponding physical organ, the pineal, is known to contain vestigial retinal tissue, and its structure is likened by modern physiology to a third, albeit atrophied, photoreceptor.

A further interesting physiological fact is that the pituitary gland (of the Brow Chakra) is connected to the *left* eye and governs the lower half of the brain, whereas the pineal, expressing the Crown Chakra, is connected to the *right* eye and governs the upper half of the brain. A marked difference is often apparent between the left and right eyes of both mediums and schizophrenics, or of people undergoing the rigours of harmonizing their aetheric with their physical systems. Thus, although this may indicate a relative 'separation' between the spiritual and bodily systems, it may also indicate a breadth of range and versatility between the two worlds, rather as wider-spaced legs permit better balance. Migraine, or 'hemicrania', in chronic cases of which one side of the face both feels, and outwardly appears, literally to be torn away from the other side, is becoming recognized by psychology as resulting from an endocrinal imbalance precipitated by a lack of parity between the patient's 'emotional ideals' and his actual life situation. For occultists, of course, it signifies a 'span' between the radiative bodies of the Brow and Crown chakras – the chakras of 'spirit' and of 'worldly integration' (see Fig. 80).

With much less practice than might be expected, these aetheric organs can be experienced, and they begin to emerge as similar to radio stations, broadcasting at different frequencies, out of whose organic lattice crystallizes the fluid and constantly changing enigma of our own bodies.

EEG Monitoring and Bio-feedback

As multi-dimensional myths can be reduced to rational, two-dimensional symbols, we also have an increasing variety of rational methods of discerning the 'frequencies' or wave-patterns which fluctuate throughout our systems. Rather as the myths of occultism refer to the chakras as organs of consciousness, instead of simply as organs of bodily functions, so too are the rhythms now being monitored in the brain by EEG meters (or electro-encephalograms) which record altered states of consciousness.

EEG monitoring has so far isolated about eight different cerebral wave-patterns, the most significant to date being 'alpha', 'beta' and 'theta' waves – frequencies which at the rational level can only exhibit their differences in tracings on a video-screen or a sheet of graph paper. It is now known that the rarer alpha rhythm is produced naturally only by specific subjects, and by others not at all, but that with 'bio-feedback' devices* some 90 per cent of *all* subjects can learn to produce cerebral alpha rhythms at will.[3] J. Kamiya, a Japanese-American researcher, writes that the best alpha producers seem to be those who practice some sort of meditation:

* Bio-feedback, or 'operant conditioning', involves rigging up a simple system to let a subject know when he has achieved a specific change in his organism: for instance, so that a light shines or a bell rings when the specific change has been achieved.

... it doesn't necessarily have to be of the zen or yoga school, or any other formal school of meditation. If the individual has had a long history of introspection on his own, he seems to be especially good at enhancing the alpha rhythm. Also, he is likely to be an individual who uses words like 'images', 'dreams', 'wants' and 'feelings'. I have come to the conclusion that there are a large number of people who really don't know exactly what you are talking about when you speak of images and feelings. To such people the words describe something that *somebody else* might have; but these people do not seem to have any degree of sensitivity to such things themselves. These people do not do well in my experiments, and fail to gain a high degree of control over their alpha rhythms.[4]

The alpha rhythm is not only particularly strong in creative people during 'inspirational' moods – the rhythm tending to fade with weariness – but it is also characteristic of a higher state of consciousness. We know that the body shows specific physiological changes during sleep (decreased oxygen consumption, slowed pulse, high-voltage and slowed EEG activity, etc.) which are of course reversed during wakefulness; but extensive research[5] has shown that in states of deep meditation the body exhibits all the signs of sleep or profound relaxation, except that the alpha rhythms – denoting full alertness – are strongly present. Further work in this field has been conducted in India, establishing the intense flow of alpha (and possibly of additional, still un-named) rhythms in the heads of Raj Yogis during states of 'samadhi' or 'blissful enlightenment'.

Bio-feedback techniques, whereby a subject can learn to produce given rhythms on demand by being rewarded with the ringing of a bell or the shining of a light when the rhythm is achieved and maintained, are now also being used to teach both animal and human subjects to alter their autonomic functions, their pulse and even their localized blood pressure.* Thus throughout America and in parts of Europe these methods are being used to train people to cure themselves of such illnesses as epilepsy, asthma and acute anxiety, which derive from an imbalance in the autonomic system. One of the early exercises for migraine sufferers is to learn to raise and lower the temperature of the hands while keeping the temperature of the arm constant. Think about it.

A wide variety of EEG meters is now being marketed for private medical or meditational use. Students of consciousness can monitor the pitch and steadiness of the alpha rhythms they produce during meditation; but once the technique is acquired they can dispense with the

* Rats have even been taught to bleed on demand through their stomach walls in exchange for 'electrical' rewards to their cerebral sexual centres.

machine, in the same way that a tightrope artist dispenses with the balancing bar once he has interiorized his sense of balance. It is precisely this 'interiorization' of consciousness with which the religious scientist is concerned.

Researchers have been intrigued by the fact that the subjects who have learned to dispense with the bio-feedback gadget, while still accurately producing the required rhythms on demand, have difficulty in describing in everyday language how they *know* they have achieved the required rhythm. Even the most articulate are reduced to vague and all-inclusive 'dream' language, similar to that of religious or poetic symbolism; for they have moved into an unfamiliar environment where the experience, and thus the language, is different from everyday perception.

Bio-feedback provides a powerful link between 'science' and 'religion' through the medium of medical research. The simplest bio-feedback device is a mirror; with this the more waggish student of consciousness can teach himself to wiggle his ears. That this is possible at all has interesting implications. The ear's mobility, in its detection of the smallest sounds of game or danger,* was a vital aid to primordial survival. When this was no longer necessary, the once conscious faculty lapsed back into the stream of autonomic control, for even today our ears continue, though almost imperceptibly, to 'respond' like those of a bat to strange or alarming sounds. What more mysterious faculties, we wonder, have been drifting dormantly, for untold generations, in the autonomic stream? What range of vision has lapsed back beneath the limen (still latent, though hovering on obsolescence) like the sleeping princess of the fairy-tale? Perhaps it is this which occasionally reaches us in a gigantic twitch of premonition or super-consciousness.

Radionics

Yet another avenue to the complex universe of our vibrationary bodies is opened by radionics, which begins with the premise (explained in Chapter 5) that all matter, whether alive or dead, radiates energy. It is not enough to call it simply 'magnetic' or 'electrical' energy, since, under different circumstances, it is both more and less than these. In the case of man, he radiates an entire field of interrelated forces of different

* From a less Darwinian viewpoint the esotericists claim that man was once fully conscious of a broader range of the electromagnetic spectrum than he is today, and his body was completely adapted to detect all its subtleties.

frequencies. With a pendulum – preferably a pear- or pyramid-shaped semi-precious stone on a four- or five-inch length of thread – we can learn to detect these energies. One way to begin is by holding the pendulum slightly away from the end of the index finger of the left hand (if you are right-handed), which is where Kirlian photographs show energy spraying from the ends of the fingers, and to observe the swing which the pendulum develops.

The pendulum's response to 'positive', 'negative' and 'neutral' energies will differ with each individual, since our natures vary as widely as blood groups. The index finger of most men, but not all, has a positive

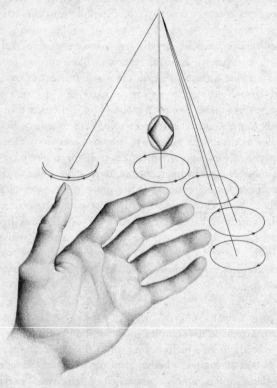

81. The direction in which the pendulum swings over the ends of each of our fingers can be used to ascertain our individual pendulum response, or 'language'. This figure shows one of the more usual response patterns, but it must be stressed that this should not influence you away from discovering your *own* – any more than a 'right-handed' culture should influence a 'leftie' from discovering his own nature.

radiation, and in my own case the pendulum responds to this with an anti-clockwise swing. With most women, however (but again not all), the situation is reversed, their energies tending to be the mirror-image of men's. But with all of us our fingers are alternately polarized (see Fig. 81), with the exception of the thumb which has its own particular force that is neither positive nor negative and, for the sake of convenience rather than accuracy, can be referred to as 'neutral'. My own pendulum responds to this in a backwards and forwards swing – although your 'swing language', although responding to the same energies,* may be quite different.

Further practice with the pendulum can be had by holding it over a healthy garden weed, such as a dandelion, where a strong 'positive' swing will develop in response to the plant's field of life force. If the plant is gently unearthed and slowly turned with the other hand, the pendulum begins to swing less lustily until, at certain degrees of the plant's revolution, it will almost stop. When it has been revolved through a complete circle, back to where it was growing at its most comfortable angle, the pendulum will resume a healthy swing denoting the happiest position for the plant. The most desirable angle, which is relative to the geo-magnetic force of the earth, differs with each species and individual of plant. Many people are now re-orienting their indoor potted plants in this manner, finding that individual plants are not necessarily happiest, as would be expected, when oriented to the strongest source of sunlight, but in relation to the subtle force-fields in which we all live.

Others use their pendulums for choosing food, for they respond to the degree of 'life force' remaining in fruit and vegetables – I have never had the courage to try it with meat. The market vendors in London's Portobello Road are becoming quite blasé about people swinging their pendulums over their fruit and vegetable stalls. One recently remarked to me while I was shopping that the best 'spiritual' lettuce had just gone, but there were two more 'good swingers' which he had kept aside for himself.

It follows that the envelope of energy surrounding the human body can also be detected with a pendulum, as can the Qi meridians of acupuncture, in the same way that a dowser traces ley lines across the country with his divining rod.

---

* In Japan, the highly industrialized chicken-farming industry has for over a decade used people trained in the subtleties of the pendulum for sexing and sorting fertilized eggs.

Radionics has developed this energy-detection to a fine art, and it should be stressed that it remains an art rather than a science, although producing many empirical by-products. Over the years radionics has developed a catalogue of the specific vibrationary frequencies (or 'rates'), expressed in numbers, not only of the essential aetheric 'radio

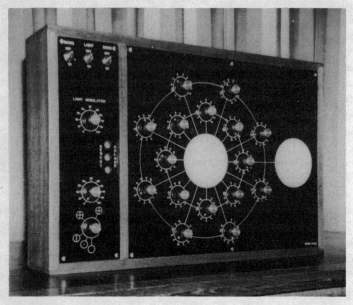

82. A Radionics 'black box' or, more precisely, a 'Mark III Centre Instrument', developed by David Tansley of the Radionics Association, in order to directly treat the chakras of the aetheric anatomy.

stations' in the body – the chakras – but also of the specific diseases which we allow to enter our systems. It is not the diseases themselves, but the vibrationary imbalance *underlying* them which is treated. This is done with a sophisticated electronic gadget called a 'radionics instrument' or 'black box', which is a source of considerable hilarity among cynics – despite a surprisingly high success rate in the curing of ostensibly 'incurable' diseases. This instrument both detects and treats the aetheric imbalances which give rise to a multiplicity of physical ills.* In

* Allopathy knows to its dismay that whereas it may lop off the branch of a physical manifestation of illness, unless the underlying cause is attacked, another branch, in the form of different symptoms, will quickly take its place.

the first instance, since it is merely a form of complex pendulum, it detects malignancies from the dents, deformations or discoloration of a patient's vibrationary aura *before* it appears in the physical body – very much as Kirlian photography shows us a 'plasma' or 'fire body' *underlying* all life-forms. In the case of treatment, a 'witness' from the patient (in the form of either a hair or a drop of blood) is placed in the instrument, and the dials are then set to the numerical equivalent of the required healing 'rate', which is then 'resonated' towards the patient, regardless of his geographical distance. This choice of a hair or a drop of blood – reminiscent of witchcraft, which also requires such a sample to control a subject (whether for good or ill) – may no longer be as superstitious as it sounds. Contemporary biology is aware that a single skin cell is a microcosm of the individual chemical, or 'vibrationary', pattern of our entire bodies, a key from which it is theoretically possible to reproduce a full-grown 'clone', or twin of ourselves – which is surely a more irrational concept than witchcraft.

It is precisely this marriage between the rational and the irrational – the flat and the multi-dimensional – which is the vaulting-pole to visionary breakthrough. In this respect the radionics box can be seen as a twentieth-century mediumistic device, an electronic 'crystal ball' through which man's intuitive, as well as rational, faculties are given equal rein. Radionics is thus a further point of fusion between the spheres of science and occultism, through whose narrow connecting point can be seen the developing terrain of interior knowledge.

The fabric of this expansive new vision which is trickling down from the higher reaches of rational science is also seeping up from the 'irrational' levels of society, where people are *intuiting* their way towards a similar perspective. These 'outer' and 'inner' avenues to the same emergent cosmology are acting like twin rudders which have barely begun to affect the immense inertia of political and moral dogma; but the culture is already discernibly altering course. Some of the most evident points of this change can be seen in the medical field, where the massive fact-accumulating body of orthodoxy is being assailed by the ancient tenets of 'supernaturalism'.

The medical fashions of an age go hand-in-hand with its religious and philosophical climate, for they invariably reflect the prevailing attitude towards 'removing pain' and 'making man whole'. We may look back with horror at the recent orthodoxies, when amputees' bleeding stumps were plunged into molten tar, and the general panacea – like an aspirin –

was the application of ravenous leeches, but it will be a while before we understand the barbarous medical fallacies of today.

'Allopathic' or 'drug-and-cut' medicine and psychology, which have been the institutionalized expressions of the age of rationalism, are only just ceasing to treat both the body and the mind as machines which can only be understood by taking apart their various cogs. Whereas allopathy generally sees man as a mechanical and chemical 'island unto himself' walking on the surface of the earth, fringe medicines recognize him as a force-field, a part of the force-fields of the earth, which is in turn a part of the weave of the Cosmic Force-Field. In this context our ills are seen to be an imbalance in our response to the invisible forces which maintain us. It is significant that the fringe medicines still farthest from orthodox recognition are those which most strongly accept man's aetheric nature, yet in certain instances, such as acupuncture, they have a validity which can be scientifically demonstrated while yet being founded entirely on 'mystical' precepts.

Acupuncture

Although it has enjoyed orthodox recognition in China for over five thousand years, few people in the West had heard of acupuncture until the 1960s, when a plethora of publications appeared describing its philosophy and practical use. Yet it was only seriously considered by doctors in the early 1970s when a *New York Times* reporter named J. Reston had an acupuncture experience which became world news. Reston was in Peking covering Dr Henry Kissinger's arrangements for President Nixon's visit to China, when he suddenly became ill with acute appendicitis. In the absence of Western medicine he had no alternative but to submit to the local standard practice, whereby he was abdominally anaesthetized with needles placed in the acupuncture points of his right hand prior to being operated on in the normal surgical way. His rapid return to health, also facilitated by acupuncture, amazed and intrigued Western doctors sufficiently to make them take a serious look at the practice.

Acupuncture seeks to balance the energies of the body by impeding, or else enhancing, the flow of Qi – a still enigmatic force which courses through the body in specific channels or 'meridians' which do not physically correspond to nerves or blood vessels. This Qi energy, or Life Force, underlies many of the Chinese and Japanese forms of re-equilibrium which are now being revived in the West, such as Aikido,

Karate, Ju-Jitsu and Ta'i Chi Chuan; and it derives from the broader yin/yang concept of symbiotic (as opposed to contradictory) opposites. In acupuncture, the balancing of Qi is achieved either by massaging, or placing needles in, the specific power points along the Qi meridians which correspond – though they may be anatomically far removed from – the physical organs of the body. The precise position of these points differs with each individual, and although they can be approximately located with a 'neurocalcometer' (a device which measures electrical skin resistance, rather like Clive Backster's botanical lie-detectors), their exact location relies ultimately on the sensitivity of the acupuncturist.

Various doctors are already combining acupuncture with their orthodox practice – despite the two systems being founded on entirely different premises. Since acupuncture can localize the killing of pain very precisely, dental surgeons in various Western capitals are now using it to anaesthetize their patients' jaws without having to put them to sleep.

It is interesting that the neurocalcometer detects normal points of maximum and minimum electrical skin-resistance which are identical to the acupuncture points depicted on the early Chinese anatomical charts. There was once a time in the Far East when all children were taught the points and meridians of Qi energy in their own bodies, rather as Western children today are introduced to anatomy. If it is indeed the 'subtle anatomy' which maintains the physical body, rather than the reverse, then the superiority of the Chinese form of education is obvious. The apparent sophistication of Oriental medicine throws our own into a medieval and superstitious light, and makes sense of the (to Western minds) bewildering custom of the Chinese doctor being paid only when his patient was well, and having in turn to pay his patient when he fell ill. If we sought to adopt the same custom in the West, before fundamentally altering our view of the basic nature of 'dis-ease', then our doctors would soon be reduced to penury.

Many ill people are still unaware that when all else has failed there is as broad a field of 'alternative medicine' to turn to as there is of 'alternative religion' – both of these parallel branches being the fresh evolutionary greenery bursting from the dying trunk of orthodox medicine and religion. In a culture of impure food, extreme tension and spiritual vacuity, allopathic medicine itself admits to being able to do little more than stem the rising flood of disease with palliatives, rather than cures. For this reason fringe medicines – such as naturopathy, herbalism, homeopathy and chiropractic – are increasingly being adopted by people who recognize the need for a deeper view of their condition.

From naturopathy springs a variety of specialized fringe medicines: on the one hand are the adepts of 'natural substances' found in herbalism and homeopathy, and on the other the bone specialists of osteopathy and chiropractic, for whom the spine is the trestle-board for rectifying health.

Naturopathy and herbalism see the human body as capable of rejecting all ills if it is but given the pure and organic food which are its birthright. Once the deficient and actively poisonous substances which Western man habitually ingests are avoided, the equilibrium of the subtle body, and thus its physical expression, adjust themselves to vibrant health. With the wisdom of the wild animal, these practices seek to return to nature's rich storehouse of cures, palliatives and tonics where nature – not as alien and hostile as civilization has come to believe – is found, like man himself, to be a cornucopia of distilled energies. The blurred definitions of naturopathy and herbalism encompass the great stream of country medicine – that blend of old wives' tales and inspired wisdom. Many of the new religious groups, from the witches' covens to the meditational brotherhoods, being already immersed in some deeper form of orientation, find that they now respond directly to herbal essences alone, and are increasingly sensitive to the alien effects of even the mildest pharmaceutical drugs.

At a more superficial level of the culture is the fad for health farms and health food shops and restaurants which – themselves a measure of the desire to return to essentials – provide treatment and brews deriving from an ancient though largely lost system of knowledge.

The subtilizing of human consciousness brings with it the awareness of 'whole systems' which unite both the invisible blueprint as well as its physical expression. When a whole system is seen as such, it is clear that it is more than the sum of its parts. Buckminster Fuller has coined the term 'synergy', meaning 'system-behaviour' as opposed to 'part-behaviour', and he has applied it to every conceivable branch of learning, crediting it with being the key to many of his more visionary scientific inventions. Homeopathy is a cogent example of 'medical synergy', involving the balancing of the aetheric body by administering the minutest distillations of physical essences. In the words of homeopathy's modern revivor, Samuel Hahnemann, who was born in Saxony in 1755: 'It is only by the power to make sick that drugs can cure sickness, and that a medicine can only cure such morbid conditions as it can produce, when tested on healthy persons.'[6]

This idea of '*similia similibus currentur*' ('like cures like') is found as early as the Hippocratic writings, and its paradoxical tenets are compelling. If, for instance, it is assumed that fever is the body's way of fighting malaria, rather than malaria's way of fighting the body, then helping the body with its fever will be the 'synergetic' way of ejecting malaria. This method is working *with* the system, rather than *against* it, as would be allopathy's standard prescription of fever-reducing drugs.

Allopathy has tended to consider the 'bone-setters' as the poor men of medicine, the 'horse-doctors' whose medical knowledge never extended beyond skeletons. The bone-setters – along with the other fringe medics – were thus also excluded from orthodox recognition and gradually evolved their art separately until it emerged again as the present-day practices of osteopathy and chiropractic. These in fact see the skeleton merely as the 'trellis' which mirrors the aetheric structure of man. The essence of this trellis is the spinal column, that almost mythological tree of vertebrae around which clings the mutable flame of the human body. Even allopathy recognizes that the carriage, the spinal curvature, can reveal at a glance a great deal about the glandular and thus the psychological balance of a patient. But the 'spine' fringe medicines carry these implications much further, and seek to help the Life Force flow unimpeded through the organism, freeing it of malfunction, by aligning the bones which have become pulled 'out of true' by subtle and interior disharmonies.

Allopathic doctors are aware that some of their colleagues, like gardeners, have 'green fingers' with their patients, whereas others seem literally to have the touch of death, despite possessing the same amount of factual knowledge. One wonders why virtually none of the millions spent annually on medical research goes into discovering more of the basis of what makes man whole – of that resonance of 'life' itself which the true doctor has unconsciously at his fingertips.

But our myopic and mechanistic research projects have gathered such momentum that a deeper look at the underlying rhythms of our nature constitutes a menace to pockets and reputations. For this reason the still prevalent belief that fringe medicines are a last resort to cranks, by cranks, is fully encouraged by doctors, whose assumed monopoly on healing is threatened, as well as by the pharmaceutical industries whose concern is, by definition, to profit financially from public 'health'. Thus the essentially 'psychic' problems – of cancer, for instance – continue to be attacked mightily from the same two-dimensional standpoint, and the statistical correlations between smoking and early death, as another example, suppress the more obvious suggestion that chronic smoking is only one possible expression of a deeper disharmony of tension which is the real trigger of fatal disease.

But the rising social pressure of inner need is causing fringe medicines to expand, their ranks being swelled by an ever increasing number of people who realize that these arts have not only kept abreast of anatomical and biochemical discoveries but have also retained the unfashionable knowledge of man as a spiritual whole.

The connections between medicine and religion are clearer still when we see that the 'priests' of pre-urban societies were also the doctors as well as the agrarian advisors of the community. The priest is ideally the scientist of invisible laws, as well as the adept of ritual who can fashion the appropriate symbolism to mediate between the world of everyday experiences and that of eternal law. By treating the immediate predicament of health within the context of cosmic meaning, fringe medicines are branches of religious science, and in their growing popularity we see a further sign of today's rejection of authority in order to turn inwards to a personal and religious dimension. Since they offer principles of curing the self, their relevance is further increased by the currents of contemporary myth which presage a massive holocaust, a sudden destruction of society as we know it, when each of us will need a personal knowledge of how to survive and flourish in the absence of doctors and priests.

The 'evolutionary lurch' of the past decade has sought first to de-condition the self, to destroy the false authority in the personal pysche – a process which is often projected in antagonism towards external auth-orities. The need has been to return the mind as nearly as possible to a *tabula rasa* on which to plant a new and indestructible authority of personal experience. Drugs were one of the primary means to this end, and young people rejected allopathy's gifts of body-changing drugs, and accepted instead those which altered the mind. From the apothecaries they borrowed the 'uppers' and 'downers' and the terrifying 'reality keys' of mescalin and LSD, and from the fields and hedgerows they culled the natural gifts of cannabis, hallucinogenic mushrooms and cacti. With these they cast themselves adrift from the landmass of inheri-tance into the ocean of inner vision, where some were wrecked in storms of disorientation, others learned to navigate and brought back their knowledge, and others still learned to live in this sea alone, forgetting, or never caring to return to, the tangible world which is also such a vital part of ourselves.

Andrew Weil, in his book *The Natural Mind*,[7] comments that loosening the perceptive framework is a natural part of human growth, an example of which is the universal practice among children of spinning round to make themselves dizzy. In 'rational' societies this habit is discouraged, and the children are told to 'pull themselves together' and act 'normally'.

An interesting example of man's fear of and resistance to the unknown is that despite a plethora of highly reputable reports commissioned to analyse objectively the dangers and advantages of cannabis – all of which conclude that the drug is less physically harmful than the culturally sanctioned drugs of alcohol, nicotine and pharmaceuticals – its use remains a felony in every country of the world. It seems to parallel the extraordinary illegality of suicide, where the assumption is that the State owns our bodies and decides what we may do with them. Escape from the dominant 'reality' of a culture, of course, is as illegal as climbing to the West over the Berlin Wall.

The co-culture continues to use drugs in two distinct ways: both as an 'escape', and as a conscious means of purifying the perception and re-orienting the self towards the whole process of living and experiencing. On the other hand, the orthodox medical profession has already begun to use hallucinogens in 'psychodelytic therapy', a form of chemical psychiatry often as frighteningly heavy-handed as their approach to surgery. To this end, the profession has in many instances been driven to ask advice of the lone explorers of the psyche, for among these 'survivors' of the drug culture a tremendous hidden body of knowledge has been amassed as to the relative dosages, qualities and merits of mind-altering drugs.

For several decades controversy has raged between those for whom hallucinogens are a key to unlock the full immediacy of man's mystical potential, and those for whom they are a dark threat both to the individual and to the moral calibre of society. In one camp we find such spokesmen as Aldous Huxley, Timothy Leary and Alan Watts who became, in some cases reluctantly, the high priests of hallucinogenic mysticism. Their opposition, backed by social inertia and articulated by such people as R. C. Zaehner of Oxford and Walter Pahnke of Harvard Medical School, argued that the drug experience was in no way 'mystical' in the traditional religious sense.

This debate has become somewhat academic over the years, since hundreds of thousands of people have already experienced drugs for themselves, and since at the level of laboratory experiment it is a clinically undisputed fact that hallucinogens can profoundly affect perception, personality and world-view. The psychologist Stephen Spinks writes that '. . . drug-induced or ascetically induced experiences can be the means by which the human personality is laid open to suggestion of the unconscious through whose primordial imagery the deeper activities of the soul emerge as a conscious recognition of the transcendental.'[8]

We can already see that a decade of hallucinogenic drugtaking, among what started as a hairy cultural minority, has now overtly altered the musical, artistic and verbal expression of the entire culture. Perhaps, through the revitalization of symbolism – facilitated by drugs – the avenues of cultural expression as a whole have been 'loosened' in preparation for an entirely new dimension of artistic forms.

Rather as fringe medicines have lent fuel to non-mechanistic views of our body, so 'fringe' or 'anti-' psychiatry is providing a whole new range of perspectives for 'getting our heads in tune' with the way things may really be. These include Bio-energetics, Gestalt, Encounter, Psychodrama and so on. In America they are articulated by such people as Rollo May, Fritz Perls and the late Theodore Reich; and in England by such doctors as R. D. Laing, who has argued that orthodox psychiatry is the prime cause of twentieth-century 'iatrogenic' disease, i.e. disease which is caused by doctors. Fringe psychiatry is a radical departure from mechanistic psychiatry in that it sees man both as an inseparable mind-body relationship and as an individual-group relationship. Implicit in this are 'invisible energies' of an individual, group and planetary kind, which is why a broad variety of semi-religious techniques have been appropriated by fringe psychiatries, such as yoga, zen and T'ai Chi Chuan – the Chinese art of moving meditation where the body discovers its internal harmony through a slow and rhythmic form of conscious dance.

Most anti-psychiatries share a view of us as victims of certain response patterns, from which we must free ourselves in order to '*be* anew'. In the case of Encounter therapy, this is achieved by 'encountering' others in groups and spontaneously 'acting out' our emotional responses to them. First responses to others – such as eye or hand contact, warmth or reserve – are used as clues for unearthing the constricted knots in the psyche. Just such clues, in fact, as have long been recognized in the occult arts of character-reading.

Gestalt and Encounter therapy emphasize 'here and now' experience (reported to be the origin of the term, the 'Now Generation'), and they see 'worry' or 'nervous baggage' about the past – and the future – as the prime impediments to personal growth. Wilhelm Reich, that strange visionary who died in an American jail for his beliefs, sought to crush his premonitionary vision into a science which was before its time, and his methods, though perhaps not his conclusions, will long be a joke to rationalists. But Reich – like Rudolph Steiner, Carl Jung and various other twentieth-century philosophers whose visions have yet to flower into touchstones for future cultures – could actually *see* the force-fields and energies which science is just beginning to acknowledge. Reich, for instance, watched 'orgone energy', the terrestrial force, moving on the surface of the sea or in the sparks which briefly flash in the blue sky.* He saw it in life-forms and foods, and even built 'orgone energizers', cubicles of electrical cables in which a patient can sit in anticipation of being revitalized with orgone energy. The fact that Reich remarked cycles of intensity in orgone energy makes one wonder what links are still to be made between 'cosmo-rhythmology' – or astrology – and the relative life-forces in plants, animals and people during certain planetary aspects.

Experience of man as a force-field connected to others and, in turn, to the force-field of the earth, where the power of attraction and symbiosis and the unstinting exchange of energy are operating, leads easily to a more rational concept of 'love'. Reich saw that when the psyche, and thus the body, constricted itself with fear and aggression, it also severed itself from the life-forces of love. He thus saw the need for regular orgasm as a prerequisite to psychic and physical health. These ideas branched into politics, where oppressive and fascist systems were seen to reflect the suppression of the orgasm and the cultural denial of love energy, an energy which is forced to burst out in the destructive vibration of war. Reich was thus the mentor of the 'Love Generation', and his ideas are crystallized in the button slogan: 'Make Love Not War'.†

* These sparks can be seen by any of us, but we have culturally conditioned ourselves to ignore, and thus not see them.
† A recent Yugoslav film, *WR – Mysteries of the Orgasm* (recently changed, perhaps by anti-orgasmic censors, to *WR – Mysteries of the Organism*), explores and spoofs at some length the political implications of Reich's sexual philosophy.

Massage and Occult Sexuality

The practice of mutual massage, which in the early seventies spread across America and into Western Europe, seeks to awaken the self, with the help of others, to the actual anatomy of the life-forces within us, and to activate their therapeutic and communicative power. Through knowledge, the tangible power of love, rather than its ideal, springs to life – like a phoenix from the miasma of wishful thinking – and with it comes the awareness of proportion and depth, the keys to true morality. What may begin as 'playing with fire', develops – in accordance with real law – into either leaving the fire alone, or else no longer merely playing.

In the age of rationalism, where everything is explained (or ignored), the philosopher cries: 'Show me a single miracle!' Yet even into the darkest abyss of myopia three perpetual miracles – birth, death and sex – reach down and touch each of our lives: yours and mine as well as the Holy Man's. Birth, which we seek to control, we have anatomically scrutinized down to the earliest fusion of sperm and ovum. Death, which we defer mechanically for as long as possible, we then ignore – for it is the point at which our otherwise neat cosmology abruptly ends with shattered sinews; and it is a wound in the cultural psyche which must be masked. And 'sex', which is together the most hackneyed of clichés and the most evocative of power words, is the guise in which, in a religionless age, ecstasy can still be experienced. Sex and love, oddly bound together, comprise a universe of meaning – touching presidents and shop girls alike – and in any universe there are the polarities of opposition, from the most execrable evil to the throne of God.

The most sinful of Christian sins (although there are fashion cycles in such things) have been lechery and promiscuity, yet today the closest we get to God – if the theological descriptions are anything to go by – is in physical love.* Today's songs and tales of love, which occupy so much of the air waves, exert more power over us than religion simply because, in this heaven-dimmed age, they are the most apparent intimations of divinity.

---

* Certainly more sinful than murder: in the middle ages, when Christian attitudes were not essentially very different from today, only more overt, it will be remembered that while the Crusader was abroad killing the heathen for Christ, his wife was at home locked in her chastity belt. The neck-to-toe nuptial gowns, of coarse fabric and with orifices at the appropriate places, designed to ensure minimal physical contact and carnal enjoyment during the necessary but 'despicable' act of procreation, have their descendants in today's loose gowns still worn by convent girls to take a bath. Their purpose is to shield the girl from the temptation of catching a glimpse of her own naked body, 'purity' presumably being more desirable than 'cleanliness'.

The Sufi mystics say: 'Man, you are asleep; must you die before you can awake?' and today it is through the joy of sexual union that man begins to stir uneasily in his sleep, and – in orgasm – almost to awake into Life.

Esotericists have always known that sex is not merely a 'base urge for procreation', but a doorway to great mysteries, though fraught, like all avenues of primal power, with seductive traps and dangers. In Tantric Yoga the knowledge of sexual energies was developed into a science of worship, where men and women became not merely the symbols of opposites, but the conscious alchemical mediums of spiritual transformation. Even today, in the Sacred Language of High Javanese the term for a man is 'half-a-woman' and for a woman, 'half-a-man'. Through practising the science of spiritual development a couple is known actually to grow together, to become a single – though invisible – entity, a palpitating super-cell which may be offered up as a sacrament to the life-giving influences – a rite which may even produce another life. The quality of a child's spiritual potential is believed to be greatly conditioned by the degree of sacred and conscious unity experienced by its parents at the time of its conception.* The aetheric unity of the pair continues to operate despite even the distant separation of their bodies, so that when the woman needs to respond to life with masculine force (which in Western terms might be the mending of a fuse or dealing with a salesman) it is the man-ness of her mate which moves through her; and the reverse is true of the man, who finds himself (if cooking, for instance) acting and moving with the feminine sensitivity of his woman. They *know* each other because they have *become* each other, and share a human soul which is greater and more versatile than it could ever be as merely a 'half-man' or a 'half-woman'.

The so-called 'love generation' swam deep into the taboo waters of eroticism to find if and where they touched the bottom of natural law. They knew that 'love', like 'religion' or 'death', is a meaningless term unless *experienced*, utterly alone; and they moved inwards on the dangerous journey to the 'golden forest' of fairy tale, seeking to bring back a golden twig to the real world of now, so that the *self* would forever possess some of the truth. Even in the most profane sexual encounters, the power of love reminds us of wholeness. A friend of mine who had consciously sought to free herself entirely of her 'Puritan conditioning',

---

* Today we see in our own culture – from the statistically higher divorce rate among the children of divorced parents – that children of broken homes have an inward though

as she put it, commented that she had discovered that '. . . it was a drag to make love to someone you didn't spend all night with, and a drag to spend all night with someone you didn't live with (since they tended to get up and leave in the morning), and a drag to live with someone you didn't love.'

She had found, on no authority but her own, that sex retains an unseverable connection with a deeper mystery, one which eventually resonates in everyone except, perhaps, the mindless profligate or the frozen ascetic.

In 'experiential' rather than 'authoritative' religion, celibacy as well as sexuality is a tool to knowledge; for ideals are pointless without knowledge of their attainment, and of where we empirically stand in relation to them. To *know* of love – rather than to dream about it – requires first learning about the energies of which we are made. To temporarily deny sexual energy – like inhibiting the flow of Qi with acupuncture – is to change the habitual balance of the body, to stand back for a moment (or a few years) so as to become aware of the forces of which we are usually the unconscious victims. In this way the power is increased and channelled beyond measure, for only someone who has practised conscious celibacy – while keeping all his physical and psychic antennae fully alive – can learn the power of physical love. From this a real freedom emerges; we are no longer chained to the 'need' for freedom, for both the constrictions of guilt and the compulsions towards 'fresher fields of the body' loosen their grip. We come to recognize that it is the force-field of another in which the 'action' lies, rather than their body, and the hierarchical chemistry of relationships becomes both immediately real and divinely simple. Thus the seekers who are really experienced in love begin to encounter 'real' moral laws, based on what *is*, rather than what officially *should* be – which of course is different for each of us at different times.

But in the technocratic West we are still children in the area of the supernatural, versed only in the physiology of love, consuming textbooks on the ABC to orgasm; and barely aware of interior energies, we nevertheless pine after their sanctity, trying to crush from the body, from the cunts and tits of pornography, the essence of what it is that really moves us. But from oriental and esoteric legend drifts the knowledge that to sleep with someone means actually to become aetherically mingled with them, to begin to fuse into what may become, after years of conscious love, a single aetheric being. No woman who has tasted some of this extraordinary sanctity can remain a tigress of female liberation, and no man a chauvinist pig; for they discover that their differences are profoundly complementary, and that they are potentially a part of each other's souls in as real a way as we are each part of our parents and our children – and of every creature which moves on the earth.

It used to be an old joke in medical schools that the specialist in the nervous system made a great lover. But what about the specialist in the aetheric and spiritual systems? What new dimensions are added to the meaning of love? The word 'to heal' derives from 'making whole', and the energies of 'making whole' – both those from which man physically springs, as a fertilized cell, as well as those which he much later discerns as unifying the whole cosmos – are the energies of 'love' in a very real sense. For the gematrician – the symbolist of letters and numbers – the only difference between 'live' and 'love' is the 'I' and the 'O'; the first being the love of the 'I' which keeps the self alive, and the second being the enveloping love of the 'O', the self's awareness of its place in the cosmos and in relation to others.

In that each single one of us is a 'makeweight' in the scales of creative evolution, we can either resist the interchange of energies, or else we can surrender to them, and be lifted high in the wind thermals of change, each discovering for himself more of the immense harmonic geography of the inner world of which our century is standing on the threshold.

7   Maps of Self-Discovery

The 'rejection of authority' among the young stems from the fact that there are now so many conflicting authorities that the concept has lost all power, and the only place to turn to for answers is the self. Beneath the apparent demise of Christian orthodoxy, which is what most of us think religion to be, is a turbulent and widespread religious revival which is characterized by the need to experience personally the reality, or otherwise, of the supernatural. That the survival of 'meaning', and thus of any future form of religion, relies on this discovery alone has driven people with a kind of desperation back to test the truths of the spiritual world which have never been forgotten by the gnostic and occult traditions. Here we find charts of how to proceed, distilled grammars of the laws of symbol which can, if we have the courage to follow, lead to the full reality of a different world of meaning.

These symbolic systems – the I Ching, the Tarot and the 'body languages' of Physiognomy, Palmistry and Graphology – are, together with Astrology and Numerology, which we have already looked at, simply tools rather than ends in themselves. They may be picked up by the curious, crushed impatiently for their sustenance, and prove dry; or they may be followed clue by clue into a deeper form of commitment; or again, as is often the case, they may be used by those already involved in a 'religious' method of self-awakening merely as touchstones for worldly guidance. With the latter, these systems can work extremely well, for they are seen within the context of a fuller hierarchy of law, and are experienced as belonging to the more temporal and limited end of the spectrum.

One of the simplest and most natural ways of access to underlying meaning is to listen conscientiously to our dreams. By listening, we remember, and by remembering we begin to see the living parts of ourselves which have become submerged. The lunar self, on the night-side of the waking ego, is not only rich in millions of years of genetic wisdom, but is also – perhaps paradoxically – the medium through which a 'higher' self can speak, a self which is part of our evolutionary future. Swathed in a cocoon of rationalism, over recent centuries we have seen fewer and fewer spirits; yet the fear of these energies – fear springing always from the unknown – has not diminished but has been projected 'outside' us into the 'tangible' energies (such as nuclear power) which are at our command while yet being beyond our control. In dreams, trance and worship, where supernatural energies still vibrate, we face the mystery and the fear, and only in this solitude can we come to terms with what we see to be malevolent *external* forces.

That we are inwardly connected to laws less fickle or fearsome than chance has been denied mainly on the grounds that we are the product of the laws of chance alone; and that we do not have an 'inner self'. But the existence of the 'inner self' – or the faculty of deeper awareness – can no longer be doubted, and it appears to be as instinctively aware of balance and proportion as are the automatic processes which direct the various chemical fluctuations in our bodies. All our racial memory points now to the need to become *conscious* of what it is that moves harmonically (and largely instinctively) both within and without us. To be unaware of the hidden self is also to be unaware of the different universe of being which it alone is adapted to know. It seems almost as if the evolutionary process, which, like all laws, functions differently at different levels, conspires to force us back to the hidden self – or else perish in the maelstrom of conflicting phenomena which our technology has unleashed.

As the man knows who has walked in the labyrinth of despair, where there is nothing but darkness, each step forward miraculously lands on firm ground and, clue by clue, we are most 'unreasonably' led back to survival. Most of us have experienced being *in extremis*, the whispered prayer in moments of great fear, the saving thread which, when every-thing is lost, catches us up into transcendence at the last moment. The transcendent, when it really happens, is usually associated with being *in extremis*, for only when we have nothing to lose – at the moment of death or great loss – are we totally vulnerable to the proverbial 'Powers that Be'. Yet these influencesare *always* operaing; we only need the same attitude of surrender – so rare when we are relatively comfortable – for them to burst into our immediate world. The old adage says that there are only two certain things in this world: that everything changes, and that eventually we die. To face death now, while well and content, is to face the essence of fear which can then never touch us for the rest of our lives. But to face it is to move voluntarily in the way the man in despair is *forced* to move, by taking a step, with all one's weight and soul in it, into the void.

People once knew this, with their minds and bodies. Now we only remember it vaguely, and it lies ingrained in our fabric, awaiting resurrection. The simplest tools have been left, disguised as games, and rhymes, as stories and shapes; to pick them up is to move inwards.

There is something sacred about real games: they teach 'integrity', the balance between the earnest and the carefree. 'Does it all really *matter*?' whispers one part of our soul about the earnestness of life; 'No!' comes the answer from the other part. 'Then need I worry, or do anything?' 'Yes,' cries the soul – for existence is both desperately urgent, and infinitely relaxed and easy. Wisdom seeks the mean between the two poles – a mean which is mirrored in games. There is no fear in them, yet they *matter*. A child's games teach him of the adult world to come; a panther cub's games are entirely playful, yet he is learning to become a panther. There are certain games through which adults can learn to become human. In *The Glass Bead Game*[1] Herman Hesse describes a game where the monks had a secret computer, disguised as a set of beads, which mirrored the laws of the cosmos. Many common games, now played with the mind alone, have roots in profounder knowledge – chess, for instance, with its polarities of black and white on the square base of matter, with its eight divisions (for the cycles of eternity) on every edge, giving the sacred sixty-four microcosmic squares. The chess pieces, in the guise of a human hierarchy, reflect the levels of power, which move differently in space: in strides, or hops, or angles. It commands such archetypal power that millions have turned to the great chess matches; Fischer versus Spassky becoming two knights waging a war of invisible forces.

There is also the pack of playing cards, the exoteric version of the ancient Tarot pack, or Book of Seth, the mirror of the cosmos with its roots in long vanished cultures. The four suits of the seasons, the hierarchical family beyond the numbers up to ten, become in a game of cards actually alive with the projections of the unconscious. They focus power to know the cunning, the intellect and the heart of other men, causing the literal loss and gain of fortunes in material wealth. The once sacred game of Mah Jong, which was brought back from China in the tea-trading days and which swept through the parlours of the West at the turn of the century, has its roots in a subtler pattern, one seen most clearly in the I Ching, the first of the systems we shall examine that are microcosmic code-books of higher law.

The *I Ching*, or Book of Changes, is a sacred game to be played with the self. In that the adage: 'all changes, and I myself die', can be reduced simply to 'all changes', the I Ching is a slide-rule of the laws governing change – in the way that the Periodic Table of Elements is a graph of all the possible combinations of physical matter. The book is now carried like a living bible by thousands of seekers, for it has endless permutations and becomes as alive – to the owner who has come to know it – as the invisible hierarchy which it mirrors.[2]

It is often said that the I Ching is built on a binary system, but it is more accurate to see it as a trinary one. In the West, still strongly influenced by Aristotelian logic, we think in terms of 'yes' and 'no': a thing cannot 'be' and 'not be' at the same time; in the East, however, it can. The oriental admits of a 'yes', a 'no' and of a 'maybe' somewhere between the two. Thus the I Ching begins with the polar extremes and maps the degrees of 'maybe' through which one merges into the other. The masculine Yang is an unbroken line ——, the feminine Yin is a broken line — —, and they represent all the possible antitheses which permeate our physical and psychic environment.

Used as a mirror, the oracle requires the casting of matter into 'chance', the void from which order is reflected. For those versed in its interpretation the discerned order becomes a continual guide to the great laws which underlie the vagaries of phenomena in which we are habitually caught. To cast into the void of chance, like releasing Noah's dove, can be done by tossing a coin.* As we know from the secret grammar of numbers, 3 is the principle of generation, and it is three coins at a time which must be thrown into chance. The fall of these three – in the strange progression of numerology – can mirror *four* possible alternatives: three heads, or three tails, or two heads and a tail, or two tails and a head. The latter two are more 'probable', and to the two heads and a tail is attributed Yin-ness† ——, and to the two tails and a head — —, Yang-ness. The three-of-a-kind are different stages of 'maybe', or change; the three heads being Yang *moving* towards Yin, ——, and the three tails being Yin *moving* towards Yang —✕—. But to conjure the 'timeless' into the present, in the way of magic, requires a

* The more traditional way is by throwing 'yarrow stalks', a more lengthy, rhythmical and satisfying ritual – often giving the practitioner time to 'centre' himself sufficiently to understand the response.
† This is if we choose to equate heads with Yang. The numerical value of each coin thrown is either three for Yang or two for Yin; so by addition, each throw of three coins can give us the numbers 6, 7, 8 or 9, from which we can quickly reach our 'moving' lines in the Book of Changes.

knowledge of how it responds, and the key is again in numbers: the number 6 being the first complete harmony in the decad, symbol of balance, we cast our three coins six times. By marking down the six symbols which appear, from the *bottom upwards* (since we begin in matter and aspire to the knowledge above it), we achieve a hexagram for this moment in time, of which there are only sixty-four possible kinds, ranging between the two polarities of Ch'ien, 'The Creative' or total Yangness and K'un, 'The Receptive', which is its antithesis. In Fig. 84 these two hexagrams are found at the top and at the bottom of the full circle.

The 'Book of Changes' itself is then referred to, which contains counsels in the form of explanatory epigrams for each of the sixty-four possible hexagrams.* If in our six throws either three heads or three tails have appeared together, then these are 'moving' lines. We have two moving lines in this hexagram: Ta Chuang, 'The Power of the Great', one in the first place, at the bottom, where the unbroken Yang line is changing into Yin, and one in the fifth place, where the reverse is happening. Thus for a deeper reading, for an extension in time of the situation being mirrored, we can read the new hexagram into which Ta Chuang is metamorphosing, namely Ta Kuo, 'The Preponderance of the Great', where there is an overbalance of density in the middle four lines, and the hexagram is less stable than if the weak lines at either end of the figure were contained by strong ones. The nature of change through the metamorphosis of one hexagram into another can be read from the 'moving lines' commentaries which are given in the I Ching.

The hexagram itself consists of the more primal grammar of trigrams, each with its own balance of meaning. The more obvious two are the top three and the bottom three lines, but in addition to these are the two further 'nuclear' trigrams which are dovetailed together in its centre, one despiring from heaven, the other aspiring from earth.

* The number 64, closely associated with the gnostic science of numbers in all cultures, is also the number of squares on the chess board. The same 6- and 4-fold qualities range through Mah Jong, suggesting that they all have a common root, not so much in China as in the universal vanished wisdom, which leaves its esoteric traces throughout the earth.

From these nuclear trigrams can be read the inner or spiritual nature of a situation, while the two outside trigrams reflect the more obvious or exoteric polarities of an event and point to guidance in more practical matters. In Fig. 84 the full sixty-four hexagrams are arranged in a circle, and the harmonics of change are reminiscent of the geometry of crystals, or magic squares.

The I Ching's influence can be traced back many thousands of years, but after the Confucian School adopted it at the end of the Chou dynasty, and when all but this school were banned from the Imperial Academy in 140 B.C., it became the established classic of Chinese culture until modern revolutionary times. Its fluid versatility has saved it from the doctrinal fate which has befallen so much of our Western sacred literature, but the counsel in the book is still heavily couched in the language of the social hierarchy of Chinese antiquity – ranging between the 'Emperor' and the 'mob'. But as even the medieval Chinese commentators suggested, these should be taken simply as symbols of the higher and lower aspects of the self: the 'superior man', so often referred to in the I Ching, is appealing to the superior man in our own understanding, and the entire book, regardless of the mantic uses to which it may be put, is a single vein of liturgical wisdom, which may be tapped for sustenance at any point.

Most of today's computers work on a binary system – of 'yesses' and 'no's' – but more sophisticated cybernetics are moving into a trinary programming phase, in which the 'maybe's' are included. These machines more closely parallel the diversity and range found in the natural world, and the simplest grammar with which they can be programmed – it so happens – has sixty-four variables – the number of hexagrams in the classical I Ching.

The Tarot, disguised as a game of cards, is a further microcosmic 'control panel' which can focus the psyche and sensitize it to those laws of which we are usually only aware *in extremis*.[3] It is the itinerant 'survivors' of the world, the gipsies, the bards, the hippies, those who always live close to the wilder shores of fate, in whom the oral and gnostic traditions are kept alive and carried like torches from age to age ready to ignite the fires of a new way of seeing. In post-revolutionary China, when the great cultural heritages were burned and reviled, the blind beggars continued to cast the I Ching, feeling the change from the faces of the coins and reciting the appropriate passages from memory. In Europe, such social pariahs as the gipsies kept alive a similar wisdom,

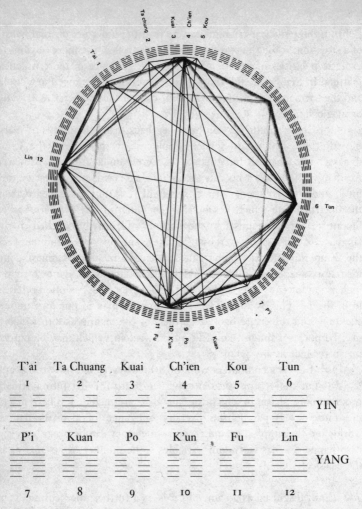

84. The circular sequence of the sixty-four hexagrams. The squares delineate the octagon contained within the circle, each of its points touching opposing symbols.

The twelve 'sovereign hexagrams', representing the twelve Chinese months of the year (beginning 5 February and ending 21 January) occur in a harmonic sequence throughout the circle, representing lines of tension and proportion, like the strings of an instrument, which may be either experienced aesthetically or analysed mathematically. They are here placed with the number of the month, and the name of the corresponding hexagram. These twelve 'sovereign' hexagrams show the fluctuations of the Yang and Yin forces throughout the year: nos. 1 to 6 being predominantly Yang, the remainder mainly Yin.

On the above circle Ch'ien and K'un alone are connected to each one of the other sovereign hexagrams.

locked in the Tarot pack – the sacred 'Book of Séth', which even in its profane version of ordinary playing cards was to exert such a fascination over later and less visionary cultures.*

With their symbolic roots in the cultures of Egypt and Mesopotamia, the 78 cards of the pack are based on a supreme union of numbers and geometry which has come to be known as the Cabbalistic Tree of Life. The Tree is indeed alive, for it harmonically multiplies itself from the infinitely small to the infinitely great, moving into three dimensions, outlining as it does so the five sacred solids, without in any way changing the proportions relative to its parts. Its numerical harmony, even in its tracing of the glyphs of the numbers which we use daily, is nothing to the immediacy of meaning and proportion it can awaken in the understanding of how we ourselves, in our pains, anxieties and triumphs, actually function.

Some of the Tarot's magic emerges if we show the first steps in constructing the Living Tree of which the Tarot Pack, and we ourselves – even the material construction of the crystals in our bodies – are the fruit.

In Fig. 85 four macrocosmic circles unfold from each other, like multiplying cells, producing four vesicae piscis – two vertical and two horizontal. In Fig. 86 we see more clearly the two vertical vesicae – representing the upper and lower worlds. But since we are not fully three-dimensional creatures, we can take but one axis at a time, and we place our four inter-penetrating circles (in Fig. 87) on the vertical axis strung between heaven and earth. Since our point of aspiration, as constructors of the Tree, begins at the more material end of the ebb and flow between heaven and earth, the three lower circles of Fig. 87 form the basis for the rest of the Tree's construction. Joining these circles' 'inner' points of contact, we get two $\sqrt{3}$ rectangles (3, 2, 5, 4 and 5, 4, 8, 7).

The 'paths of Power' are generated from the 'navel' of the lower rectangle (which is number 6 for the 'harmonious centre') and extend

---

* There are of course many different Tarot packs, with differing numbers of cards, such as those of Florence, Seville, Transylvania, etc. One of the earliest known European packs was painted in 1393 by the Cabbalist Jacquemin le Grigonneur for Charles VI of France. Its seventeen surviving cards are all of the Major Arcana still used in the so-called Marseilles pack of seventy-eight cards. Despite modern variations, such as the A. E. Waite and Aleister Crowleypacks – and even more beautiful recent ones – the Marseilles pack has been and still is most widely used, probably for its symbolic as well as geometric equilibrium.

85. The four vesicae produced by four macrocosmic unfolding circles.

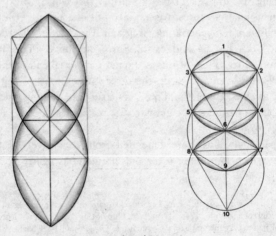

86. The two vertical, interpenetrated vesicae.

87. The four microcosmic circles on the vertical 'cross'. The points of connection of the lower three produce the ten Sephira of the Cabbalistic Tree of Life. Note the $2\sqrt{3}$ rectangles circumscribed by the Sephira 3,2,5,4, and 5,4,8,7.

to the remaining nine of the ten points, or Sephira, of the sacred decad. The glyphs of the decad – 1 to 10 – can be seen traced on the tree in Fig. 88; we see this numerical progression beginning in the supreme unity of the 'Crown' at the top of the tree, and descending like 'the lightning bolt' of spirit down through the numbers to 10 at the bottom, the 'Kingdom', the world of divine multiplicity on earth.

The Tarot pack, which symbolizes in primal archetypes the movements and points of rest in this Tree of Life, has four suits – Sceptres, Wands, Cups and Swords (which in the seventeenth century became the Clubs, Hearts, Spades and Diamonds which we know today). These represent the four Elements, or worlds of the four circles on our vertical tree. There are thus four court cards in each suit: the King, symbolizing the higher spirit in man, the Queen, the 'soul' of the inner pattern of the metaphysical self,* the Knight, the personal ego or form of self-expression and the Knave, symbolizing the personal vehicle of the body. After these, in each of the four suits, come the further minor trumps, numbered 1 to 10 (like playing cards – for the 10 Sephira of the decad), comprising a total of 56 minor trumps. There are a further 22 major trumps, for the 22 'paths of power' between the numbers. Each is symbolized by an archetype reflecting the 'vibrationary frequency' existing between the 10 numbers; and they correspond to the 22 letters of the Hebrew alphabet.

The tree has three vertical trunks, or pillars (see Fig. 88). On either side of the central, androgynous pillar of mediation are the pillars of the male and female polarities. Only on the central pillar are to be found the Godhead of everything in one, and at the bottom, its converse, complete material multiplicity, and the harmonizing principle of 6 together with the 'foundation' of 9. The paths between the numbers obey integral laws, like physics: there are no direct paths, for instance, between 3 and 7, or between 2 and 9, for the qualities of these pairs of numbers are inharmonious unless passed through the equilibrium of 6. It is often assumed that such symbolic thought is so fluid that it has no laws and may be used as one will; but with discimination and training, very definite laws

* There is a general confusion, only obscured by orthodox religion, between the concepts of 'spirit' and 'soul'. In practical occultism the distinctions become much clearer. The 'soul' in this context, symbolized by the Queen, is that part of us which, unlike the essential 'spirit', is conditioned by astrological influences. It is the still more 'material' aspects of us, as symbolized by the Knight and the Knave, which are conditioned by merely sociological and environmental forces.

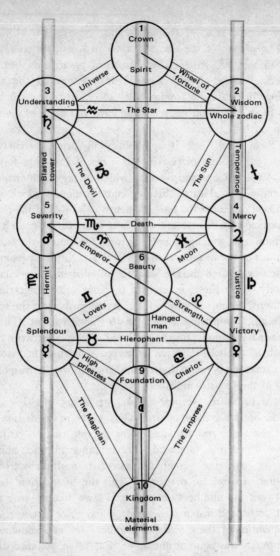

88. The Tree of Life, with its 10 Sephira and 22 'paths of power', and how they traditionally relate to the 7 major planets and the 12 signs of the zodiac. The 'Three Pillars' (on the vertical axis) are suffused by the 'Lightning Bolt' of spirit which descends from the One down through the numbers 1 to 10. The 10 Sephira are named for their archetypal 'qualities'. The 22 'Paths of Power' are symbolized by the 22 letters of the Hebrew alphabet, as well as representing the 22 major trumps of the Tarot pack, whose names appear on the paths in this figure.

emerge, which, though more subtle, are just as integral as those used by science.

To use the Tarot as a mantic or inspirational medium the neophyte first places himself (as with the I Ching) in a state of submission, quietening his mind and desires. He then shuffles the symbols into the void of chance, and the patterns which return, like the snowflakes which come out of the chaos of the night, are full of symmetry and meaning.

Occult systems such as the Tarot and the I Ching are psychic analogies to visual puzzles and illusions; they show us that the way we generally *see* things is not in fact the way they *are*, since the way the world appears at one level is only part of a highly complex and yet precise blending of being at another. When the turning of the Tarot cards, or the fall of the yarrow stalks, begins to mirror situations very precisely, it is not an 'outrage of chance', since the laws of probability (which are 'rational') are external to the inner self, and inward laws – as each of us knows – are very often totally contrary to those of 'probability'. Our very existence, if we reflect 'rationally' for a moment, is highly improbable. These occult grammars merely project the psyche and its interior order on to the outside world, and thus bring some of the transcendent balance (which is not to be confused with determinism) to the exterior chaos of our lives. The miracle – or rather its perception – is always *inside* us, and the wiser and more 'religiously' oriented learn eventually to dispense with these mantic devices of external projection, rather as the meditator learns to dispense with the alpha-meter once he has learned to achieve a state of 'clarity' on his own.

The Body Languages

Another of these subtle maps is the human body itself, which in its fluid and geometric harmony is a key to the various occult 'body languages' of physiognomy, palmistry and phrenology. One of the most exhilarating of today's hidden themes is the rediscovery of the miraculous, and the most immediate of miracles is the body we walk around in. The medical and psychiatric professions – which for over a century have been attempting to categorize the mind and the body as determinist machines – are reduced to leaving the cure to 'the wisdom of the body' when there is no more to be done for a patient. What is this watery ghost of flesh –

this 'goodly frame of aether', as Shakespeare called it? It harbours the people we love and those we fear; and we ourselves look out from and touch the world with it.

All human bodies, in proportion and size, have but a shading of measurable differences between one another, but from a thousand faces we instantly recognize the one we know. Yet it is by the shape of the nose, the turn of the mouth, or do these merely mirror something else which we recognize?

To re-see the miracle of the human body we can go back for a moment to trees. It is assumed that the tree grows *upwards* out of the earth from its roots, somewhat like a hosepipe with water-pressure in it. But this is a two-dimensional concept: 'tree's point of beginning' is really all around it with the chemical interaction of elements. Its leaves and branches grow 'outwards' into visible, multi-dimensional space, rather than 'upwards' from the earth. Drawn by chemical and photoelectric influences trees 'appear' in space, hundreds of feet high, emerging into the visible from an unseen blueprint, rather as frost-ferns – in two-dimensions – crystallize on a window-pane.* The many chemical elements constituting the tree's 'mask', the shroud it wears while swaying in the material world, obey the laws of chemistry – the basic elements of which are standard throughout the world. But the invisible 'blueprint' which conditions the species, while allowing an enormous variety of individuals, obeys a different set of laws, those which we have barely begun to discover. It is these which are nevertheless mirrored in the physical bodies of trees, those musical blends of invisible essence with hereditary and environmental chemistry. Moving inwards from rationalism, which examines the visible components, we approach the invisible life-essence in ourselves.

The twentieth-century Russian mystic G. I. Gurdjieff once said that although human bodies vary only within narrow limits the human soul ranges from minnows to whales in comparative 'size'. Occult tradition has long maintained that the human body – like the tree – is only an exteriorization of invisible energy whose traces can be discerned in the body like the ripples on a pond left by the wind.

In these traces can be detected not only the quality of vibration underlying an individual here and now in time, but the probabilities of

* To an ant, whose concept of time and physics is limited, the frost-fern also begins at the 'bottom' and grows 'upwards' – but in fact constellates into the visible at all places simultaneously – its organic integrity already implicit 'elsewhere' in the unseen dimension.

its expression in both the past and the future.* The parts of our bodies which are most characteristic of the human species – the overall form, the hands, and the eyes – are also the most sensible to the imprints of this individual energy.

Physiognomy explores the face as a mirror of character. In the art of phrenology, the cranium, with its proportions and lumps, is seen as expressive of the entire underlying fabric of character, but in physiognomy this has spread to cover the features and proportions of the face. The face, though perhaps the most familiar of objects, continues to be one of the most mysterious. Mr A. Taylor has recently written on the immense amount of tacit or 'unconscious' information we receive from a person's face on first meeting them.[4] Most of us are inveterate face-watchers, for through them we sense the enormous range of interior worlds in which mankind lives, and this in turn throws some light on who and where we are ourselves. The art of physiognomy brings this information from the instinctive to the conscious level.

The eyes alone disclose a far wider range of personality information than would seem possible from their slight differences in colour, shape and size. Taylor writes: 'The individuality of a man's countenance is almost destroyed by marking the eyes . . . it is the quality and illumination of the eye itself which stamps each and every human being differently.'[5] Although the 'light' of the human eye cannot be quantified, it is recognized as a key to individuality by the entire human family, as reflected in the criminal who masks his eyes, or the scandalous photographs where only the eyes are blanked out to prevent recognition. At the ordinary level, states of grief, being stoned or being afraid – all clearly discernible in the eyes – are masked with sunglasses. Various military and police régimes of the world, such as the Ton-Ton Macoute of Haiti, also use sunglasses, which shroud the wearer's soul, and act as instruments of fear and tacit reminders that here is a man or a body of men unconnected with the human brotherhood, and of whom therefore any merciless action may be expected.

The whole range of relationships with others, from merest acquaintance to deepest love, is expressed by the degree to which we open our eyes to them, for sight – the instrument of consciousness – carries power, a power which most of us have instinctively learned to check,

* Prediction, with knowledge, is not so strange, but it remains an art, due to the variables. Farmers, economists, you and I in our own fields, subsist on tacit and largely accurate predictions every single day.

only fully opening the diaphragm of their strength to those we trust and love. Beauty, that unquantifiable magnet in people which draws and stills others, is above all a quality of the eyes and of the voice, for these most nakedly mirror the invisible energy of which the body is merely a fragile and temporary shadow. As all the occult arts are concerned with equilibrium to a perfect 'mean' of proportion, the positioning not only of the eyes in the face but of the irises in the eyes, is seen as a key to the inner nature. Both Oriental and Western Mystery traditions speak of how a very material soul often carries its physical irises high in the eyes as if the body should in fact be slightly 'higher' to fully accommodate them. These are the 'diabolic' eyes often seen on gargoyles, the grotesques in Hieronymus Bosch's painting or the demons of Bali. In corpses, which have relinquished the soul, the irises are often rolled

upwards, as if their eyes were trying to escape back to the sunlight world from which they came. The average 'mean' is to have the irises in the

middle of the eyes, a surprisingly uncommon attribute in most of today's city-bred people; whereas the sign of spirituality is to have eyes like the rising sun.

Early portrayals of the Buddha have such eyes, as do young babies, whose souls are brighter and larger than their bodies, and are 'rising' in them in an upward stream of evolutionary growth. The schizophrenic, the ill person or even the 'mad artist', not infrequently have each eye and its iris (as we saw in Chapter 6) in different relationships to each other, reflecting a disharmony between the vibrational sources of the 'crown' and 'brow' chakras.

Once a primal diagnostic aid to medicine, the shape and quality of a face is still used by that profession as indicative of glandular and functional imbalances, for the face is particularly 'soft' to the inner force. The notions of Mercurial, Lunar or Saturnine faces, even in a supposedly de-mythologized age, still conjure up a clear picture: the generosity of the mouth; the laughter lines running down the cheek; the sensitivity of the nostrils which can flare like those of a horse; the pendulous or constricted form of the ear-lobes (those apparently useless pearls of blood); the way the eyebrows either extend across the bridge of the nose, or are divided, with balance; all have their special meaning, and hint at a far subtler and more exact art of character analysis.

Palmistry. The hand too, like the foot, face, ear or bodily form, is a miniature map of the inner man. For over a decade it has been known that a single skin-cell carries the chemical key to the entire bodily make-up – giving rise to the possibilities (expanded fully in science fiction) of creating, as we have already mentioned, a complete copy of an individual, or 'clone', from one of his cells alone, just as hermaphrodite micro-organisms produce multiple replicas of themselves. In palmistry, therefore, it is not so strange that the hand, with its markings and proportions, can accurately indicate the physical and psychic qualities of its steward.

Looking at the phalanges of the curled index finger we see them spiral into diminution in the 'golden mean' proportion:

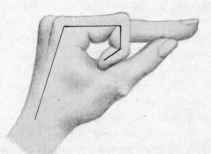

The closed fist is the size of the heart, the open hand the size of the lungs. In Japanese palmistry the grip of the closed fist is related to the 'strength of the heart'; it is possible to gauge, by the strength of the fist's grip on first waking in the morning (the time when we are most 'yin' and receptive to our inner nature) how the heart is recuperating from emotional as well as physical weakness. In Chinese symbolism the palm is the masculine 'yang' polarity of the hand, in opposition to the sensitive 'yin' of the fingers. For this reason people with longer fingers than palms tend to be more yin – artistic, thoughtful, etc. – and people with longer palms than fingers, more yang and more physically and practically oriented. But this balance may be outweighed by other factors, such as the curvature inwards of fingers, which is more yang, or outwards, which is more yin, and so on.

These polarities of 'expansive/contractive' are in turn refined by the basic archetypes which underlie the spectrum of occultism, but until the twentieth century has provided a new language for the subtle world – which it has only just begun to do – we are still constrained to refer to the symbols in their ancient or medieval guise. Each finger is seen as reflecting an archetypal vibration, or element, and the proportions of their three joints to one another mirror the triplicity of 'spirit', 'soul' and body, as – complementarily – do the three lateral divisions of the whole hand. Between the fingers and the 'mounts' on the palm run lines which may be seen as analogous to the 'paths of power' in the Tree of Life – the resonances or 'notes' between different sources of energy. Each of us stands in a different relationship to the golden mean of harmony between all the energies and elements, and the degree to which we individually vary from this 'mean' is immediately detectable in the hand.

As we instinctively judge character from faces, so too do we judge from the texture and quality of a hand-shake. Hands, together with faces and bodily proportion, have been from earliest antiquity the constant themes of art and sculpture, for they are the 'musical instruments' through which vibrates the power which maintains us.

The permutations of the hand's grammar, though composed of the same essential elements, are so infinite that no two hands, or even fingerprints, are identical. The police forces of the world are strongly supported by forensic science which, in the area of fingerprints, has collected much of its data from the traditional archives of palmistry and chirognomy. As the occult arts and empirical sciences draw closer together, although each loses something – in the manner of any compromise – their union is gestating an emergent area of knowledge which is potentially greater than both.

A highly specialized branch of diagnostic medicine, calling itself dermatoglyphics, is currently being exhumed from the wealth of chirognomantic tradition. Research by Menser and Purvis-Smith[6] at the Royal Hospital for Children in Sydney, Australia, is providing correlations

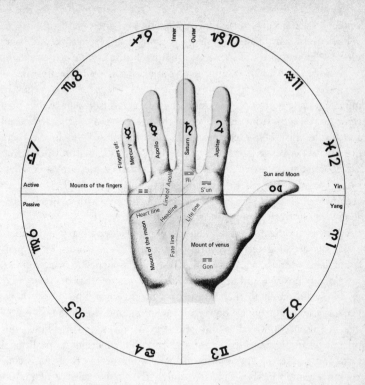

91. A simple 'inter-disciplinary' view of the hand, showing the underlying connections between diverse systems. Notice the two primary polarities of the hand: the upper half being 'active' or Yin (in the sense of 'fluid expansion'), and the lower half being 'passive', or Yang – in the sense of 'hardening contraction'. The Mercury finger side of the hand reflects the 'interior' qualities of the character, while the thumb side shows the nature of its 'external' expression. Superimposed on the horoscope we see the significance of the fingers as they fall in or between the astrological houses. The First house, where the thumb lies, denotes the ego and 'worldly strength' of the individual. The eleventh and tenth houses – respectively of 'higher aspirations' and of 'ambition and career', cover the finger of Jupiter, which denotes the blend of these two qualities in an individual. The tenth and ninth houses cover the finger of Saturn, which reflects the qualities of 'ambition and career' combined with the ninth house's 'philosophy, deep thought and distant journeys'. The eighth and seventh houses, of 'rebirth and regeneration' and of 'marriage and close associations', cover the finger of Mercury, which mirrors the combination of these qualities. Further correlations emerge between the trigrams of the I Ching, Oriental palmistry, and the palmistry of the Western Mysteries Tradition. Had we used the left hand, instead of the right, then we would see the first house of Aries in the more traditional place on the left of the figure.

between the markings on children's hands and their susceptibility to such apparently unrelated problems as mongolism, leukaemia and heart defects. Abnormalities of the heart are mirrored in certain tell-tale signs in the finger of Apollo, where the wedding ring is traditionally worn – the finger named after the patron god of the arts, the venusian equivalent to emotional expression. Early anatomists believed that an artery ran directly from this finger to the heart – and apothecaries used carefully to mix their medicines with this finger so as to infuse them with creative love. A later, more materialistic medicine, on discovering that no such artery existed, was quick to denounce these mystic beliefs as quackery, but the recent revival of subtle medicine has shown that an acupuncture line of Qi energy, clearly detectable with a neurocalcometer, runs directly from the ring-finger to the heart.

A further interesting correlation exists between palmistry and radiesthesia, the art of detecting subtle vibration with a pendulum. A pendulum held over the end of each of the four fingers in turn produces alternatively positive and negative swings, suggesting that the fingers are oppositely polarized to their immediate neighbours. The thumb however has a neutral, though powerful, radiation; and the thumb in palmistry represents both the Sun and the Moon together. Thus this apparently ambiguous duality of the thumb's function in traditional chirognomy (like the ambiguities in many other occult systems) is thus becoming more clearly resolved through the young science of radiesthesia.

Graphology. Perhaps the most successful emergence from the attics of 'superstition' is the judgement of character by handwriting. Like fingerprints, the signature has long been known to be the stamp of a man's identity, but now the study is being revived of *what*, in his identity, makes him who he is. In the way that a person's gait or odour carries a unique and immediately recognizable code, so too do the shapes of our written 'a's' and 'f's'. For over thirteen years in America and Europe serious graphological agencies have been operating specifically to advise business companies on the characters and capacities of their potential employees, from their handwriting alone.

Connections

A number of organizations have recently emerged, such as the 'Society for the Correlation of Physiological Patterns', which specialize in the connections *between* the different occult systems. For instance, where a person has a strong astrological influence from Venus in his natal chart, as well as a pronounced palmar mound of venus (at the base of the thumb), and a strong 'venusian mound' on the cranium, then he figures as one of the scores of samples which statistically support the underlying connections between astrology, palmistry and phrenology, and thus their probable validity.

For over a decade diagnostic medicine has been probing our bodies with sophisticated electronic devices; it is now beginning to stand back a bit, and to look more carefully at the contours and proportions which brush the body's surface. Through 'body languages' each one of us can now begin to read the fluctuations of energy in which we are held – for no one is the steward of our bodies but our own selves.

If we look at our nails we can see horizontal and lateral wave-forms on them, like the surface of flowing water. Today's doctors still use the blemishes and quality of a patient's nails as diagnostic aids, a technique which stems from the magical origins of Western medicine, prior to the Enlightenment, when it was recognized that the entire body – the hands and nails in particular – mirrors the fluctuations which have already taken place at the level of subtle vibration. Legends in China and Thailand tell of magicians who wore their nails extremely long, like lengths of graph-paper extending from the ten vibrationary 'nozzles' of their hands; from these they could read at a glance the harmonic oscillations in the 'plasma field' which invisibly maintained them.

The present revival of occultism is seen at one level as merely the immature reversion of our culture from the pressing reality of rationalism, back to the consolation of atavistic superstition. That these occult systems superficially seem to differ so widely from one another (as do religions) is often taken to confirm their essential falsity, but their underlying symbolism shows them all simply to be different fruits of the same vibrationary tree. Their shared patterns, like the proverbial different pathways leading up a mountain to the same peak, lead also to the deeper, yet similar, mysteries of 'religious' commitment. It is these underlying patterns, when relatively freed from the stylized symbolism of long-passed cultures, which are gradually emerging as the network on which the future Aquarian Religion is being founded.

8   The Religions of Experience

In the absence of knowledge, is not certainty close to lunacy?

JACOB NEEDLEMAN

In previous chapters we have watched how the once solid ground of scientific rationalism is beginning to melt, like ice-floes, back into the rhythms of an underlying cosmology. The chaos and alienation brought about by our culture's obsession with reason persist because of our reluctance to change our 'depth of vision' and to view the universe of fact in a deeper dimension.

Rather as these two-dimensional shapes:

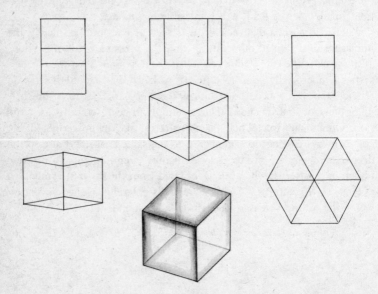

reveal themselves to be but different facets of a single three-dimensional organism, a cube, so too do the disconnected icebergs of 'fact' which have cluttered our horizon since the Scientific Enlightenment dissolve into a single ocean of vision when viewed from a deeper dimension. Sir Isaac Newton wrote in his diary shortly before he died: 'I do not know what I may appear to the world, but to myself I seem to have been only a boy playing on the sea-shore, and diverting myself in now and then finding a smoother pebble or a prettier shell than ordinary, whilst the great ocean of truth lay all undiscovered before me!'[1]

The clues to this 'truth', as we have seen in previous chapters, are in certain shapes, numbers and patterns which determine the growth not only of the *outside* world of crystals, music and living things, but also of the *inside* world, of the very structure of mythic and symbolic thought. This hitherto conflicting duality of the 'outside' versus the 'inside', is now beginning to fuse even at the most physical level. For several decades neurosurgeons have known that the *left-hand* hemisphere of the brain is adapted to deal with the physical and rational world of everyday experience, but now, paralleling the general cultural search for renewed religious meaning, they are entering the 'dark continent' of the brain's *right-hand* hemisphere, and finding that it is specifically adapted to deal with the deeper, more abstract dimensions of perception.

The earth – as a macrocosm of the human mind – also consists of a right-hand and a left-hand hemisphere – the East, which excels in religious and transcendent areas of consciousness, and the West, which excels in technology and manipulation of the material environment. Until recently, this duality was unreconciled, but now it is beginning to merge, both in the cross-fertilization between the global East and West, as well as between the left and right hemispheres of our individual brains, which means that 'religion' and 'science' need no longer be spoken of in different breaths.

The rhythmic patterns of energy, which we are finding underlie all matter, are leading us ever inwards towards a simpler and yet vaster Order, to the awesome place of '*re-ligare*' with our source. The more we look at the world's 'Great Religions' in the light of the 'new science', the more they emerge as giant edifices which have corrupted around a miraculous thread of knowledge. We see ourselves as savages wandering among the ruins of a vanished technological civilization; our priests, in the crumbling power stations, intoning the fading instructions on the walls and making gestures with the long-disconnected levers. 'Outer' religion is a religion of 'faith', of hoping that the electrical energy, if one gets the ritual right and repeats it often enough, will again flood through the corroded machinery. But 'inner' religion is the experiential awakening of *knowledge* of the actual power which makes things work. This rediscovery, among the ruined power stations of our spiritual heritage, is being pursued by small groups of twentieth-century alchemists, who are continually experimenting in the laboratories of themselves – even if like Edison with his first attempts at making a bulb, achieving only but a brief flicker.

Whereas everything in the natural world still dances to the vibrationary music of its source, man alone seems to have branched out into a waterless desert of externals, one which he is only just realizing threatens his very existence. Sumatran myths tell how the more separated man became from his inner source, the longer he had to sleep, for only through dreams could he remain connected to the inner world. Once, in the golden age of myth, when he barely slept and lived for centuries, before he knew the 'shame' of God's rejection, his inner self was still linked to his waking awareness, and the stiffening of his penis – as the sceptre of creative worship – was as much under his conscious control as is today the raising and lowering of his arms.

But today we are schizophrenics, the lower half of us – like the allegory of the Pan God – obeying the laws of biology, while the upper half does not. Dream and symbol, myth and legend, through which the rhythms of sacred order reveal themselves, have been ignored and allowed to wither in the heat of rational progress. Even 'innocence' is now cynically assumed to be naïveté – but what is innocence if not the primal tool of submission, of quietening ourselves to the harmony inside us.

As children we are briefly allowed to live in the world of dreams and fantasy where invisible myths are alive with meaning. Having come so recently from the unseen world – which our culture oddly assumes to be pre- or unconscious – children are still closely attuned to it, and just before they cross the 'bridge of tears' into adult chaos, their transparent questions and observations gleam with what most of us have buried and forgotten. Children are a constant reminder of the alchemists' saying that 'we are surrounded by colours we cannot see, by sounds we cannot hear; and we see as real what is unreal, and cannot see what *is*'.

Of all the natural kingdom man shares with only a few insects and amphibians the strange deformity (or transitionary stage) of never quite reaching adulthood. Like these odd hybrids the limbs of our inner being no longer fully develop, and as adults we are still mostly children – but without the child's innocence and vision.

As a child I remember listening to classical music and remarking that the instruments were too coarse to express it properly, and I wondered if anyone in the world had made instruments fine enough to interpret what the music *really* was. But as I hardened into maturity I realized that violins and flutes were the best there was; it was *their* sound which became the music itself, rather than the music's imperfect shadow. Words too began to condition thought, rather than to express it.

'Become ye as little children' was no injunction to return to infantilism, but to rediscover *consciously*, as adults, what as children we knew instinctively. How often have we thought, or rather allowed ourselves to *know*, that we are citizens of another dimension who, by some impenetrable trick, have been press-ganged and transported to awake in a distant and alien land – with only vague memories of our halcyon origins to sustain us?

Plato allegorized this '*gnostalgia*' by writing that before man was born he lived on a star. Looking over the star at the earth of matter his curiosity overcame him, and he fell towards incarnation, where he spends the rest of his days trying to get back to where he came from.

Man strives for the Real, for the *meaning* behind the shadows, and this re-connection is achieved through symbols – which is why anthropologists have described him as the 'symbol-making creature'. The archetype of the 'search' which runs through all mythology is the search for more transparent symbols which mirror the self's quest for the 'star from which we came'.

This pursuit is projected into countless external endeavours: the will to make money (the accumulation of power and freedom), the explorer's quest for uncharted lands, the lone sailor's conquest of his own frailty in the grip of the elements. The racing driver and the occultist alike seek the ultimate razor edge which divides them from death and insanity, for what we are can to some extent be discovered by learning the point at which we break. In spectator sports, the masses project this interior battle on to the pugilists in the ring, or the football teams in the stadium. It is only the outer symbolism of the odyssey which differs, for whether in the inky entrails of the earth or on the battered heights of Everest, the spelunker and the mountaineer alike pursue the same goal.

When Sir Edmund Hillary was asked why he bothered to climb the world's highest mountain, he repeated the well-known answer: 'Because it is there.' It is *there* for each one of us, yet it seems that only a small percentage of the sleepwalking human race responds to the supreme challenge of what *is* there. Thus, although many of us today have lobotomized ourselves from the whisperings of the psyche, and doggedly rise each morning to face the routine of living, for others the need for meaning has broken the bounds of curiosity. It is no longer enough to be sensitive to the myths of change, to cast the I Ching or to study the subtle maps of character. They seek to learn how to live while there is yet life, to transform every sleeping and waking moment into a sacrament to meaning. It is these people who begin to be drawn to the new religious groups, the central well-springs about which hover the mists of myth and occultism.

Now that the new religions, or 'Ways', as the Sufis call them, are as accepted a part of our culture as the disintegration of Christianity, they are still no better understood. The mass media, extracting every shred of newsworthiness from their more sensational and eccentric aspects, publicly air the new 'ways' with a kind of patronizing disdain. For the academics they have become objects for psychological and sociological dissection, in the mistaken belief that such 'objectivity' will lead to the roots of religion itself. But to drag this interior mystery into the outer world is like dragging the branched seaweed from the ocean, where it lives suspended as a tree of gauze, and laying it on the beach, where it falls shapeless and inert. To understand either the weed or inner religion, we must experience them in their own dimension, for life can only be studied *in vivo*.

Our rational conditioning prevents us from noticing that there is an 'inner' and an 'outer' to all things, from a blade of grass to a carpenter's guild. Nowhere is this duality more apparent than in religions, whose outer structure, rooted in the political and economic world of the secular, totally differs from their inner and secret nature, which leads the self to the music of our individual purpose. Inner religion transcends the general rules which authority (whether of an old or a new religion) gives to the mass of humanity which demands to be told what to believe. If the secrets are brought out into the open for all to see (which is what has happened recently), they still remain 'secret', for the gullible and the cynical alike continue to interpret them as they please, while only the few 'with eyes to see' recognize them as tuning forks for freedom.

Inner religion is the most powerful and desperate of adventures, where the ultimate prizes of sanity and freedom are at stake, but it is not a spectator sport. It involves abandoning everything we had believed to be true; the whole shell of one's personality with its beliefs and visions must utterly disintegrate before a new, more complete belief can emerge. Initiation into a true brotherhood is not only a new birth, but the first link in a whole chain of rebirths: the hair is cut, the name is changed and we are left naked and alone in forty-day deserts. This continual shedding as we ascend towards completeness is consistent with reason, for – to transpose J. S. Haldane's remark about the universe – God may well be not only queerer than we suppose, but queerer than we can suppose, and we must be broken, altered, uplifted and broken again before we can even taste the nature of Truth's intensity.

The great movement of the young towards Eastern religions, which has puzzled and outraged the ministers of our Western Churches, has occurred quite simply because the East still nurtures avenues of 'experiential' discovery of God, catering for *individual* inner needs of a kind which have long been suppressed in the West by orthodox Christianity.

This Western estrangement from inner religion is rather curious. In Oriental religions the 'outer' and 'inner' forms manage to coexist peacefully. In slam, for example, there are the two paths of Tariqu'a and Shari'a. In the first, the average man is assured of salvation if he simply obeys the laws of the Koran and gets on with his life without asking questions. The Shari'a way, however, which includes the multiple Sufi brotherhoods, provides the secret means for experiencing what lies *behind* these laws, for *knowing* God, rather than merely believing in him. Thus Islam – which perhaps after Christianity is the least tolerant of the great religions – is simultaneously both dogmatic and open-ended, and can accommodate everybody, even the more critical and experimental pursuers of truth.

But in Christianity the 'secret' tradition, which was once nurtured by the Heseychasts and such other gnostic brotherhoods as the Templars and the Albigensians, was suppressed as early as the fourteenth century when Pope Pius III declared Heseychasm a heresy. With this, the secret sciences were driven underground, and as the Church became encrusted with dogma its spiritual claims rang hollow against its secular pursuits. The giant façade of repetitive ritual lost its soul, and became vulnerable to commonsense: the Emperor's clothes became transparent until, for all the children with innocence enough to see, the body of the Church emerged as less mysteriously meaningful than the new visions of rationalism. Galileo, Mendel, Darwin brought tidal waves of living symbolism which quite easily eroded the Church's hard-fought monopoly on universal meaning.

For the average man the choices of religion expanded beyond the various denominations of the Christ myth to include, without fear of heresy, both atheism and agnosticism. Later, with the growth of the social sciences – the 'looking beyond' of our own culture – the choices again expanded, like multiplying cells, into a profusion of alternative symbols through which the inner nature of religion could actually be *experienced*, ranging from the most atavistic pantheism to the most intellectualized faith.

Though many of us ache with the need for spiritual orientation, we are unaware that there are now almost as many 'experiential', as opposed to 'authoritative', religious choices as there are temperaments; for whereas until recently in the West there was but one religion for everybody (and the few who hungered for its secrets had to practise heresy) there are now many religions for the few.

The gnostic embers of Christianity are being fanned to life again in the the new magical and witchcraft groups of the Western mysteries tradition. There are the imports from the East, where the green shoots of secret wisdom still flourish, uncropped, among the weeds of superstition. The life in these is a blood transfusion to our own mysterious revival, and this cross-fertilization has spawned a whole variety of hybrids between the ancient forms of occultism and the contemporary myths of science for, as Bryan Wilson has written, '. . . in a society where intellectual criteria dominate, it may well be that what cannot be intellectually accepted cannot be emotionally reassuring'.[2]

Yet many people are driven by this indefinable hunger into the occult book shops, where they quickly lose their purpose in the confusion of titles and categories. Others still – the spiritual 'frogs' – leap from group to group trying to cull the electric pearls from each one, but are disoriented further by their differing surfaces. With religion, as with sexual relationships, it is promiscuity which appears to offer the greatest spice, but it is this which also blinds us to the vistas of richness which lie beneath, in the depths of commitment to a single person or Way.

A Persian proverb advises us on how to seek a spiritual teacher:

He who knows not and knows not he knows not, is a fool; shun him.
He who knows not and knows he knows not, is asleep; wake him.
He who knows and knows not he knows, is a child; teach him.
He who knows and knows he knows, is Wise: follow him.

Yet depending on who we are, on our personal landscape of vision, what is a fool for one, for another is a wise man. Which means that really there are no fools, for a fool to me will be a true teacher to another. In this sense all the ways are 'true', and the truth of the different claims rests on how successfully a particular way discloses meaning to those who have submitted to it. For this reason virtually all the groups enjoin novitiates to 'forsake all others and follow me', for they know that 'mixing ways' leads to confusion, and that although all roads can lead to the Rome of the Self, we can travel but one at a time. When our own chosen method, whatever it turns out to be, is entered in depth and with commitment, then all the others can be seen to lead in the same direction, however divergent and 'absurd' their outer symbolism may appear. Thus the groups and gurus which have recently emerged into view from the dark recesses of our culture are like the tips of icebergs whose real significance – and connection – extends deep beneath the surface of 'objectivism' into the moving forces of cultural change, which only the subtle and subjective faculties can know.

Groups

We may ask why, if inner religion is ultimately a subjective experience, there is any need for a group? Why can't we go it alone, choosing what suits us from the full spectrum of myth and practice? Although man is born and dies alone, in the intervening period he is a corporate creature. In groups even spelunkers and mountaineers achieve more heroic goals than they could by going solo, for groups reflect a power greater than the sum of their parts, becoming living libraries of pooled resources which ferment myth and orientation of greater depth and sustaining power than would be possible alone. Groups are macro-organisms, having natural hierarchies, senses, alimentary canals. They defend themselves from attack like organisms, with anti-bodies and defensive and offensive ploys; they are imbued with the instinct of growth and survival, which draws its sustenance only partly from its adherents. Whether street crowds or management committees, groups are larger and more strangely autonomous creatures than people, but whether angels or evil giants still depends on the individuals which constitute them. For although in groups we may be capable of more than we could ever achieve alone, we may also commit acts more heinous, of a moral calibre lower than the lowest of the group's individuals.

There is a parallel here in the realm of biology, where science is finding that the distinction between groups and individuals is becoming increasingly blurred. A certain species of amoeba, for instance, lives as individual spores until there is a shortage of food; they then aggregate into a single slug, a slime mould, which migrates through the forest in search of fresh sustenance; when it finds this it splits again into its constituent cellular spores which now begin feeding on their own again.

Religious groups, however profane their symbolism, respond altogether, like heliotropic plants following the sun through the sky. In the seven years that I have been studying them, I have noticed that they appear to respond in specific cycles, to such things as concentration on 'rules', 'death', 'making money' and so on. It is as if some power, working through these movements, is leavening human consciousness in specific areas at specific times. Members of a group discover that they are more than themselves. 'And if ye mingle your affairs with others, ye shall become as brothers,' says the Arabic proverb. In a true brotherhood 'love' becomes a tangible and miraculous energy; people dream each other's dreams, sense each others's despairs, protect each other from their weaknesses.

But a hairline balance must be maintained when becoming part of a group, for in order to flower in it we must accept its myths, submit to its ideals and disciplines, and yet not lose sight of where it is carrying the *self*, and at what cost. Don Juan's advice to Carlos Castañeda was above all to find a group which had 'heart', for if after one had followed it to the bitter end one found it without heart, one might never be able to leave it and grow further. If the self is utterly surrendered to the group, rather than to its direction, then instead of becoming sharpened into clearer vision it may become erased and subsumed by fanaticism. These two sides, of conscious brotherhood and mindless zeal, coexist in all groups, however divinely inspired. In some the ideas are greater than the people following them; in others the people are greater than the ideas. Either way, we should resist being put off a group by the quality of the particular people we meet in it.

A friend of mine recently remarked that he found it difficult to join groups because most of the people in them were 'emotional cripples', 'loons' and 'losers'. The same criticism was levelled against early Christianity, for in a desert parched of religious meaning it is the most thirsty, the halt and the lame who are the first to cluster round the new waterholes. It is these motley circles which we see first, and we often wander on without noticing the glowing well of mysteries which they surround.

Personal Experience

With the awareness of our need for meaning, and the range of symbolic alternatives now available, the search for our own particular 'way' can begin. In this each one is on his own, for although there are many proficient guides within the individual groups, there are no guides as to the choice of a group in the first place; but there are two traditional methods of finding a Way – one magical, the other 'practical' – and they are the very same by which we consciously or unconsciously find a marriage partner.

The first, which may be misinterpreted as 'fatalistic', requires remaining quite still inside, consciously consolidating the awareness of our need, and patiently continuing to live normally. In this way we 'attract' a teacher (or a mate), since our internal need distils itself into a clarity which has its own power, and through it we can *recognize* the 'returned King' (or Queen) even if they enter our lives disguised as beggars. Much of our confusion comes from not being *still* for long enough to consolidate the recognition of our needs, so that we often overlook the perfect opportunities even when they stare us in the face. The Sufi proverb says: 'for he who is ready, the teacher will be there'.

The second method is more exoteric; we rationally examine to the best of our ability the kind of person we are, and deduce from this what kind of teaching we would be able to give ourselves to; we then begin consciously familiarizing ourselves with all the alternatives, finally settling for the most appropriate – even though, like a wife or husband chosen by this method, it may at first not be outwardly perfect. Both of these methods require considerable single-mindedness, as well as faith in one's self.

'Faith' and 'superstition' are two loaded terms which need redefining. A Ceylonese mystic, when recently asked the meaning of superstition, replied that it was superstitious to believe that a spirit lived in a certain tree when it in fact did not; but if it *did* live in that tree, then despite the fact that others might not be able to see it, the belief was not superstitious but a simple statement of fact. On the other hand, faith may be a kind of superstition; it may be used to perpetuate myopia, as in the case of the 'flat earth' theorists who still continue to have 'faith' that science is mistaken in calling the earth 'round'. Or else faith may be used as a 'technique' to alleviate myopia, to lift by the bootstraps, to walk quite blind across the gulf of no 'positive feedback', sustained only by hope and humility, towards a broader horizon of vision. Creative faith is thus simply confidence – springing from depths far beneath our worldly faculties – that everything is really just fine, and the universe is unfolding as it should.

It is among the new mystical groups, where in many instances faith and reason are combined, and where intense energy is devoted to the experiential pursuit of an ideal, that the bright seedlings of Aquarian religion are hiding. If there is any truth in Aldous Huxley's prophecy that 'We are all on the way to an existential religion of mysticism', then its embryonic anatomy must surely be found among these twentieth-century alchemists who are continually experimenting with the power of living symbols, and whose lives are dedicated to the articulation of a new framework of meaning.

At the start of my research on 'alternatives to orthodox religion', I came to these groups only partly as an outsider, since I was already a member of Subud, and it was my own commitment which I used as a kind of touchstone in the ordering of the other groups I was to encounter. This meant that some of the beliefs were more appealing to my own particular temperament and, to me, the group 'souls' had totally different vibrations – some powerfully uplifting, some dizzy-making and some positively frightening.

I have not listed all the groups here, since they change, flower and decay as continually as a coral reef, and because outer descriptions of their differences do not lead to their inner meaning – for that can be sensed by the *self* alone. But according to their inner, symbolic natures, the full spectrum of choices can to some extent be categorized in terms of the six primal 'mythic perspectives' through which the new religions 'see', and thus pursue, their goals. In Chapter 2 I described how all 'truth' must be reflected through certain symbols, and though the symbols change with the fashions of the times, the pursuit is the same. From the outside, these beliefs appear as different as the faces of the flowers in the field, each one adapted to attract a different species of insect, but all are part of the identical process of pollination. The myths, like the flowers, can be seen in terms of genus and species, the six basic categories of which can be described as:

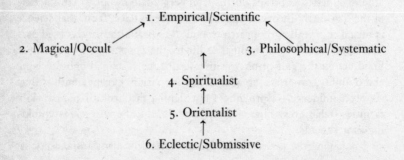

I shall describe each of these types in turn, and the kinds of groups which are found in them, but it should be remembered that these are only, as it were, 'primary colours', and each group is always a mixture of colours, in the same way that people are astrological combinations of the Four Elements: some mainly 'cerebral', others mainly 'feeling', etc. Thus each individual group is a mixture of the six primary mythic strands, and is categorized under one of the above headings by virtue of its dominant strand, or theme. Certain groups may equally well come under two or even three of these headings at the same time; and it becomes even more complex when certain levels of the same group – say 'novitiates' and 'inner brothers' – alter their mythic emphases as they ascend through the hierarchy of the group myth. This is therefore only a loose grid, to be placed over what is really an entirely 'fluid' matrix of myth, to help the seeker feel the range and scope of alternative religions.

1. The Empirical/Scientific

This area is at the most 'grounded' end of the spectrum: it is rational and scientific in its approach to the transcendent, viewing reality in the focal depth of 'objectivity' – the fashionable mythic perspective of our times. It is this area which tends more towards inquiry and classification than inner experience, yet it is the vital link between the phenomenal and the metaphysical worlds, and the 'proof' of the latter's existence. It is the 'pseudo-scientific' area, where science is being used as creative poetry, the thin end of the wedge into our rationally conditioned minds and the area to which I have given most time in the preceding chapters.

It includes 'paraphysics' proper, of the kind pursued in Russia, for instance in clairvoyance, telekinesis and dermoglyphics. In Britain there is the Paraphysical Laboratory, with its sophisticated electronic devices for measuring and tabulating the physical manifestations of hauntings, poltergeists and the other phenomena which for over a hundred years have been carefully documented by the British Society for Psychical Research. Uri Geller, the Israeli telekinesist and clairvoyant, is a 'prime' control for the groups in this heading, but there are also those who research into other aspects of subtle vibration: the Radionics Association; the British Society of Dowsers; Hygeia Studios in Gloucestershire, which measure the various effects of form, colour and sound on the human psyche; Chladni's and Jenny's correlations between vibration and form; Backster's on plant empathy and response to music. In the same field is the research into 'bio-feedback' and the connections between brain rhythms and altered states of consciousness. There are the 'bio-rhythmic' research organizations, the astrological lodges, the pyramid researchers – all those areas where the 'invisible' world can to some extent be 'measured'. Here is the beginning of the 'new science', but its tools are still largely 'objective'; it leads towards, although it is not yet fully afloat in, the subtle areas of direct cognizance, for – like science – it relies on the five senses, or their synthetic amplifications, and thus the Empirical/Scientific category is farthest from 'religion' as we are conditioned to understand it.

From this first focal depth, which works from the five senses of the body (perceiving through what can be touched, heard and seen), branch two different focal depths: (2) that of the 'emotions', the Magical/Occult variety, and (3) that of the 'intellect', the Philosophico/Systematic variety.

2. *The Magical/Occult*

This category includes those groups which work with the 'feeling' tools of archetypal symbolism. They have moved a step inwards from the tangible, objective world, though of course they still use it alchemically as an instrument of ritual. Their strength is drawn from the seething stockpile of the racial unconscious, from the earliest pantheistic unions with the wild forms of nature to their later ritualization in the secret brotherhoods. Here are found the whole range of witches and sorcerers, from the blackest self-seeking and coercing of natural law for personal ends – the 'Process', the Satanists, the 'New Hellfire Club', the orgiastic revellers in the primal life-force – to the most elevated wisdom of 'white witchcraft'; from the Dionysiac sorcery of rural Wicca covens to the truly secret contemporary groups that are rekindling the occult power of the Western Mysteries tradition. In Britain there are the revived Druid cults which circle round the pre-Celtic sites of power – Iona, Glastonbury, Stonehenge – while in America similar groups revolve round the archetypal wisdom of their early peoples, the Indians, the Way of Don Juan, the visions of the Eskimo shamans and so on.

A good deal of contemporary European magic is based on the distillations of the Order of the Golden Dawn, which in turn was distilled from Christian Cabbalism in the late nineteenth century. These ritual archetypes fed the imaginations and lifestyles of such differing though influential people as Macgregor Mathers, W. B. Yeats, Dion Fortune,

Israel Regardie and that 'monster' of a man Aleister Crowley. 'The Great Beast', as he would doubtless like to have been called, was an almost superhuman explorer of ego-based magic – of the psychological heavens and hells. Much of his contemporary revival may be due to the titillating drama and fear which early encounters with the soul can awaken in the ego. Carl Gustav Jung, commenting on the dangers of spiritual stature, mentioned that the higher the mountain then the longer the shadow it casts. It may be that our present psychological perspective gives us a better view of Crowley's extraordinarily extended shadow than the height of the mountain needed to cast it.

3. *Philosophical/Systematic*

From the empiral myth of science (the extension of the body) branches on the one hand the spectrum of 'feeling', and on the other the spectrum of the intellect. This category includes those groups which see their world in terms of reason, and which attract the cerebral types. The power of abstract reasoning is the ground from which they start, and their world-views and practices tend to be highly structured and often tightly disciplinarian. They seek to awaken 'consciousness', the reasoning mind, to the process of spiritual evolution. In certain cases they seek to put into practice the systems of the great philosophers (as do the Pythagorean Society and the New Platonists) and however abstract their ideas, they always try to ground them in the needs of everyday living.

Here too is the 'Work' started by G. I. Gurdjieff, who died in 1949, and around whom a world-wide literature is developing. His system and world-view embrace, re-interpret and extend the findings of modern science in harmony with the perennial teachings of esotericism. Gurdjieff's basic teaching is that man is born as a 'seed', but that the development of his 'higher bodies' depends on intensive personal effort within the framework of a highly technical esoteric discipline. The best account of his teaching, outside his own strange saga *All and Everything*, is that written by his pupil, P. D. Ouspensky, *In Search of the Miraculous*.[3]

The Work's many offshoots include the 'School of Economic Science' in London, where its ideas have blended with sociology and view man's inner nature in the context of the forces which govern society. Here too is Scientology, that vigorous, almost secular organization which so fully used the communications media and 'bio-feedback' meters, that it is (even if only at the lower levels of the occult) well in advance of many other groups in its consolidation of outer form. Scientology's wealth, drive and demagoguery have – as traditionally happens – aroused the fear and hostility of the culture at large.

Also included here are the giant 'softies' of occultism, Theosophy and Anthroposophy. At the turn of the century, when Science, with its simultaneously bleak and inspiring horizons, was in deadlock with Christianity, Theosophy was the first major alternative to orthodoxy. At its numerical peak, in the 1920s, it had several thousand members, drawn mainly from the ranks of the 'leisure classes' of Europe; and its history and later schism into Anthroposophy is a textbook example of the way groups flower, change and throw out new seeds.

At the height of the Scientific Adventure, in 1892, when it looked as if the spirits were about to sink for the third time beneath the tide of Rationalism, they suddenly burst forth again in a Vermont farmhouse belonging to the Fox sisters. The tappings, apports and ghostly happenings which began to occur around these two young American girls achieved immense publicity, and the world's imagination, reluctant to let the reality of spirit die altogether, was ignited with new hope. Thus spiritualism sprouted throughout the Western world – its rebirth happening to coincide with that of its rational counterpart, clinical psychology. Hence at the turn of the century man broached the inner world on two fronts simultaneously – via 'intuition' on the one hand, and the 'intellect' on the other. Among the curious who flocked to witness the happenings around the Fox sisters was a remarkable Ukrainian woman, H. P. Blavatsky, who met there two eccentric Americans: the lawyer William Judge, and a Colonel Olcott. Blavatsky was already widely travelled – being probably the first Western woman to cross Tibet alone – and was personally familiar with various Oriental centres of occult power. She, Judge and Olcott were interested in a more 'religious' focus for the spiritualist revival, and they travelled together to India to gather what further knowledge they could from the secret traditions which still flourished unhindered in the thicket of Hinduism. Thus the three of them formed the Theosophical Society. Theosophy (which means, as its name implies, 'God-centred knowledge') was to evolve into a great movement which expressed itself through the perspective of Orientalist and Spiritualist myth, before grounding itself in later years in a more 'structured' philosophy.

In 1920 the leaders of Theosophy, now including Annie Besant,*

---

* Annie Besant, who had been Bernard Shaw's mistress, actually became Krishnamurti's adopted mother. Her book, *The Ancient Wisdom*, though rather dated, is still a classic of eclectic Aquarian thought.

discovered a young Indian boy named Krishnamurti, whose quality deeply attracted them. They brought him to England, educated him at Cambridge and nurtured him to become the new Messiah and the leader of the Theosophical movement. But the young man's vision and integrity blossomed into more than they had bargained for, and at the age of twenty-one, before a vast gathering of Theosophists, he officially renounced his position. In a memorable speech, he told the gathering that to 'lead' them was to encourage the sheep-like adulation which had traditionally stifled the 'experiential' essence of religion; and that he was a leader only in so far as he could awaken the inner teacher in every individual, and that since the inner teacher was different with each of us, it could only be discovered alone. At this he walked off the podium, and began his many years of travelling round the world talking of God and moving on hurriedly before anyone could project on to him their need for a guru.

The Theosophists fell back in confusion, pondering and regrouping. It was some years later that another remarkable man, an Austrian Jew named Rudolph Steiner,[4] rose from the ranks of Theosophy to challenge its world-view. Reacting against its 'God-oriented' other-worldliness, Steiner sought to see things from a more practical, man-orientated perspective, and he led the breakaway movement of Anthroposophy, a kind of mystical Humanism which sought to find God within man himself, rather than seeking man within God.

Steiner accepted, and sought to integrate into his spiritual system, every step which science had taken. He was a visionary pioneer in seeing science as corroboration of the existence of spirit, rather than negating it; and his Anthroposophical Movement continues today as a powerful current, with specialized branches in the practical development of the 'subtle' faculties, as well as 'inner' healing and education for both adults and children. As a 'structured' admixture of spiritualism, oriental and pseudo-scientific myth, Anthroposophy – like Theosophy, the 'Work' and other movements – now falls into this heading of Philosophical/Systematic groups.

4. *Spiritualist*

While the physical, scientific approach of (1) gives rise to the 'feeling' and 'intellectual' myths of (2) and (3), beneath and between them lies the faculty of mediumistic clairvoyance. The groups in this category derive their teaching and orientation from personalized spirits which speak through certain 'contacts' or mediums. Thus the worldly leaders of some of these groups are simply the mouthpieces of (ostensibly) a higher, invisible leadership. In certain instances the guiding spirit of a group is still physically alive, but absent – 'Koot Humi', for instance, who in the early days was an incarnate monk in Tibet. But generally these spirits have either ceased to be incarnate, or else are too 'large' ever to have been contained by a human body.

Mediumship requires the stilling of the conscious ego, which may either be 'put to one side', and continue to function without interfering with the spirits which speak through the still-conscious medium, or else is altogether suspended, as in 'trance' mediumship, where the medium cannot monitor and recall the words which came through him. Seership and trance have existed in all religions, and they raise in our practical minds the problem of the dividing line – if any – between the subconscious and the superconscious. The subconscious, that mysterious genetic ocean millions of years deep which we all share, is as full of chaos as it is of supernal wisdom, for it harbours memories both of the evolutionary 'dead-ends' which led us nowhere, and of those ascending avenues towards light which, somewhere in our history, we abandoned. By putting aside the crust of consciousness, information from this reservoir beneath it can erupt, and the eruption usually clothes itself in such archetypal imagery as the Red Indian, the Egyptian, the Chinese and the Medieval Nun. Sometimes, however, the eruption is virtually naked and comes from the Beyond – the Totally Other, as Otto has called it. It has been argued that this is what happened, for instance, to Moses when he copied the Commandments on the Mount, or to Smith when an angel directed him to found the Mormon faith.

When a medium is 'spoken through', whether from beneath or above, our concern with discerning the 'source' of the speech usually distracts us from hearing its 'quality'. One wonders how influential the Koran would have been if, instead of coming through the Warrior Lord, Mahommed, it had been vocalized by some little old lady during a parlour seance. The quality of the teaching appears to be only partially dependent on the quality of the medium through whom it comes: and for this reason the whole outwardly rather musty area of spiritualism tends to be overlooked, instead of 'sifted' for the nuggets of truth and poetry so often concealed in it.

The large spiritualist organizations, such as the Spiritualist Association of Great Britain and the Spiritualist National Union, comprise many mediums through whom speak equally many spirits.

Although some of these spirits claim 'superior wisdom', most of them specialize merely in healing the sick, recovering lost objects and carrying messages between the dead and their living next-of-kin. With many smaller groups, however, such as the White Eagle Lodge, or the School of Universal Philosophy and Healing, it is the teachings of 'larger-than-life' spirits which form the central axis of the groups. In the former case, it is the great, wise spirit 'White Eagle' who speaks through the medium Grace Cooke (or, when in trance, 'Minesta', as White Eagle has dubbed her). Mrs Cooke is merely the 'worldly' leader of the group and not, she insists, the roots of its inspiration. Such spirits' symbolic clothing ranges through all the familiar archetypes mentioned above, from Red Indians to the forest Devas and Nature Spirits (which guide the Findhorn Trust in Northern Scotland), to interstellar angels (as in the case of the Aetherius Society).

The Aetherius Society is an interesting example of the fusion of yogic trance mediumship with that of advanced scientific technology. The Master Aetherius is an advanced Venusian Intelligence who is among a number of Cosmic Masters from Planets within this Solar System who are trying to save mankind from himself. Although these Masters, one of whom is The Master Jesus, could make their presence known to all men, they choose to speak through the mediumship of Doctor George King, Founder/President of The Aetherius Society, so that their message can be propagated to the world through this organization.

The Aetherius Society sees itself as the primary channel for Interplanetary communicators, and it seeks to prepare the way for the New Age using methods which are a breakthrough in modern science, and yet are based on the most ancient philosophies on Earth. Nineteen mountains around the world have been charged with Cosmic Energy by the Interplanetary Masters, and are regularly climbed by Aetherius Society pilgrims in order to radiate prayer energy to the world. Via the yogic trance mediumship of Doctor George King, Transmissions, sometimes involving several communicators from other worlds, have been tape-recorded and preserved for present and future generations. The European Headquarters of The Aetherius Society in London holds regular courses of lectures on different aspects of the space message.

This entire Spiritualist category is vivid with topical mythology and, like the other new religions – even if only at one level – it is an invaluable cultural gallery of imaginative artistry.

5. *Orientalist*

This perspective includes all those groups which have turned to the symbolism of the Oriental religious tradition. The first step for a seeker who has the courage to abandon his inherited religion is often to turn to another form of orthodoxy, but one beyond his own culture. This fresh and totally different perspective may then lead back again to the discovery of the unseen truth in his own religion, or it may cause him to relinquish all 'outer' forms of religion (even the rich tapestries of orthodox Islam, Buddhism and Hinduism) to strike out on his own into the secret labyrinths of 'experience' which underlie them all. Thus the Orientalist category includes those groups in the West which continue to practise an Eastern orthodoxy as well as those groups which pursue the 'inner' paths offered by Eastern traditions.

This category covers the largest overt part of the religious revival, from the 'hobbyists' of religion who merely adopt the Eastern trappings of diet, vocabulary and dress, to the committed explorers (such as the Sant Mat Brotherhood) who meditate for no less than three hours a day, abstain from meat, fish and eggs, and from any sexual contact which may not produce children.

This category includes the wide variety of gurus, from the peripatetic and elusive kind – like Krishnamurti – who travel like comets from place to place, awakening their listeners to the truth within themselves, to isolated mountains of thaumaturgic strengths, gurus like Balyogweshar Sant Mat, who encourage their thousands of followers to recognize them as the sole personification of God on earth. Some of these gurus never move beyond their Himalayan confines, while others have stormed the outside world – such as the Maharaj Ji of the Divine Light Mission, whose following in the West has grown in four years from a mere handful of devotees to something over a quarter of a million.

The archetype of the 'oriental sage', with penetrating eyes and a voice like dark honey, first ignited the West in the person of a young Indian named Yogananda, who after ten years of self-imposed hermitage in Bengal was sent by his guru to Boston in 1923 to represent India at the International Conference of the World Federation of Churches. Yogananda spoke with such power and humility, and with such unrhetorical eloquence, of the need for syncretism between all religions, that virtually overnight the hitherto patronizing humour with which the Eastern hierophant had been regarded was transformed into the realization of the vitality which Oriental philosophy could bring to the ailing concepts of Western religion.

Thirty days after Yogananda's death (in California, where he had made his home) his body was still as sweet-smelling, according to the doctors, as a bunch of roses – something which did little to reduce the posthumous hold which he still has over his devotees in the Self-Realization Fellowship. The mysterious vistas afforded by this new perspective prepared the ground for subsequent tidal waves of oriental mysticism. Seldom have we been further from Rudyard Kipling's view that 'East is East and West is West, and never the twain shall meet' – for what historically have appeared as contradictory opposites are now symbiotically feeding one another: the East, under the tuition of the West, becoming more outwardly practical and technological, and the West, under the tuition of the East, re-familiarizing itself with the interior domain of the spirit.

After the First World War the media's undiscriminating tentacles spread throughout our culture, the gurus of different shapes and pretensions were brought to the public's attention – without any accompanying yardstick for distinguishing their relative sanctity or benevolence. In the 1960s, when the Beatles joined – and later left – the Maharishi Mahesh Yogi, it seemed that the ultimate public acclaim for a spiritual leader (short of the Pope) had been achieved, and equally quickly discredited. But had it?

Ideas take root proportionate to need, and one thing which the 'secret' tradition of the Orient supplied the West was forms of meditation which offered strictly practical means of toning up the body and reducing stress. The Maharishi's brand of devotion (Transcendental Meditation) actually presents itself to the public as, initially, a means of learning how to relax – something which it certainly does more effectively (and at less cost) than drugs. Of the many forms of yoga, each tailored to the different levels of the human self, from the body up through the mind and emotions to the higher faculties of consciousness awakened by Raj Yoga, it is understandably the more bodily levels (Hatha Yoga) which have been the first to take root in the West. Yoga, and related forms of meditation, are now being taught at schools, universities, women's institutes and businessmen's conventions. The fact that breath control alone can lead to a revitalization of the whole body – even changing its proportions – is an indication of the extent to which the higher forms of yoga can quicken the 'unknown' side of man into conscious immediacy.

Many people ask why the young are turning towards the East when they have a perfectly good religion at home. The answer is that the experiential forms of meditation which existed in Christianity died with the excommunication of the gnostic traditions; and thus whereas Christianity was largely emasculated, the creative techniques of occult knowledge – though often heavily disguised – live on in the East. This flood of orientalism into the West not only breathes new life into the embers of our domestic tradition – since it supplies rational corroboration for what must otherwise be taken on faith – but also illuminates the secret threads which underlie all forms of worship.

The staple rituals of religious practice, such as fasting, sexual monogamy, prayer and the giving of alms, which in the habitual Christian context have for many become quite devoid of 'meaning', are being quickened to a new life by the spring rains of Oriental mysticism. These practices are re-experienced as being as important a part of life as the maintenance of a bank balance or a regular intake of protein, for they keep us aware of the second-to-second immediacy of the inner as well as the outer dimensions of living. Religion again becomes the obvious and practical key to human existence, for it is *'ordered'*, taking the *whole* of us into account, and makes us constantly aware of the cyclical flow of the energies which maintain us.

6. *Eclectic/Submissive*

This final mythic perspective is the most subtle and difficult to define, since it is so transparent that it is usually the other perspectives which we see through it, missing this one altogether. Under this heading belong those groups which base their faith on unconditional *receiving*, on 'opening' themselves to the Powers above them – though they may well find themselves confronting those below. These groups are almost totally unstructured; what 'form' they possess is the minimum necessary to constitute a corporate vehicle of 'receiving' – rather as giant radio dishes need only be skeletally structured to receive signals from the chasms of space.

While every group, as already mentioned, is a composite of these six primal themes of mythic perspective, and is categorized by virtue of its *dominant* emphasis, in all the groups there is some area of total submission (beyond even the 'structure' of prayer or mantra) to the Cloud of Unknown Energies which burgeons just beyond even our inner grasp.

All religion is to some degree a matter of 'mediumship' in its higher sense, of raising the self in the palms of the hands to the influences of Life which cannot be rationally understood. The faculty of 'understanding' is axiomatically too coarse an instrument to respond to the deeper vibrations of life, and must be held in suspension either by sacramental drugs or internalized ritual,* so as not to interfere with the process of receiving. As the coarser self begins to become finer – perhaps only after years of practice – it becomes more like a drum-skin (instead of rhinoceros hide), which responds to the patterns of invisible energy. It is then that the conscious self can come into play, can awaken from its sleep to *see* and *feel* the qualities of its new environment – and at last the 'left hand' begins to know what the 'right hand' is doing. But these patterns, or Chladni figures, which appear on the drum-skin of the inner self are the myths and symbols of religion (as constant in form as sacred geometry) and though exquisitely beautiful, they are still merely two-dimensional, and not to be confused with the multi-dimensional world which they only partially mirror.

By definition, the groups which fall into this category are almost invisible, like the transparent larvae of fish which are only identifiable once they have matured into colour and form. They include groups of only a few individuals, as well as enormous, invisible brotherhoods. Subud began by belonging to this Eclectic/Submissive category, and in some countries where it is still practised in its original form of neither a 'religion' nor a 'teaching', but simply a 'receiving' – it would still belong here. But as Subud developed demands were made on its leader, Bapak, to articulate doctrinal guide-lines, and round these grew the mythic clothing of Javanese Islam, placing the group closer to the Orientalist category.

A group which still remains under this heading is 'Triangles' which, although originally derived from Alice Bailey's 'Arcane Society' (of the Magical/Occult category), developed into a specialized practice which is barely group-structured at all. What structure there is begins with the concept of the Triangle as a 'power-shape'. Three people, who may never have met one another, agree to form the three points of an invisible triangle, whose sides may be hundreds of miles long, depending on the distance between their homes. At predetermined times, the three seclude themselves and each concentrates on forming a bond with the other two. Envisaging their mutual bond of love, they consciously

* The psychologist might well refer to this kind of internalized ritual as 'auto-hypnosis'.

render their aetheric triangle as a channel through which Divine Energy may resonate into the world.

Throughout the globe there are now many thousands of these interlocking triangles, most of them burning into life in synchrony and pumping a leavening harmony into the world of chaos and pain. 'Triangles' is but one of the many forms of 'unstructured' receiving which a seeker may discover for himself, and to which he may perhaps add the energy of his own submission.

To place ourselves in a state of 'unconditional surrender' without some preliminary guidance, however, can be both dangerous and unpleasant. As a child of eight in an English prep-school dormitory I once had an overwhelming desire to break out of my accumulating darkness. After the others in the room were asleep, I ritually surrounded myself with pillows and blankets, composed myself in a position of prayer and from as deep a place as possible I tried to sutrender myself. But the darkness settled closer, filling with the phantasms of despair, an ancestral army of sad ghosts marched through me until I was weeping with uncontrollable desperation – an experience which I was at a loss to explain to the indignant matron who came to quieten me. I have heard similar experiences from others, and it seems wiser to acquire first some guidance and orientation before this kind of surrender – or we may move downwards into the dark layers of our inheritance, rather than upwards towards the Light.

Yet all religion is ultimately submission – whatever the mythic guide which leads us there – even if only submission to the possibility that we can be touched by power beyond our ken, and resurrected from the myopia which breeds stagnation and fear.

The solitary key, for solitary people, is to practise regularly the 'awareness of the presence of God'. This means to sit, lie or stand quietly, and actually *feel* it; feel the soft miracle of immediacy both within and without us, and let the sensation form a reservoir of awareness which cannot leak from our countless fissures of mis-directed energy. It is this reservoir which powers our vision into different dimensions of space and time.

Some twenty years ago a traveller in Nepal encountered an entirely isolated group of mystics. For generations they had been simply practising this 'awareness of the presence of God'. To the traveller's question of what possible good they could do in meditative seclusion while the rest of the world was crying out for positive action, the monks replied that as a brotherhood their destiny was simply to keep the 'doors open' between the two worlds. They were merely channels, they explained, together with the world's other scattered and invisible brotherhoods, through which – when the time was ripe – the next influx of sacred energies could flood the earth. They saw their geographical position, their overt presence, as truly 'immaterial' to their function, for when the Rebirth took place it would anyway occur far from their lands, in the deepest cauldrons of materialist ignorance.

9 Time Now

He who cannot see himself within the context of at least a 2000-year expanse of history is all his life shackled to days and weeks.

RILKE

Is this change which is taking place around us purely illusory – or is every tree of our social environment showing the first buds of a fundamental change of thought? Is what was the 'unimaginable' a few decades ago now seeping into our lives in living colour?

When I returned to England from Mexico and saw my father for the first time in seven years, I was surprised that he was my father. Throughout my first meal with him I thought: 'How odd, he is my own sire, his blood runs through my veins, and yet we are strangers to one another.' Only at the end of the meal did I catch sight of his hands, and the hair stood up on my neck as I recognized them as identical to my own. He had always been rather fey, telling me when I was a child of his experiences with ghosts and poltergeists, but when I now told him of my strange experiences in Indonesia he became alarmed, and eventually retreated into saying that he believed only in ghosts and poltergeists, since he had experienced them both himself.

I left him that evening feeling sad: since recognizing his hands as my own I had wanted to communicate, but had only succeeded in widening the gap.

Several nights later, staying with friends in London, I had a disturbing dream. I 'awoke' in my dream and could see everything in the room, from the position of my sleeping body to the book I had left on the floor by my bed. I felt uneasy, and as I watched, the pictures on the walls began to tilt, and the doorknob to turn, then the book ascended from the floor by my bed annd shredded like snowflakes over the room. I ran down the hallway in my dream to my brother's room (both he and my mother were in fact still in Mexico) and said: 'Poltergeist!' He was disbelieving until we watched thhe pictures tilting in his room as well; I continued to my mother's room where she met me with the words: 'I know, it's a poltergeist'. Then I was back in my bed again,, knowing I was asleep, and that the pictuures were shifting, but not wishhing to wake myself lest I should see them. The dream was so deeply disturbing that next day I took it to several of my friends for interpretation, but we were all puzzled.

The following night I again awoke in my dream, seeing again the whole room; just to the right of my bed, an arm's length from my sleeping body, was a luminous, man-sized form. So real was my perception of being both asleep and aware of the waking environment that I knew that if I forced myself to wake, to remove the covers from my head, I would *see* the form with my eyes. Alarmed by this, I stayed as I was, watching the form in my sleep until it gradually dissolved. A few moments later – at six a.m. as it turned out – I dreamed the phone rang, and within moments of that my hostess in 'fact', came into my room saying she had some bad news for me. I awoke immediately with the words: 'My father is dead.'

My stepmother had just found him dead in his sleep from a heart attack, and had immediately telephoned the house where I was staying. Remembering that my father had finally declared his belief in the super-natural as extending only to poltergeists and ghosts, I was later able to tell my friends that my dream had been partially solved by its sequel. The 'inner' dimension, of course, is not constrained by time as we habitually experience it, but extends both forwards and backwards from an inner event, like ripples from the stone cast into a pond; and I often regretted being too dense to understand the first dream enough to drive down to the country to say my inward goodbye to my father the day before he died.

The true messages from outside time are again beginning to get through to us in the symbolism of dreams, the mantic arts and the states of mind altered by drugs and meditation. A hundred years ago, when our clairvoyant faculties were sharper, I might well have been awake when I saw the pictures move on the wall, and the ghostly form – although just as fearfully unconscious. Now it seems that such information finds it harder to reach us, and we must be asleep – or deeply 'quiet' – before we can respond to the faculties which teach us of connections in a different dimension of time – connections of the kind, for instance, that I was to discover existed between my father and myself at a far deeper level than the mere similarity of our hands.

It is when more and more people begin to experience 'reality' in a different dimension that the dominant world view begins gradually to form a totally new cultural basis of belief.

If beliefs are changing, as they are said to be, then what do *we* believe? Can we discern our personal threshold of belief or its changing patterns when we are not quite sure what beliefs are sustained by, or sustain, even our own culture? The great disparity between what we think others believe and what they in fact do, and the ease with which we can be caught by the mass currents of acceptance or rejection, are usually as unexamined as the beliefs themselves. Freeing ourselves from the magnetic tides of these beliefs – in order to experience our *own* – can generally be done only through great strength, or great innocence – as with Hans Andersen's child who cried out that the emperor was naked. But few of us are that innocent any more, and the courage to interpret information for what it really is comes only from caring enough about *meaning*.

Only the tiniest percentage of each culture is consumed by meaning, and it is the solitary voyages of a few artists, scientists and explorers which become – perhaps generations later – the tacitly accepted beliefs of a culture. These few stand alone at the bows of the evolutionary voyage, pressed against the galactic void, while the rest of us, living more domestic lives in the engine rooms or first-class lounges, remain largely oblivious of where the ship is going, or why. The beliefs about our course and its values are mainly gossip, passed among the passengers, and thought to come from the bridge. But the bridge, when it is examined, proves to be strangely empty of officers – for there is no-where to turn for guidance but inwards. Hints of the inward visions to which a civilization responds come from that handful at the bow whose cries of the water ahead can barely be heard against the cacophony of mindless debate, on the lower decks of courage, which occupies the rest of the culture.

But the rhythms of 'metanoia' – those total changes in our 'ways of seeing' – move majestically forward through an expanse of history greater than we can imagine. Thus our universe changes as we ourselves change, not always gradually but often in sudden tidal waves of new and fearful vision.

The early Europeans (says the schoolroom myth) believed that to the West there was merely a great sea which ended in the edge of the world. The first tales of a massive continent there produced fear and ridicule, for it threatened the dominant world-view. More terrifying still was the later discovery that the whole earth was merely a fluid pearl wheeling in a space so infinite that its centrality in the universe became laughable – and the geocentric belief was engulfed by the vision of boundless suns and time.

It is easy to burn the bearers of apocalyptic news, to quell the rumours spread by the first sailors to actually run the sands of America through their hands, or by the cranks who had witnessed through their own telescopes the planets irreverently orbiting *across* their biblically ordained courses. But have we the imagination to know whether, if we had lived then, we *personally* would have been among those (like the Vatican pontiffs) who turned *away* from Galileo's telescope lest it reveal a universe too great, too awesomely destructive of everything we had hitherto lived and fought for?

The challenge is precisely the same today, for we are on the crest of an even greater metanoia – one which, like all profound events, has sent its ripples both forwards and backwards in time. To respond to this we must first sense where we are still caged by false myths, and where we are being quickened by the subtle insights of new belief. Although we may be no more capable of seeing our historical environment than, as Herbert Marcuse puts it, the fish can see the water in which he is suspended, we can at least sense the power which rational conditioning still has over us. Charles Davis writes:

'The cultural context in which a technocratic society lives and acts is bounded by the detached objectivity of reason – chiefly by its lower and less imaginative form of technical expertise. The attempt is made to bring everything . . . under the manipulation of the technical reason. Anything that refuses the limits of [this] formalizing control loses any status as real, because it does not conform to the criteria of hard fact. Thus consciousness is contracted in a way that excludes the spiritual and the transcendent from reality.[1]*

For several years we have known that our technological processes are overtaking the concepts which gave them birth. We have engendered a massive machinery, both interior and exterior, too momentous to check – a dilemma which is symbolized in one of the great contemporary myths: Frankenstein. Count Frankenstein, in the original story written by Mary Shelley at the height of the Industrial Revolution, was the

---

* The psychologists refer to this condition of separation as 'alienation', and the sociologists, as 'anomie' – terms which they proceed to apply, somewhat paradoxically, to those segments of society which do not *share* the mother culture's massive aanomie and alienation froom the interior rhythms of univeersal knowledge.

creator of a foolish and relatively harmless automaton. The Count, with the full knowledge of 'specialization' at his fingertips, sought to create a perfect man from the 'best' parts of the 'best' dead bodies; but the premise was its downfall, the brain was damaged, and with the loss of organic cohesion the result was a powerful moron. In the popular imagination – that compost bed of myth – the name Frankenstein came to refer to the monster itself. The creature has eclipsed its maker and become the international symbol for the sinister destroyer. The many literary and cinematic expressions of this myth echo the fear of having created (albeit with altruistic intentions) a soulless mechanical culture which exerts a cumulative and uncontrollable force over its creators. The sociologist Harvey Cox writes:

In Western Civilization we have placed an enormous emphasis on man as worker (Luther and Marx) and man as thinker (Aquinas and Descartes). Man's celebrative and imaginative faculties have atrophied. This worker thinker emphasis, enforced by industrialization, ratified by philosophy and sanctified by Christianity, helped to produce the monumental achievements of Western science and industrial technology. Now, however, we can begin to see that our productivity has exacted a price. Not only have we gotten it at the expense of millions of other people in the poorer nations, not only have we ruined countless rivers and lakes and poisoned our atmosphere, we have also terribly damaged the inner experience of man. We have pressed him so hard towards useful work and rational calculation that he has all but forgotten the joy of ecstatic celebration, antic play and free imagination. His shrunken psyche is just as much a victim of industrialization as were the bent bodies of those luckless children who were once confined to English factories from dawn till dusk.[2]

It is over this 150th-year period that our isolation from the Miraculous has increased. Our factual machinery became increasingly estranged from the interior universe, so that each generation of children had to inherit a progressively more alien and chaotic world. Merely six generations of this rising tension produced a 'children's revolution'; its cry, like the slogan on the doors of the Sorbonne in 1968, was 'Imagination has seized power'.

The archaic legend of Spring against Winter – Senex versus Puer – had come to life, and the Saturnian influence of authority was rejected again (as it has been cyclically throughout history) in favour of the Neptunian vibration of myth and fantasy. This 'Zeitgeist', or 'spirit of the age', reacted against the dogmatism of religion – where God and the Map to Him are unalterable capitals – as well as against the dogmatism of science, that 'cold cosmology' where everything is but the chance union of atoms, the body of man merely another determinist machine, and the spark of speech and consciousness no more meaningful an attribute than the colour blue on a kingfisher's wings. But beneath the culture, among the young, the travellers and romantics – those spirits still loose enough to respond to the incipient 'Tsunami' of change – there fermented dreams and fantasies of a vaster dimension of freedom. Fed by the long-suppressed currents of supernatural wisdom, these myths – as all live myths must do – began to crystallize into realities. Astrology, once the resort of superstitious old ladies, has emerged as an embryonic science of stellar rhythms. Palmistry and graphology, the former tinselled penny-pullers of the fairground, are now being used as integral tools in the selection of colleagues and business associates; and the I Ching, no longer the quaint Oriental party game it used to be, is proving itself as a grid for the most sophisticated computer programming. So too, as science enters the rarefied mirrors of self-projection, do the mythical and symbolic currents of the past return to us in vivid colour, and infuse religion – in a new guise – with the depth and lustre of significance once enjoyed by science in the mid-seventeenth century.

Rather than a reformation, the movement was an 'evolutionary lurch', born perhaps of some atavistic survival instinct, back towards the irrational grounds of subjective experience. It appears in two main guises: the extroverted, which seeks to change others through radical politics, and the introverted, which seeks change by changing the self. Whereas the former, in America, has swept up the rungs of the culture and actually shaken the Capricornian president off his throne, the latter is the powerful international matrix where the new patterns of religious awareness are gestating. Since many of us are still adjusting to the fact that there are still people alive today who remember the first powered air flight by the Wright brothers, we have barely had time to countenance the still more recent and pressing revolution – the unpowered flight of the human soul.*

It is this current of thought which reacts against the 'objective' myth, where the only real meaning is that the world is 'out there' and I am out there with it. It turns inwards, reversing – like the Tarot's Fool – the

---

* Concurrent with 'inner flight' has coome the outer knowledge of how to carry man's body, in the muscles of the air, on the wings of a Hang-glider. With the principles of technology and aerodynamics whittled to a fine frame of silk, wire and aluminium struts we can again, in this archetypal sport, climb the wind-thermals of the sun like happy Icaruses, sustained only by our knowledge of air and design. Hang-gliding has even helped revive the forgotten mythology of the sect of Tibetan monks who once, for their novitiate trials, leapt from Himalayan crags to glide for thousands of feet on wings of embroidered silk.

grounds of meaning; it seeks, in Rudolph Otto's words, to reside again at the very source of Primordial Reality, at the place where the world was in *statu nascendi* and everything was as the First Day. It senses the stifling constriction of calendar time, the loss of contact with the rhythmic cycles of the inner seasons, knowing that we are hourly goaded by our clocks to our places of business, to perpetually reinforce the illusion that 'objective' truth is more important than subjective happiness.

Yet there is a kind of consistency of this irrationalism, and what started in the early 1960s as a mere feeling, a resonance, among a hairy minority, has now begun to erode every aspect of the mother culture, from food, dress and medicine to architecture, music and language. The primary effect of this Zeitgeist is to restructure expression more closely around the immediacy of visionary experience. It is a process which shows how just the resonance of an idea 'whose time has come' begins to bear tangible fruit as it echoes through every level of a civilization.

Our clothes, after long decades of the grey uniformity of suits and ties, have suddenly blossomed into colour and variety: the body is rediscovered through its reflections, for in a universe reverberating with filtered light it seems fitting to dress – or undress – in response to the full magnitude of the spectrum. From awareness of the body sprang the philosophy of touch and feelings. The clarity of feeling, or 'vibration', was seen as related to its purity, and people turned to the purity of sensuality, and of foods, recognizing that the life-force in food affects the life-force of the body which eats it: 'You are what you eat.' Awareness of this sensitized them even to the qualities of the earth which bore the food: their palates became constant reminders of ecology; with each mouthful they could taste the vitality or corruption of our globe – that breathing leviathan which is the indulgent, though not inexhaustible, host to the parasite man.

Macrobiotic, vegetarian and health foods, like other sacraments of the co-culture, have since been adopted and profaned by the megalithic corporations which now sell the same lifeless, de-ritualized food under the labels of 'health' and 'purity'; but these counterfeits are readily discernible to those who are practised in the sanctity of food.

Thus orthodox medicine, both mental and physical, also began to change its countenance, to give way to the ancient medicines which recognize that to re-harmonize the body or the mind requires an understanding of the aetheric and vibrationary fields which maintain it.

With the sensitivity to quality rather than quantity, social and economic forms have begun to change. Currency began to be sensed as a symbol of value which is usually absurdly disproportionate to the 'qualities' of the objects it is linked with. People returned to the manual skills, to bartering and trading with tangible products, whose intrinsic value in terms of the work required to produce them is less obscured by the fluctuating illusion of the value of money. Thus social distinctions such as class and wealth have begun to give way to qualitative meritocracies, to the real, rather than traditional, hierarchies of human and economic value.

The nuclear family has in certain areas begun to dissolve into communes, into group families where the responsibility of influencing children is spread and balanced – as in those primitive societies where the children refer to all women as 'mother' and to all men as 'father', so that the personal prejudices of only two parents can less easily distort the child. The adults, as well as the children, are fed, cuddled and supported; they put themselves – like their plants – in a barely structured earth and watch themselves unfold. They seek to listen, to be passive to the influences which maintain, trusting that submission to these will reveal an order, rather than a chaos, of the kind so evident in the vegetable and animal kingdoms.

For this reason the terms 'flower children' and 'drop-outs' symbolized how the co-culture itself believed. The weapons of the children's revolution were flowers – symbol of the heart, that petalled faculty of feeling which unfolds only through a passive response to natural and invisible influences. Rather than 'dropping out' of responsibility – as many assumed they were doing – they took the more courageous step of questioning what 'responsibility' meant: a response to what? They sought to *respond* to the miraculous, to release the imprisoned mind so that it could see and feel as if for the first time.

Drugs were used to break through the congealed perception, to throw the users into the immediacy of reality – with all its dangers, Marijuana – at least at the core of the movement in the early communes – was above all the substance which could be taken and given quite freely. Although precious, its value was in its sharing, and its giving was as contagious as its receiving; for the depths of pleasurable communication between people who took it revealed that its value was not in its material possession.

For many, the taking of drugs, rather than being a mindless escape, was a conscious vehicle inwards towards self-knowledge – as it was for Aldous Huxley[3] – and required, particularly in the case of the stronger hallucinogens, the courage of desperation. Unlike alcohol, which merely breaks down the inhibitions and dulls the senses, the softer drugs break down the barriers to 'communion', throwing the inhibitions into relief so that their foundations or otherwise can actually be *experienced*. They awaken the full power of the feelings which are usually held in check by the intellect, in such a way that the intellect gradually becomes their instrument, rather than their master. What in some instances is a total 'flight from reason', in others is merely an early oiling of the rusting faculties of the heart preparatory to a change even within the dimensions of reasoning. Already discernible is the 'post-drug' society: people who have been awakened to the reality of the interior world through drugs, and who now seek to expand it consciously through natural and meditative means.

At one time or other the priests of nearly all religions have found in their hands a new 'sacrament' – a substance which conducts power, and a catalyst for renewed perception. T. E. Suzuki, the Japanese philosopher and mystic, once commented that the difference between the Zen Buddhist and the Christian paths – both equally valid although different – was epitomized in their sacramental substances. For the Christian (the Western imbalance tending more towards over-intellectualism), the Way was through the emotions – since religion is awareness and awareness is balance – and their sacrament was wine, which softened the mind.* The reverse was the case for the practitioners of Zen, whose Oriental temperaments naturally disposed them more towards 'feeling' and introspection, and whose Way was thus through the mind, and the laborious training of the intellect. Their sacrament was tea, which sharpened the mind and stilled the feelings. Timothy Leary goes further and suggests that in a culture so heavily gripped by the world of objective facts, so estranged from the experiencing self, little short of psychedelics could loosen the shell, and it is LSD which will be remembered as the sacrament of the Aquarian religion – the chemical channel for the visionary conversion of a whole generation.

Music is the integrative ritual of this metanoia, the tapestry of harmony which bypasses the intellect and directly touches the feelings. The

* This is not to suggest that the Christian must become besotted on sacramental wine to suffer a revelation: symbolism, as we have seen, may be no less powerful than chemistry – if indeed there is ultimately any difference between them.

wordless music carries the listeners who submit to its power to the weightless area of pure experience, and they begin to resonate together, as an entire generation, not only to the same rhythm but to the same thought-patterns. Through its sheer volume the music of the sixties and seventies has served to soften the conditioned mind and also, with its lyrics, to seed it with the poetry of a new teaching. Certain musicians now have the same symbolic role that specific saints have in Latin America: they bridge the two worlds and ignite the people's senses with the meaning of transcendence. Stereo-sets have become the altars at which the young resonators to the Aquarian Age remain tuned to the rhythms of change. The music festivals have replaced the traditional holy functions, pilgrimages being made for hundreds of miles, often on foot and in cold rain, to the living sources of celebration. Here, within the cataclysmic atmosphere, and smuggled among the high-decibel music, flourishes the real contemporary poetry – always close to the language of religion. It speaks to an enormous and receptive public of fears and passions, of transcendent insights: it nurtures the feeling of other worlds in a language curiously alien to the traditional articulation of the sacred. In music we have the movement into a new time, with the syncretism of archaic and heraldic symbolism with that of space-age technology. In Neil Young's songs we hear the hunger for the incipient age of inner as well as outer light and purity:

I dreamed I saw the knights in armour coming saying something about a queen;
There were peasants singing and drummers drumming and the Archer struck
    the tree.
There was a fanfare blowing to the song, there was floating on the breeze.
But now look at Mother Nature on the run in the 1970s.
I dreamed I saw the silver spaceships flying all around the chosen ones.
All in a dream, all in a dream, the loading had begun.
Flying Mother Nature's silver seed to a new home in the sun.

Cat Stevens sings:

> Can't you feel a change a coming, from another side of time,
> Breaking down the walls of silence
> Lifting shadows from your mind? *

Where world-views change, language also changes, and the present Zeitgeist seeks above all to free itself of cliché. Michael Polanyi, a

* © Freshwater Music Ltd. *Changes IV* by Cat Stevens.

contemporary philosopher of language, has clarified the concepts of 'tacit' and 'explicit' knowledge. He shows how the root of thought – referred to as tacit knowledge and experience – lies *beneath* the threshold of conscious, or explicit knowledge. He describes the distinction by saying '. . . we may say that we always know *tacitly* that we are holding our *explicit* knowledge to be true.'[4]

Polanyi further shows how language springs from the tacit area which lies beneath the explicit and conscious threshold: 'Our whole articulate equipment,' he writes, 'turns out to be merely a toolbox, a supremely effective instrument for deploying our inarticulate faculties.'[5]

When explicit language becomes too separated from its tacit roots in the psyche then it degenerates into the kind of mechanical cliché used in clerical and legal circles or, with only slightly more colour, by the general public and the mass media. But the language of the co-culture, which has already leaked into our dictionaries, springs directly from the tacit dimensions of feeling. It mines its symbols from the 'beat' poets and jazz musicians of the 1950s, from the arcana of mysticism and visionary–drug-experiences. The argot bubbles out like glossolalia around the immediacy of sensuality: the music which 'blows one away', the rituals of surfing and skiing – those supreme unions of man's intuitive balance with the elements, when the feelings are so fully in the body that they are somehow beyond it.

With the change of language also comes the change of mediums of artistic expression. People have begun remembering their dreams, and with their remembering the strength of mythic language returns. Books of legendary cosmology – such as those by C. S. Lewis, J. R. Tolkien and Carlos Castañeda – have enjoyed a great revival. In the communes long hours, in Britain particularly, are spent reading again fairy stories from Celtic and Arthurian legends where flourish the great battles between the knights of self-discovery and the dragons of fear and self-doubt.

The plastic arts have begun to blend romanticism with science – sculpture being moulded with vibration, with electrical fires climbing sinuous tentacles of steel. Computerized animation weaves forms of light from different voltage strengths producing spiralling images in hypothetical space. It is in the visual and emotional kinetics of animated film, with its weightlessness and impossibility, that the release from gravitation – both physical and conceptual – is most keenly sensed.

Whereas the music conservatories and museums of the mother culture are largely mausoleums for what was once the vital artistic expression of ages no longer our own, the contemporary mediums of the new 'tacit' art and thought are still largely without temples, and move beneath the surface of the 'pop' psychedelia. They are becoming less literary and more visually and kinetically orientated and are often disguised as a kind of ferocious play. There are the new comic books, the cartoons and fantasy films, spontaneous puppet-shows and street pageants.

Underground comic books, or 'head comix', have transcended their 'super-hero' and anthropomorphized animals variety – which we remember with Batman and Mickey Mouse – and become articulate expressions of the archetypal struggles between today's values. They usually appear in a graphic and literary guise so emotional and direct that the mother culture sees them merely as violent, obscene or absurd, and it suppresses them with greater vigour than it does the hard-core pornography of the sex-mag trade. Though a taste to be acquired, as with any new literary medium, they are quickly transparent as the listening-posts for contemporary myth. Today's pilgrims' progress through the maze of gurus and spiritual systems comes to life in such series as 'The Kingdom of God is Within You Comix', and the problems of survival in a world decimated by pollution or nuclear holocaust are fantastically and humorously explored in such series as 'Last Gasp Eco-Funnies'.

All the better comics, with their colloquial language and surreal graphics, which are dog-eared from being exchanged among the subterranean cognoscenti, throw into relief the readers' attitudes towards sexuality, racial prejudice, drugs, estrangement from interior meaning – all those areas which are usually ignored or obscured by factual and analytical language. The versatility of the medium, its already disreputable form as a mere 'comic book', gives it freedom to capture the entire spectrum of myth which moves in the contemporary psyche. In the future it is the head comix of the sixties and seventies which will be remembered as a more accurate – because more archetypal – literary pulse of our times than the superficial and hysterical legacy of newspapers.

In this metanoia a different order of time is sensed. There is an increased tendency to dwell in that area referred to by R. C. Zaehner as 'sacred', rather than 'profane' time. The latter, experienced by the outer self, is the horizontal world of consecutive events, where 'profane history' extends no further back than our chaotic and limited vision, and to which we are addicted in the daily newspapers and the media, which, reflecting our own condition, bombard us with violence, silliness and contradiction.

Inner or 'sacred' time, however, is vertical and non-consecutive; it contains everything in the present, extending its tendrils both forward and backward in time, and with its sacred memory it encompasses far greater horizons than those of profane history. It knows, in its mythic language, that there was once a time when man was a divine creature, perhaps coming from the stars or from the higher reaches of inner space; when his cities and technology reflected an understanding which dwarf those of today; when he stood fully erect, like a stringed instrument, mediating the harmony between the polarities of spirit and matter. This memory senses that we are nearing the end of the period referred to by the Hindus as the 'Kali Yuga' – the real Dark Ages, the cycle of greatest estrangement from God, when man is plunged into the depths of *matter* and sees only the reality of the phenomenal world.

Dr J. Hillman, director of the Jungian Institute in Zurich, writes of profane history:

The fantasy we call 'current events', that which is taking place outside in the historical field, is a reflection of an eternal mythological experience. An historical analysis of these events – Old Mao and the Red Guard, the hippie flower youth, the sociology of ageing – will not lead to their meaning. We can no more grasp the soul of the times through a study of the newspaper than we can understand the soul of a person only through the events of his case history.[6]

He goes on to suggest that a possible redemption from the addiction to profane history from which we 'suffer' might come from a different ordering of the way in which we experience events:

. . . but this reorganization first requires a change in memory itself, so that one asks each day not 'what happened?' but 'what happened to the soul?' For this way of remembering events memory needs to return again to its reminiscence of primordial ideas, to its original association with the archetypal root metaphors of human experience.

The core of the cultural metanoia is doing just this,* for the great

* In recent years people have again turned to charting the anatomy of 'inner' time. Peter Simester, for instance, has produced the *Phenomenon Calendar* and the *Bard Diary* (Bib 10). The former publication aligns all the world's major time systems into a coherent whole for the years 1974/5; and shows how out of phase are the 'fixed' time systems, with those of the spiritual energy periods during which the ancients held their festivals. The 'Bard Diary' allows us to monitor the effect, for each day in the year, of the changing resonances of astrological time. It is the simplest possible guide, for those with the patience to fill it in each day, for observing what actual effect repeating lunar phases and planetary aspects have on our own individual lives.

variety of symbolic vehicles which we have touched on in previous chapters all lead back to the essential 'root metaphors' of meaning.[7]

Through the lens of but one of these metaphoric vehicles, astrology, even with the barest familiarity with its symbolism, we can glimpse the vast expanse of inner time, and the tracks it leaves in outer, historical time. In the purest sense astrology is a great clock-face, whose hands and numbers are the 'root metaphors'. From these can be discerned not only the resonance mixtures of individual characters, but also of historical duo-millennia – somewhat over 2000 years long – which are influenced by particular astrological signs, and their opposite polarities on the zodiac. Twelve of these 'Ages' make up a Sidereal Year, somewhat over 26,000 years long. This cyclical process which begins and ends Sidereal Years – always in a new plane on the evolutionary spiral – is due to the 'precession of the equinoxes', a regular astronomical pulse of variation between the solar system and the pole star.

To scan but four of our recent duo-millennia (and neglecting for the moment their opposite and contributing polarities on the zodiac), 8000 years ago began the rise of the Age of Gemini, ruled by the communicative and dexterous planet Mercury. It was when cuneiform writing was developed in the Mesopotamian valley, when the picture glyphs of the early Egyptians and American empires blossomed into a written language, and when their artifacts acquired an unprecedented precision and finish. What we know of the religions also tends to be dual – like the Geminian twins – Zoroastrianism in Persia, Set and Ra in Egypt, representing the Dark and the Light Kingdoms, the Yin and Yang of China, and in Europe the early pagan dualities, one of whose expressions has survived in Romulus and Remus – the twin gods in whom ancient Rome was eventually to be founded.

The Age of Gemini, characterized by the largely restless and wandering tribes of the earth, was followed about 6000 years ago by Taurus, the sedentary Earth sign which is ruled by Venus. The people settled permanently around their agrarian, earthy interests, building megalithic cities – which today we associate with the great periods of Egyptian and American culture – consolidating strength, husbanding the earth and enjoining people to multiply. It was an age of stabilizing, and the religions clothed themselves with Taurine imagery, from the sacred bull-dancing of the Minoans of Crete to the 'Golden Calf' of the Old Testament tribes. In India the cow acquired a sanctity which echoes down to the present day.

Close to 2000 years B.C. Taurus was followed by the age of Aries, the

Cardinal Fire sign, ruled by the warring and creative Mars. Mars, symbolized in alchemy by molten iron, presided over the rise of the Iron Age, in which immense battles were waged with swords and armour by such fiery militants as Empress Wu of China and Alexander the Great. The Fire signs are associated with the sun, and in the great cultures, particularly in Egypt and America, the religious symbolism became dominantly solar, reflecting the flaming energy of Aries – and great

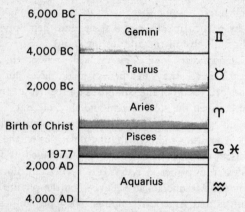

93. The Aeons, Ages or Duo-millennia in which 'vertical' or astrological time sees the vast expanse of our history. This section covers merely 10,000 years.

sacrifices, both in blood as well as in the subtler human substances, were made to the sun. The Judaic god Yaweh is a specifically martian deity in his aspect of the avenging patriarch, the uncompromising judge whose influence we still detect in Christianity despite Christ's revolutionary injunction to 'turn the other cheek'. The bull symbols of the Taurine Age had given way to the Ram – such as that found by Moses in the thicket. In Classical Greece we have Jason's quest for the Golden Fleece, and elsewhere in Europe Pan stalked through the forests of the human psyche as the great horned god with the hooves of a ram. This was the new guise of man's duality. Pan, like man, was also strung between two worlds, his hairy animal shanks springing from the earth, melting into the torso of a man and finally flowering into the wreathed and music-making head with those magnificent horns, horns which, as recognized in the occult symbolism behind heraldry, are the antennae inversely rooted in the aetheric world, drawing sustenance from invisible sources of power.

At the end of the preceding Age of Taurus, the equivalent half-human half-divine duality had in Crete degenerated into the fearful image of the Minotaur; and similarly, with the eclipsing of Aries by the Age of Pisces, the Pan god became inverted to the cloven-hoofed Goat of the Underworld, the Devil of Christianity, for a new age had dawned, and the past symbols were sloughed lest they obscure the new.

Pisces, ruled by watery, mystical Neptune, is the second great dual sign, and its aeon, like the others preceding it (on which we have not had space to elaborate here) resonated to its opposite polarity on the zodiac – Virgo, the fixed Earth sign which is nevertheless ruled, like Gemini, by Mercury – giving it a precise and formalizing intellect. These past 2000 years have seen the travelling of the seas, the collating and structuring of knowledge. With Christianity we see the mystical, loving and devotional nature of Pisces checked and formalized by the Virgo intellect. Pisces loves with an overflowing, barely discriminating sentiment, which is purified and de-passioned by Virgo. Fish symbolism flowered through Pisces religion – the Fisher of Men, the vesica piscis (the geometrical principle on which the Gothic cathedrals were built), the bishop's mitre in the form of a fish, and the baptismal font, or 'piscina'. Later in the age, when the revolutionary Piscean messianism had become caged and vaulted, through Virgo's increased influence, in the magnificent structures of ecclesiastical architecture and theology, the symbol of the Virgin Mary began to emerge more dominantly. Christ was the first Great Fish of the Piscean Age, and was doomed to be sacrificed as the last ram (or lamb) of the dying aeon of Aries which preceded it.

Where do we stand today in this thread of symbolism? We are well into the last third of this century, and but one generation from the twenty-first, which is nearer to us now in horizontal calendar time than the nineteenth century, and those signposts of our cultural identity such as Beethoven, Hegel and Darwin, and the first progenitors of scientific rationalism. The concluding third of our century is also the concluding thirtieth of the Age of Pisces: fifty-nine generations stand behind us, and less than one ahead before fully entering the Age of Aquarius – the great pourer of the Waters of Life, the 'scientist' drawing his meaning from *scio*: 'I know', but knowing the *inner* as well as the outer nature of man.*

* For this framework of thought I am also indebted to the inspiration of Dr James Hillman.

We are already responding, each to his own capacity, to the still inchoate moving forces of this incipient age. While around us are crumbling the husks of what once fully contained the life of a previous age, among the people there is a presentiment of a different order of knowledge. The more inwardly oriented we become, the more we are estranged from the 'profane facts' of the outer world and the more strongly we respond to the awesome resonance of the Aquarian Dawn. Yet from this 'outside' alone, it seems that we merely stand among moral and hierarchical ruins, at the blackened end of the world. In Yeats's words:

> The falcon cannot hear the falconer,
> Things fall apart; the centre cannot hold;
> Mere anarchy is loosed upon the World.
> The blood-dimmed tide is loosed . . .
> The best lack all conviction, while the worst
> Are full of passionate intensity.

Yet the 'revelation', the 'second coming' which is at hand can also be glimpsed through astrological symbolism. Aquarius is a fixed air sign, abstract and broad-ranging, ruled by Uranus, the disruptive, psychic and electrical planet. His philosophy draws people together in a single revolutionary purpose, the earth moves into the first stages of being experienced as a single organism, and all mankind as a single family. Aquarius masters the air and all it symbolizes, from material aeronautics to the attenuated substances of invisible force – the gaseous, aetheric and electrical phenomena of 'fixed air'. His science moves more deeply into the subtle energies which underlie matter. In these brief few centuries we see how progress in technology – contrary to general belief – has been merely the progress of simplification. Large engines with little power gradually become smaller and more potent. Electric generators shrank to batteries, and finally to transistors which can barely be seen with the naked eye. The emphasis on mechanics has shifted more towards physics and the forces which *subtend* matter, and the enormous impedimenta once required to contain and canalize energy are gradually becoming extinct. Whereas the first clocks were great caskets of inaccurate cogs, today we can carry on our wrists precision watches driven by atomic oscillators. By becoming simpler and more subtle, technology is getting closer and closer to the body of man, in such a way that eventually it can be seen merely as an invisible extension of his own knowledge.

It is this barely beginning Aquarian science which is progressively releasing us from the domination of matter, freeing us into the dimensions of free flight – of which we have dreamed so vividly for centuries. Symbolically, it was the deeper understanding of natural laws which made it possible to build an engine small and powerful enough to lift us mechanically into the air. The levitating fakir, though seen as a humorous fairy tale, is less outrageous when viewed in the context of knowledge of subtending forces, and in this myth of the unwashed holy man hovering benignly over his Himalayan cave we can sense how ferociously cumbersome and primitive is the helicopter as a means of flight.

The subtilizing of Aquarian science brings man ever closer to the laws which subtend the universe, and of which he himself is made, so that with his *under*-standing he can begin to fly and to feel within himself alone. Whereas our outer, rational memories show us only a brief span of the surface of history behind us, our inner memories – through myth and symbol – detect the currents of meaning beneath the future as well. A forthcoming book by David Coxhead called *An Oral History of the Future*, for instance, is a compilation of dreams, drug-induced and spontaneous experiences of people from all walks of life, which taken together can be seen as a premonitionary relief map of the world we are entering upon. Our architecture, our art, our ideals are already metamorphosing into a different mode of enlightenment; people are responding to the future with premonitionary dreams of the earth as a spherical organism, brushed with gaseous vibrations of colour, nurturing man as a conscious steward of its sacred homeostasis.

The first burst of Aquarian enthusiasm experienced by the young in the early 1960s has for many subsided into a disenchanted apathy, and many former 'flower children' complain that the Movement seems to have lost its momentum and purpose; that the military and political oppression practised by establishment forces is as strong, if not stronger – than it ever was. But rather as the idea of a work of art is conceived in the first ebullient flush of ecstasy, which later subsides as the hard work to realize it nears completion, so too can we see that the decade-old dream – like a seedling planted with blood – has actually put forth its first tangible shoots, preparing to flower into a tree of unimaginable fruits.

The *outer* chaos and confusion of our time is but the disturbance which characterizes the metamorphosis of all great rhythms, or aeons, into a new one; but *inwardly*, the iron-filings of a special kind of related knowledge are already polarizing themselves round a new pattern of Meaning, revealing that a deeper knowledge of universal laws is contingent on a deeper knowledge of the self, and the schism between the two worlds of science and religion is beginning to heal and to merge into a single majestic river of vision.

Notes

CHAPTER 1

1. There are about a dozen fairly scarce books on Subud, the best introductions being: Edward Van Hien, *What is Subud?*, London, Rider & Co., 1963; Tarzie Vittachi, *A Reporter in Subud*, New York, Dharma Book Co., 1963 and the less easy to read, but more authoritative *Sushila Budhi Dharma* by the organization's leader, 'Bapak' M. S. Sumohadiwidjojo, London, The Subud Brotherhood, 1959.
2. H. Benoit, *The Supreme Doctrine*, New York, Viking, 1970, p. xiii.

CHAPTER 2

1. Bertrand Russell, *The Problem of Philosophy*, Oxford University Press, 1912.
2. John C. Eccles, *Facing Reality*, London, Longman, 1969.
3. ibid., p. 52.
4. One of the key books in Alice Bailey's prolific output on 'esoteric psychology' is her *Treatise on White Magic*, London, Lucis Press, 1970.
5. C. W. K. Mundle, *Perceptions: Facts and Theories*, Oxford University Press, 1971, p. 55.
6. Anton Ehrenzweig, *The Hidden Order of Art*, London, Paladin, 1970, p. 31.
7. C. Lévi-Strauss, *Structural Anthropology*, London, Penguin, 1956, p. xii.
8. Arthur Koestler, *The Roots of Coincidence*, London, Hutchinson, 1972, p. 53.
9. J. R. Oppenheimer, *Science and Human Understanding*, 1966, p. 40.
10. C. F. Von Weizsacher, *The History of Nature*, trans. Wiek, London, 1951, p. 63.
11. From the *Tao-Te'h Ching*, Chapter 11.

12. From the *Isha Upanishad* of the Vedic Scriptures, V. 5. L. C. Beckett's two books, *Movement and Emptiness* and *Neti-Neti – Not This; Not That*, London, Stuart & Watkins, 1968 and 1969, compare the extraordinary similarities of language now being used by astro- and nuclear physicists to that of Tibetan Buddhism and the Lankavatara Sutra, the sacred Hindu text which dates back over 2000 years.

13. Aniela Jaffe, *The Myth of Meaning*, London, Hodder & Stoughton, 1967, p. 42.

14. John Bleibtreu, *The Parable of the Beast*, London, Paladin, 1968, p. 20.

15. J. J. Bachofen, *An Essay on Mortuary Symbolism*, quoted in T. C. Stewart's *The City as an Image of Man*, London, Latimer, 1970.

16. See the visionary and imaginative anthropology of Colonel James Churchward, such as *The Children of Mu* and *The Lost Continent of Mu*, New York, Paperback Library Edition, 1968.

17. I. Velikovsky, *Worlds in Collision* and *Ages in Chaos*, New York, Dell, 1967.

18. More rational, but perhaps less meaningful, reconstructions of myth prefer to place the Sunken Atlantis somewhere between Africa and Europe in the Mediterranean Sea. See Andrew Tomas, *Atlantis – From Legend to Discovery*, London, Hale, 1972.

19. E. Von Daniken, *Chariots of the Gods?, Return to the Stars*, London, Souvenir Press, 1970.

20. G. Adamski, *Flying Saucers Have Landed*, London, Methuen, 1925.

21. Books on the geometry of megalithic sites in Britain range from the careful surveying work of Professor A. Thom in his *Megalithic Lunar Observatories*, Oxford, Clarendon Press, 1971, to the more liturgical pursual by John Michell of the significance of such architecture in his *The View Over Atlantis*, London, Sago Press, 1969, and *City of Revelation*, London, Garnstone Press, 1972.

22. C. Watkins, *The Old Straight Track*, London, Methuen, 1925.

23. Robert Graves, *The White Goddess*, London, Faber & Faber, 1952.

24. Guy Underwood, *Patterns of the Past*, London, Museum Press, 1968.

25. Maurice Freedman, *Geomancy, Proceedings of the Royal Anthropological Institute of Great Britain and Ireland for 1928*, London, Royal Anthropological Institute, 1969.

26. Jorge Luis Borges, *Spherical Animals, Io: Alchemy Issue*, New York, Grossman, 1968.

27. Carlos Casteñeda, *The Teachings of Don Juan: A Yagui Way of Knowledge*, *A Separate Reality* and *Journey to Ixtlan*, New York, Simon & Schuster, 1968, 1971 and 1972.

28. Bryan Wilson, *Religion in Secular Society*, London, C. A. Watts, 1966, p. xvii.

CHAPTER 3

1. Teilhard de Chardin, *The Phenomenon of Man*, London, Collins, 1959.

2. J. H. Nelson, 'Shortwave Radio Propagation Correlations with Planetary Positions', *R.C.A. Review*, Vol. 12, March 1951; 'Planetary Position Effect on Short Wave Signal Quality', *Electrical Engineering*, Vol. 71, No. 5, May 1952.

3. For an interesting synopsis of the work carried out by the Foundation for the Study of Cycles, see E. R. Dewey and Og Madino, *Cycles – The Mysterious Forces that Trigger Events*, New York, Hawthorn, 1971.

4. Quoted by Derek Parker in *The Question of Astrology*, London, Eyre & Spottiswoode, 1970, p. 148.

5. *Science Magazine*, 4 December 1959.

6. G. Picardi, *The Chemical Basis of Medical Climatology*, London, G. T. Thomas, 1962.

7. Reported in *Nature*, 18 July 1959.

8. Edward Dewey, *Cycles*, op. cit., p. 139.

9. J. A. West and J. G. Toonder, *The Case for Astrology*, London, Macdonald, 1970.

10. An excellent introduction to a serious study of astrology in Julia and Derek Parker's heavily illustrated *The Complete Astrologer*, London, Mitchell Beazley Ltd, 1971. For a simple and direct learning method for the fundamentals of casting a chart, see Jeff Mayo, *Astrology*, London, Teach Yourself Series, 1964.

11. See Michel Gauquelin, *L'Influence des Astres*, Paris, Denöel, 1955, and *L'Astrologie devant la Science*, Paris, Planète, 1965.

12. See Alice Bailey's *Esoteric Astrology*, Lucis Publishing Company, and her numerous other works.

13. Dane Rudyar's books include *The Pulse of Life*, Berkeley, Shambala, 1970; *An Astrological Mandala*, New York, Vintage Books, 1973; *The Lunation Cycle*, Berkeley, Shambala, 1971; *The Planetarization of Consciousness*, New York, Harper Colophon, 1970 and 1972;

Rania, San Francisco, Unity Press, 1973; and *The Rhythm of Human Fulfilment*, Palo Alto, Seed Center, 1966.

14. Jiu Purce, *The Mystic Spiral*, London, Thames & Hudson, 1974, is an intriguing and imaginative guide to the whole subject.

CHAPTER 4

1. See John Michell, *The View Over Atlantis*, London, Sago Press, 1969, and *City of Revelation*, London, Garnstone Press, 1972, from which books I have attempted to synopsize but a few of Michell's many interesting observations.
2. Piazzi C. Smyth, *Our Inheritance in the Great Pyramid*, London, Isbister, 1880.
3. John Michell, *The View Over Atlantis*, op. cit.
4. Keith Critchlow, *Order in Space – A Design Sourcebook*, London, Thames & Hudson, 1969.
5. For this framework I am indebted to Elizabeth Leader's article, 'The Avalon Apple Isle', in *Britain – A Study in Patterns*, London, RILKO Publications, 1971.
6. W. S. Andrews, *Magic Squares and Cubes*, New York, Dover Publications, 1960.
7. Oliver Whicker, *Projective Geometry – Creative Polarities in Space and Time*, London, Rudolph Steiner Press, p. 243.

CHAPTER 5

1. John Stewart Collis, *The Vision of Glory – The Extraordinary Nature of the Ordinary*, London, Charles Knight & Co., 1972, p. 18.
2. S. Ostrander and L. Schroeder, *Psychic Discoveries behind the Iron Curtain*, London, Abacus, 1975.
3. For a lush and electrifying book of photographs of matter responding to wave forms, see Hans Jenny, *Cymatics*, Basel, Basilius Press, 1966.
4. Lyall Watson, *Supernature*, London, Hodder & Stoughton, 1973, p. 105.
5. Plato, *Cratylus*, Loeb Edition, p. 175.
6. See *Journal of the British Society of Dowsers*, Vol. XXII, No. 153, September 1971, p. 233.
7. A. Glazewski, 'The Music of Crystals, Plants and Human Beings', reprint from *Radio-Perception*, September 1951.

8. Ostrander and Schroeder, op. cit., p. 200.
9. ibid., p. 212.
10. Lyall Watson, *Supernature*, op. cit., p. 149.
11. John C. Eccles, 'The Experiencing Self', *The Uniqueness of Man*, ed. J. D. Roslansky, Geneva, North-Holland, 1969.
12. Quoted in Dick Kirkpatrick, 'Do Plants Think?', in *National Wildlife*, February/March issue, 1969, pp. 20–21.
13. D. Kirkpatrick, reprint in *Science of Mind*, June 1970, p. 22.
14. Lyall Watson, *Supernature*, op. cit.

CHAPTER 6

1. See D. Tansley, *Radionics – And the Subtle Anatomy of Man*, Rustington, Sussex, Health Science Press, 1972.
2. ibid.
3. A valuable book which thoroughly documents recent research in this and other areas of changed perception is *Altered States of Consciousness*, ed. Charles T. Tart, New York, Wiley, 1969.
4. Joseph Kamiya, 'Operant Control of the EEG Alpha Rhythm and some of its Reported Effects of Consciousness', ibid., p. 514.
5. Wallace, Benson and Wilson, 'A Wakeful Hypermetabolic Physiological State', *American Journal of Physiology*, Vol. 221, No. 3, 1971.
6. S. Hahnemann, *Organon of the Art of Rational Healing*, London, 1913.
7. Andrew Weil, *The Natural Mind*, London, Cape, 1973.
8. G. S. Spinks, *Psychology and Religion*, New York, Methuen, 1963.

CHAPTER 7

1. Herman Hesse, *The Glass Bead Game*, London, Cape, 1970.
2. The most informative book on the I Ching is still Richard Wilhelm (trans.), *The I Ching or Book of Changes*, London, Routledge & Kegan Paul, 1968. Foreword by C. G. Jung.
3. Two highly recommended books on the basis of the Tarot are Frater Achad, *The Anatomy of the Body of God*, New York, Samuel Weiser Inc., 1969, which examines its geometrical structure, and Charles Ponce, *Kabbalah*, London, Garnstone Press, 1974, which goes deeply into its mythological symbolism.

4. A. Taylor, *The Occult and Scientific Correlations of Religion, Art and Science*, New York, Vantage Press, 1968.
5. ibid., p. 26.
6. Spectrum, *The Times*, 29 June 1969.

CHAPTER 8

1. From Brewster's *Memoirs of Newton*, Vol. ii, Chapter 27.
2. Bryan Wilson, *Religion in Secular Society*, London, C. A. Watts, 1966.
3. G. I. Gurdjieff, *All and Everything*, 3 vols., London, Routledge & Kegan Paul, 1974, and P. D. Ouspensky, *In Search of the Miraculous*, London, Routledge & Kegan Paul, 1950.
4. Rudolph Steiner's prolific output examines the esoteric basis of almost every area of human endeavour. Whether philosophy, education, colour therapy or architecture, are all entered in depth, and you would be well to choose one of his volumes with your subject of interest in the title. Nearly all his works are published by the Anthroposofic Press in New York. For a cogent biography of Steiner see A. P. Shepherd, *A Scientist of the Invisible*, London, Hodder & Stoughton, 1954.

CHAPTER 9

1. Charles Davis, 'Religious Pluralism and the New Counter Culture', in the *Listener*, 9 April 1970, p. 479.
2. Harvey Cox, *The Feast of Fools*, Cambridge, Mass., Harvard University Press, 1969, p. 12.
3. For Huxley's lucidly described experiments with drug-altered states of consciousness see Aldous Huxley, *The Doors of Perception*, London, Constable, 1915, and *Heaven and Hell*, London, Chatto & Windus, 1960.
4. Michael Polanyi, *The Study of Man*, the Lindsay Memorial Lectures, London, Routledge & Kegan Paul, 1958.
5. ibid., p. 25.
6. James Hillman, 'Senex and Puer – The Historical Present in View of Archetypal Psychology', from *Art International*, Vol. XVI, 20 January 1971.
7. Peter Simester, *Phenomenon Calendar*, Phenomenon Publications, 1973; *Bard Diary*, Bard Publications, 1974. New edition forthcoming from Croom Helm.

Additional Relevant Bibliography

Stanley Krippner and Daniel Rubin (eds.), *The Kirlian Aura*, New York, Anchor Press/Doubleday, 1974.

An Index of Possibilities, Aylesbury, Great Britain, Clanrose Publishers/Wildwood House/Arrow Books, 1974.

Peter Tompkins and Christopher Bird, *The Secret Life of Plants*, London, H. R. Rowe, 1973.

John C. Lilley, *Centre of the Cyclone*, New York, Bantam, 1973.

Lyall Watson, *The Romeo Error*, London, Hodder & Stoughton, 1974.

Davidson & Aldersmith, *The Great Pyramid: Its Divine Message*, London, William & Norgate Ltd., 1948.

Carlos Castañeda, *Tales of Power*, London, Hodder & Stoughton, 1975.

W. S. Andrews, *Magic Squares and Cubes*, New York, Dover, 1960.

Peter Tompkins, *Secrets of the Great Pyramid*, New York, Harper, 1973.

Index